THE FIRST-TIME
gardener

THE
FIRST-TIME
gardener

Everything the Beginner Needs to Know to
Create, Maintain and Enjoy a Garden

JONATHAN EDWARDS

CARROLL & BROWN PUBLISHERS LIMITED

To Liz and Sonja for all their help and support

First published in 2001 in the United Kingdom by:

Carroll & Brown Publishers Limited
20 Lonsdale Road
Queen's Park
London NW6 6RD

Editor Caroline Uzielli

Art Editor Gilda Pacitti

Designer Vimit Punater

Photography David Murray

A CIP catalogue record for this book is available from the British Library.

ISBN 1-903258-12-X

Reproduced by Colourscan, Singapore

Printed and bound by New Intelitho Italia SPA

First edition

Foreword

Gardening is infectious – once you have been bitten by the bug you will be an enthusiast for life. From the day you buy your first plant or sow your first seed it is a continuous learning experience.

The beauty of gardening lies in the fact that you don't need extensive knowledge to get started and yet you can spend a lifetime absorbed in the passion, learning more and more about the subject each day.

Like life itself, gardening has its ups and downs. Of course, you may get the occasional disappointment, but you can be certain that you will always get another chance to get it right. One of the great joys of gardening is that it never fails to surprise. At the very heart of its appeal is the excitement and uncertainty of what may be appearing just around the corner. No matter how experienced you become or how often you carry out a particular task, there is always something new and fascinating to learn.

Gardening is an evolving pastime that grows along with your knowledge – not only in the literal sense, as your garden matures, but the range of challenges you set yourself will extend as your skills increase. Indeed, the completion of your first garden should be viewed as the starting point of your learning experience; something that will evolve and develop seamlessly with your changing needs and interests. Above all else, gardening should be enjoyable.

Jonathan Edwards

contents

introduction

As a novice gardener, you may be overwhelmed by all the available information on this enormous subject. Not only might you have to cope with a barren plot or overgrown jungle, but also with finding a helpful guide that will explain everything you need to know to get started and to make gardening less of a chore.

The First-time Gardener has been specifically written with you in mind. While it concentrates on the creative aspects of designing with plants as well as the practical science of growing them, it also contains many special features (see the list opposite) to make this information readily graspable and easy to put into practice.

The structure of the book

Chapter 1 describes how to plan your garden from scratch or renovate and improve an existing garden with confidence. There are lots of ideas for making dramatic improvements from day one. It also includes tips on choosing and buying plants for your garden as well as advice on the essential tools and useful equipment that will save you a lot of time and effort.

The essential features of a garden are outlined in chapter 2 – what your options are when covering the ground, the various types of boundary available, and which plants to choose to get colour and interest all year. It also explains how to make the most of patios and water features within your design. Each section in this chapter is accompanied by case studies which describe how representative First-time Gardeners have put expert advice into practice. Some are new gardeners who have tackled completely empty gardens from scratch – creating an established-looking design that meets their particular needs. On pages 50–51, for example, Joe and Marsha produce an easy-care garden with a lawn and paving to suit all the family, while on pages 68–69, Judy and Chris create a perennial paradise in a shaded town garden.

There are also examples of First-time Gardeners who have made drastic improvements to existing

Facing the challenge

This barren plot is very long and narrow and has an unsightly wall at one end (right), which dominates the garden design and spoils the view from the house. What's needed here is a design that focuses the eye within the centre of the garden and makes the most of available space.

This ingenious design (far right) transformed the look and feel of the garden. It has solved the problems by disguising the boundaries with plants and incorporating a large ornamental pond as the main central feature. Changes in colour and texture from the sunny terrace to the shady border at the bottom of the garden are linked by an eye-catching blue-stained pergola.

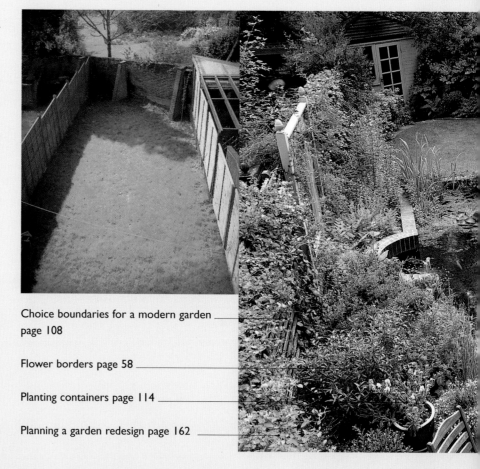

Choice boundaries for a modern garden page 108

Flower borders page 58

Planting containers page 114

Planning a garden redesign page 162

designs, either by adapting or changing features to suit their own taste and lifestyle or by completely renovating an overgrown jungle. On pages 106–107, for example, Meg and Paul tackle a plot crammed with overgrown shrubs and create space for a wider variety of plants as well as a sun-deck. In the water gardening section, an old garden is transformed by Kevin and Joanna into a contemporary design with the addition of a dramatic water feature, novelty seats and a sunken patio area (see pages 142–143).

Each real-life example illustrates how a barren plot or overgrown chaos can be transformed quickly, easily and within any budget. Here is proof that you don't have to be an expert to make genuine improvements to your garden.

Chapter 3 explains how to keep your garden looking good all year, listing all the essential tasks for each season as well as handy hints on solving common problems that might occur.

All the basic techniques you need to know to get started are detailed in the final chapter. It includes an easy-to-follow guide to planning your garden, improving your soil and recycling waste materials. There are also tips on caring for your plants, with advice on feeding and watering, plus the best ways to tackle weeds, pests and diseases, including an at-a-glance guide to identifying many common plant problems.

Help is at hand
Throughout this book, special boxes highlight essential information that will make gardening quick, easy and efficient for the Virgin Gardener.

FAQs—Frequently Asked Questions
Anticipating those questions a new gardener is most likely to ask, here are straightforward answers in easy-to-understand language on those subjects you need to know when you start gardening for the first time.

Steps to success
Essential information about the project at hand is summarised in these quick-reference guides.

First-time Gardener's best bets
Recommended trouble-free plants giving the best displays are listed; these are grouped according to their cultural needs, to help you choose the right plant for your garden.

Expert tips
Simple techniques, tried and tested by the experts, have been highlighted throughout the book – these tips will save you time, money and a great deal of effort.

Green tips
Where appropriate, handy hints are provided to help you garden in an environmentally friendly manner.

Planting and supporting climbers page 76

Constructing arches and pergolas page 92

Making a mowing strip page 49

Reshaping lawns page 46

Adding plants and fish page 138

Building a new pond page 136

Using colourful paints and stains page 30

Easy-care garden surfaces page 50

Creating a private terrace page 122

jargon buster

USEFUL TERMS

Algae A primitive plant that forms a green slime over paving and containers that remain damp for long periods. One form of algae causes pond water to turn green and a floating type, known as blanketweed, covers the surface.

Algaecide A chemical used for the control of *algae*.

Alpines Plants adapted to growing in the mountains, usually low-growing and compact. They are traditionally grown together in a special rock garden, but also can be used to fill gaps between paving slabs.

Annual A plant that takes a year to complete its life cycle: the seed grows into a plant, then flowers, produces seed and dies in one year.

Aquatic plant A plant that lives in water.

Bedding Plants that are often used in large quantities as temporary additions to a garden to provide a seasonal display.

Biennial A plant that takes two years to complete its life cycle: forming a mature plant during the first year, then flowering and setting seed and dying during the second.

Biological control A method of controlling pests by introducing a natural enemy of the pest which is harmless to other insects and the crop.

Bog garden An area either constructed or natural that has marshy soil which can grow moisture-loving plants such as rushes. Often associated with a pond or water feature.

Bud A growing point that can produce either leaves, stems or flowers during the growing season.

Bulb A generic term used to describe any rounded plant storage organ, including true bulbs such as daffodils, *corms* such as crocus, *rhizomes* such as bearded iris, and *tubers* such as cyclamen.

Capillary matting An absorbent material that holds water. Plants in containers that are placed on the matting can draw water from it by capillary action.

Chemical control A method of controlling pests and diseases using specially formulated chemicals.

Climber Any plant that can grow up a vertical surface. They can be self-clinging, such as ivy, or twining such as clematis, but also include plants such as climbing roses that need to be tied onto their support.

Cloche A protective cover made from glass or plastic, which can be moved around the garden to protect vulnerable plants from weather.

Compost bin A special container designed to make garden compost from organic waste materials.

Compost, potting A material in which plants are grown. Various types are produced, often based on peat or soil. There are special formulations for different stages of growth and for special needs, such as ericacious compost for acid-loving plants.

Conifer A tree or shrub, usually evergreen, that produces its seed in cones.

Corm A solid, underground stem that stores food during the dormant season. See also *Bulb*.

Crocks Pieces of broken terracotta or stones that can be used to cover large drainage holes in a container to prevent soil from washing out.

Crown The area where stems and roots meet at ground level.

Cutting A short piece of stem used to propagate a new plant.

Damping off A disease which causes seedlings to flop over and die.

Deadheading A method of removing old blooms from a flowering plant to prevent seeding, tidy the display and encourage a further flush of flowers.

Deciduous Plants that lose their foliage in the autumn.

Division A method of propagating large, established clumps by splitting the roots.

Dormant period The time when plant growth slows as temperatures fall during winter.

Evergreen Plants, of any colour, that don't lose their foliage in winter. The leaves are still shed, but not all at once, so it usually goes unnoticed.

Fern A non-flowering plant which reproduces by spores.

Fertiliser A material that is added to the soil to improve plant growth.

Foliar feed A fast-acting dilute fertiliser applied to the leaves of a plant.

Frost A layer of frozen condensation that may form on plants and other surfaces when temperatures fall below 0°C (32°F).

Fungicide A chemical formulated to kill fungal diseases.

Garden compost An organic material produced by the decomposition of plant waste materials from the garden. Usually in a compost bin.

Garden fleece A porous fabric designed to be laid over young plants and seedlings to protect from cold and act as a barrier against flying pests. It also can be used to wrap established plants to protect them in winter.

Germination The sprouting of a seed.

Groundcover plants Low-growing ornamental plants that produce dense growth used to cover the soil and suppress weeds.

Hardening off A method of gradually acclimatising plants raised in warm or protected areas to the harsher conditions outside.

Hardy A term used to describe a plant that can survive cold; plants, however, vary greatly in their cold tolerance (see page 160).

Herbaceous plants Perennials that produce soft, non-woody growth and die down to the ground each winter. New shoots are then produced each spring from the underground root system.

Hessian Sacking material that is used to line aquatic planting baskets.

Hormone rooting powder A compound that is used to stimulate cuttings to produce roots.

Insecticide A chemical used to kill garden insect pests.

Layering A method of propagating by rooting stems while they are still attached to the parent plant.

Leafmould Fallen leaves which after composting, are useful for using as a *mulch* or for improving the soil structure.

Manure An organic material made from decomposed animal and plant waste that is used to improve soil structure and add essential nutrients for a plant's growth.

Mowing strip A permanent edge or narrow paved border around the perimeter of a lawn and level with its surface, so that a lawnmower can mow straight over the edge.

Mulch A material laid on the surface of the soil to suppress weeds and prevent moisture loss through evaporation. There are three types: loose organic mulches, such as *leafmould*, wood chips and grass clippings; loose inorganic mulches, such as gravel and pebbles; and fabric sheet mulches made from permeable materials.

Organic A system of gardening that uses natural materials. Or any chemical compound that contains carbon. Organic fertilisers, such as fish emulsion and bonemeal, are derived from natural sources; chemical fertilisers are man-made.

Perennial A plant that lives more than one year, usually applied to a plant that produces hardy, non-woody growth. Most are herbaceous and die down in winter, but some are *evergreen*. Tender perennials are killed by frost.

Pressure-treated wood Specially prepared softwood timber that has been impregnated with a wood preservative and does not require any further preservative.

Prune To control the growth of a plant by cutting its stems back.

Rhizome A horizontal underground stem. See also *Bulb*.

Rootball A term used to describe the root system of a plant grown in a container or that of a plant grown in the ground when dug up with the soil intact around its roots.

Rootstock The root system onto which a more ornamental variety is attached. Rose cultivars, for example, are often not grown on their own roots but joined onto the root system of an easy-to-grow but less desirable relative.

Scarifying Raking out of dead grass stems from the lawn.

Shrub A plant which produces woody stems but no central trunk.

Slow-release fertiliser A fertiliser that is coated in a special resin so that it releases nutrients over a period of time. The amount released increases as the temperature rises and with moisture levels, so plants get more food when growing rapidly. Also known as controlled-release fertiliser.

Standard A plant with a rounded, bushy top, grown on a long straight stem.

Subsoil The layer of soil which lies underneath the *topsoil* and contains less nutrients and organic matter and is less well aerated.

Sucker A shoot produced from the roots or *rootstock* of a woody plant. Roses and lilacs often produce suckers.

Tap-root A succulent anchoring root, like that of a carrot.

Tender A plant that is killed by cold. As with hardy plants, the degree of cold tolerated varies from one species to another.

Thatch A term for the dead organic material that forms a dense mat at the base of grass blades in a lawn.

Thinning A method of increasing space between seedlings by removing seedlings that lie in between.

Three-four-five triangle A triangle made from rough timber with sides in the proportions of 3, 4 and 5, and with one corner of exactly 90 degrees. This is useful for checking right angles when constructing squares and rectangles in your garden.

Topsoil The surface layer of soil, which is most fertile.

Transplanting The term given to the moving of plants from one position to another to give them more room to grow.

Tuber A swollen mostly underground stem that bears buds and serves as a storage site for food. See also *Bulb*.

Turf A section of grass including its roots, cut for the purpose of making a new lawn.

Variegated A term used to describe parts of a plant that have two or more colours.

Vermiculite A natural substance which forms very light, air-filled granules after heating. Useful when growing plants from seed (see page 178).

Windbreak A barrier that protects an area from the prevailing wind. It can be made from a fence, hedge or a shelter belt of trees and shrubs, and even fabric.

making plans

designing your garden

Garden design is one of the most challenging, yet most exciting, pursuits for the First-time Gardener. It is rather like designing a room in your house, since the same principles of balance and harmony, sense of proportion and use of colour and texture apply. Your garden, however, differs in one fundamental way – it changes with time. Unlike interior design, you have to take account of how the garden will look during the different seasons and how it will evolve over the years.

The definition of a well-designed garden is one that contains a com- bination of features that gel together in a way that reflects the individual personality and lifestyle of its owners and meets their particular needs. This means that every garden design is unique. All successful garden designs, however, conform to a few basic principles which are good starting points when design- ing your own garden.

Using shapes and contrast

All garden designs, no matter how big or small, how traditional or modern, are made up of simple interlocking shapes. These shapes should complement each other and

3

1   **2**

Focal points and vistas

To create a well-designed garden, you also must include points of focus which help to provide definition. Statues and ornaments make good focal points, as do plants with bold outlines. Don't be restricted to focal points within the garden. If you have a stunning view, for example, incorporate this into your garden design.

Small features also can be made into focal points by emphasising them. For instance, you can lead the eye to a simple sundial using an attractive path, or make the most of a small statuette by framing it from a distance through an arch.

Focal points can be used in other ways, too. They are useful for highlighting certain features, such as a pond or a rockery, or drawing the eye away from unsightly sheds or compost heaps. They can add intrigue and mystery to a garden, inviting the casual viewer to explore further. This works particularly well when the feature is partially hidden from view.

Exploit what you've got

A design will be all the more effective if it is developed with the garden's surroundings in mind. In an urban situation, for example, there may be more need for privacy or to hide an ugly building – in the garden pictured opposite, a fabric canopy provides a modern solution in a contemporary design. In a country location, however, you might want to preserve a view or keep out a sharp wind.

When choosing materials for any garden features, it is worth noting that they look far more striking if they are made of similar materials used elsewhere in your house.

It is also worthwhile making the most of any existing features such as slopes, walls or established trees and shrubs. Even seemingly problem areas can be turned to your advantage by choosing the right plants to grow in them (see page 72).

You should also consider how much time and money you can afford to spend both building your garden and maintaining it afterwards. Different styles and features as well as the plants you choose can have a big impact. Also, think about the sorts of tasks you will be able to carry out yourself and which you may prefer to leave to a professional gardener or builder.

When to start work

Building work is best scheduled for a period of settled weather. Leave planting until spring or autumn. If you are redesigning an existing garden it is worth leaving it for a year before making any large changes so that you can note down the good and bad points during all the seasons. By doing this, you will make fewer mistakes when drawing up your new garden design.

combine to achieve the same central theme or style. Your overall design should be clearly defined, whether you want a formal garden with bold geometric shapes or an informal one with flowing curves.

A common problem with many gardens is that they are confusing to look at, especially when filled with an uncoordinated mass of colour, form and texture. To appreciate any particular feature, you need to bring some sort of order to the chaos so that the overall effect has cohesion and individual elements stand out from the crowd. Choose features that both complement and contrast with each other – combine plants and features that offer different outlines, textures, colours and overall sizes, so that each can be appreciated in its own right.

Striking designs
This secluded informal patio area **(1)** provides a focal point for the relaxing colourful planting scheme; fabric canopies and awnings provide privacy for this roof garden **(2)**, while mood lighting, decking and minimal plants create a calming, yet modern environment, ideal for entertaining; strong, geometric shapes and architectural plants form a highly contemporary garden style, which requires minimum upkeep **(3)**.

designing with plants

Choosing the right plants is the key to any successful garden design. The plants need to be able to cope with the conditions in your garden, however (see pages 20–23).

Plants can be used in many ways to create a variety of effects. Some are there to provide a permanent backdrop and to form the backbone of beds and borders. These include hedges, evergreen climbers and specimen trees and shrubs. Others are more decorative, producing brilliant flowers, colourful foliage or berries. They are often short-lived, taking the limelight for just a month or two. Most annuals, herbaceous perennials, bulbs and some flowering shrubs and climbers fall into this category. A garden is not complete without a few reliable filler plants that hold the design together – evergreen plants and many shrubs are good examples.

Creating structure

When choosing plants for your garden, consider what function you want each to perform and how you perceive the end result.

If you are looking for a dramatic effect, architectural plants with spiky and fountain-shapes such as yucca, phormium and pampas grass are perfect. For even more drama, look for tall, narrow, upright-shaped plants such as columnar ornamental trees and conifers.

Low-spreading plants, such as ground-hugging prostrate conifers, heathers or mat-forming herbaceous plants can create a more calming atmosphere. So too can climbers and wall-hugging shrubs, which help break up the stark appearance of walls and fences.

To add bulk and form to your design, include rounded, dome-shaped plants, such as hebes, evergreen berberis and viburnum. If it's humour you want, there are several unusually shaped or coloured plants you could choose, such as corkscrew rush, contorted hazel and zebra grass. You should use these with discretion, however.

Mood planting

A garden should be a sensual experience and so you need to consider how your chosen plants will appeal to the various senses. Colour is perhaps the most important, but texture and scent should not be neglected.

To choose colour combinations, think logically and in stages. The predominant colour in most gardens is green, so use this as your background colour. Then add colours that appeal, but how you organise them will have a significant effect on the mood you

1

create. To make combining colours easier, separate the colour spectrum into two groups: blues, deep reds and purples; and yellows, pinks, bright reds and oranges. If you want to create a harmonious scheme, combine colours from the same group. If, however, you prefer clashing, vibrant schemes, choose colours from both groups. White can be combined with any shade.

Textures are easier to combine because the worst effect you can create is no effect at all. To make an impact, put together plants with strikingly different textures, such as frothy grasses or soft ferns next to plants with strong outlines – a bold hosta or castor-oil plant, for example. It's not just foliage that can provide texture since bark, stems, flowers, seedpods and berries can also be used.

Place scented plants where they can be appreciated – next to a seating area, near an entrance or alongside a well-trodden path, for example. Avoid exposed sites as the fragrance will be carried away in the wind. The plants you choose should be a matter of personal preference. As a general rule, however, those that produce a strong scent, such as *Lilium regale*, mock orange and wisteria, are best appreciated from afar where their alluring perfume can be carried toward you by a breeze. For a sheltered corner or by the patio, plants with less over-powering scents are better, such as primroses, dianthus and clematis.

Imaginative planting ideas
A large, rounded statue and curved pots combine with spiky bronze carex and *Agave americana* 'Variegata' **(1)** to form a bold design in this seaside garden; bamboo conceals an Oriental statue and creates a mysterious Eastern mood **(2)**; a mass of colourful plants produces a traditional-looking country garden **(3)**, but a modern 'twist' is provided by the sculptural metal arch in the background; architectural forms dominate this contemporary roof garden **(4)**, which has a simple planting scheme focusing on a strikingly colourful bougainvillea.

growing your own food

For the First-time Gardener, having your own garden opens up many opportunities and one of the most exciting is the chance to grow some food. Contrary to popular belief, you don't need a vegetable plot or fruit garden to do this – a whole range of fruits, vegetables and herbs can be grown in normal borders mixed in with the flowers, and many others can be grown in containers (see page 126).

There are drawbacks to mixing crops in with your flower borders, however. Perhaps the most important is that the crop will be in competition with other plants for soil moisture and nutrients. This will slow the crop's development and reduce potential yields. Access is also poor, making it more difficult for you to plant, tend and harvest your crops. When a leafy vegetable such as lettuce is harvested, it can also leave an ugly gap in your flowering display. Fortunately, all these difficulties can be overcome by choosing the right crops for the right locations and adapting the way you grow them.

Productive borders

At the back of a flower border you could try planting an apple tree. Choose a relatively easy to grow variety, such as 'Discovery' or 'Katy', and the tree will not only be productive, but will also offer decorative displays of blossom in early spring and colourful fruit in late summer. To get the best crop of tasty apples you need to prevent competition from the surrounding plants until the tree has become well established. Don't plant any nearer than 1 m from the tree and cover the ground around the tree with a piece of sheet mulch (available from garden centres) to prevent weeds and keep the soil moist. Fan- and espalier-trained fruit trees are a better choice at the back of a shallow border where there is a suitable fence or wall. Runner beans and other climbing vegetable crops such as squashes are also worth planting in this position, where they can be trained over canes or other supports. With all back-of-the-border crops, lay stepping stones to make training and harvesting easier.

Edging crops

Some vegetables, such as ruby chard, carrots and frilly leaf lettuce, are so attractive that they can be used as a summer bedding substitute at the front of a border. A

Attractive harvests

Strawberries and drought-tolerant herbs are combined in this collection of terracotta pots on a balcony **(1)**; pumpkin squash 'Baby bear' has been trained along a low paling fence **(2)** with passion flower; add flowering plants to a dedicated vegetable plot **(3)** and you can turn it into an attractive feature.

few crops, such as ruby chard and salad bowl lettuce, can be used in formal schemes because only the outside leaves are harvested, leaving the plant to grow on. If you want to grow crops, such as hearting lettuce, where the whole plant is harvested, create a less organised feel to the border by mixing up crops, so any harvested plant will go unnoticed. Perpetual strawberries are also worth growing at the front of your borders where they will be more easy to harvest.

Attractive vegetable plots

You can make an attractive feature out of a vegetable plot by adding flowers and herbs. Some, such as marigolds, rosemary, lavender and the poached-egg plant *(Limnanthes douglassi)*, are not only attractive but may also reduce the incidence of common pests. They either confuse the pests by masking the smell of the crops they feed on, or provide food for beneficial insects that naturally prey on the pests.

where and how to buy plants

The plants that you choose for your garden can make or break its overall appearance. To create reliable, long-lasting displays, you should choose plants that suit your garden's soil type and situation, as well as varieties that are hardy in your area. To get the greatest choice of plants you will need to visit a reputable garden centre. If you want specific varieties or something a little out of the ordinary, however, you may need to visit a speciality nursery or buy by mail order or the internet. Plant fairs and garden shows are also good sources of plants. You will find the best selection in the spring.

Choosing a garden centre

Before you buy your plants, first inspect the various garden retailers in your area. Supermarket-like garden centres are good places to start. They don't grow their own plants, but instead buy them from wholesalers. This means they can offer a wide range of plants usually categorised into types to make locating what you want a lot easier. The main area for outdoor plants is usually dedicated to an A–Z selection of shrubs (by their Latin name) with smaller zones for other categories such as alpines, herbaceous perennials, trees and water garden plants.

A good garden centre should take into account a plant's requirements. For example, shade-loving plants, such as azaleas, camellias and ferns, should be displayed where they are protected from the sun. Tender plant varieties should be displayed inside away from cold draughts.

The outside display area of a good retailer should look neat and well-stocked. All container plants should be kept on a well-drained surface, ensuring that plants don't become waterlogged after periods of rain. There should be all-weather paths that are paved and uncluttered to make moving about with a trolley more convenient. Beds should be clearly labelled, and groups of the same plant kept neatly together. All plants should be clearly labelled, too, and preferably

Steps to success when buying plants

- Make a list in advance of the type of plants you want to buy.

- Choose a reputable garden centre or plant nursery.

- Check that the plants are healthy and correctly labelled.

Green tip

Protecting native plants
Wildlife gardens have become very popular and are often of particular interest to the Virgin Gardener. Many native plants are offered for sale by reputable nurseries, who have raised the plants from seed. Don't be tempted to dig up wildflowers in the country yourself, and do not accept or buy wildflower plants from other sources. Not only is this trade contributing to the destruction of the native wildflower populations, but the plants are less likely to thrive than plants propagated in a nursery from seed.

alongside a colour photograph and detailed planting and care requirements, which is an important source of information for the First-time Gardener. For this reason, it is essential that you make sure that plants have been correctly labelled before you buy them.

Good garden centres care about their customers, and often provide information desks where you can get advice about different plants. This can be a good place to ask about plants that will suit your particular requirements, or to check whether the plant you have chosen has been correctly labelled. Don't be afraid to ask. You will invariably receive a well-informed answer. Many garden centres also have reference books available.

Plant nurseries

Most of the plants at local nurseries are grown on site. These nurseries are a tremendous resource of local knowledge, but they can be daunting places to visit as they are not always laid out in a logical fashion and, in general, are less user-friendly than garden centres.

Display beds are often poorly laid out and plants tend to be more variable in quality and less well labelled. It is still worth visiting the local nursery, however, because you can be certain that all the plants for sale are suitable for growing in your area. The staff are usually very well informed, so nurseries are good starting points if you have a problem with a specific plant.

Some local nurseries specialise in a particular group of plants, such as herbs, conifers or perennials. Again, they usually grow all their own stock, but as specialists, they may sell a lot of their plants by mail-order. Despite this, you still can usually visit the nursery at set times or on particular days, but call before

you go to check their opening hours. Also look for the large mail-order specialists who produce informative catalogues, as these can be a good source of information.

If you do want to buy plants by mail order or via the internet, start by asking gardening friends where they get their plants and check out the advertisements in the press. Then, call the nursery and ask for a catalogue, price list and order form. Once you have made your plant selection, call to check the availability of the plants you want before submitting your order. Remember to check the sizes of plants with the nursery if it is not stated in the catalogue and keep a copy of your order so that you can check the plants when they reach you. When they do arrive, open the package immediately to check that your order is complete and the plants are satisfactory. If there are any problems, contact the nursery as soon as you can, to tell them of your complaint. If not, plant as soon as weather conditions allow.

Garden shows

A good way of visiting a variety of specialist nurseries in one day is to attend a garden show. Retailers often bring a range of popular plants to sell at very reasonable prices, so bring plenty of boxes and make the most of the special offers.

Neighbourhood and church sales and charity bazaars also can be good places to purchase common plants cheaply. Gardening clubs and societies also are worth joining, too.

FAQs – BUYING PLANTS

Q **How can I tell if the plant is suitable for my garden?**

A First check the plant label. These days, most plants are supplied with colour labels which clearly state the plants' soil and cultural requirements, as well as how big they will grow. If in doubt, ask an assistant for advice.

Q **When is the best time to buy plants?**

A Most garden centres have the widest range of new stock in spring when sales are highest. It is always worth checking when the retailer is due to get their next delivery, so that you have the best choice. This is particularly worthwhile if you want small plants, such as varieties of annuals and vegetable plants, that are sold for a short period only. As a general rule, try to visit your local garden centre before the weekend rush.

Q **Which is the best size to buy plants?**

A It is worth buying large specimens of slow-growing plants, such as flowering trees and Japanese maple, especially if they are to be used in a prominent position, such as a focal point, in the garden. Most other plants are best bought as small, vigorous specimens that will be quick to establish and put on new growth.

Q **Are plants worth buying in flower?**

A Although beautiful displays of flowering plants can look tempting, it is generally best to buy plants before they are in full bloom. However, it is sometimes helpful to know what a new plant looks like in flower – when matching it to an existing a colour scheme, for example. Also, some plants, such as potted bulbs, are worth buying as they come into bud to add an instant splash of colour to your garden.

choosing healthy plants

Improvements in the production and care of plants in recent years has meant that the majority of specimens that reach garden centres are in peak condition. There are exceptions, however, so it is important to know what you are looking for when you buy plants.

Bulbous plants

These are ideal for the First-time Gardener because they are guaranteed to flower in the first year provided they have not been badly treated and are stored correctly.

Your garden centre will sell bulbs either loose or pre-packaged. Pre-packaged bulbs are particularly useful because they are clearly labelled with colour photographs and a complete set of instructions. Loose bulbs, on the other hand, are often cheaper, but can be more variable in quality, so you will need to be more careful in selecting them. You also can buy bulbs by mail order from bulb specialists. This is particularly useful if you want specific or unusual varieties.

If you are buying bulbs loose, check them over carefully first. A good bulb should not feel light or hollow, but should be firm when squeezed between finger and thumb. There should be no sign of growth from the growing tip and the skin should be blemish-free and intact. The base of the bulb should be firm with no new root growth. Look for large 'single nosed' bulbs rather than 'multi-nosed' ones because the former will produce larger flowers and create a more reliable display.

Bedding plants

Hardy winter and spring bedding plants, such as winter-flowering pansies, double daisies and forget-me-nots, are available as potted plants from mid-autumn onwards. As when buying any potted plant, make sure these hardy bedding plants look vigorous and healthy so that they can be slipped into the garden for instant effect.

Tender summer bedding (some of which are really tender perennials) and patio plants are sold from early spring at every stage of growth from seedlings to large flowering potted plants. The increasing popularity of these plants means that garden retailers are stocking an ever-expanding range of varieties packaged in increasingly tempting ways. They are usually given their own sales area, which should be protected from cold winds and the frost. Many varieties are also available as seedlings or tiny plants by mail order from seed specialists.

All bedding plants transplant best while young and not in flower. The clamour for instant colour in recent times, however, has led to most varieties now being available in bud if not full bloom.

With very small plants, any buds that are forming are best pinched off before planting so the plant puts all its energies into getting established. With larger plants, look for lots of buds rather than flowers that have opened; it is the buds that will provide the display in your garden.

Don't buy plants with yellow leaves, which are signs of starvation, and avoid those with a bluish tinge, as this indicates stress caused by cold weather or a lack of water and nutrients. Try to avoid tall, lanky plants because this means that they have been grown too close together.

Hardy perennials

These plants are usually organised alphabetically by their Latin name in garden centres. Although they are available all year round, most are sold during the spring as small specimens when the fresh new growth emerges, or in the autumn as large well-established plants. Plants delivered in early spring can still be on sale during late summer,

so it is worth looking for signs of neglect, such as faded labels and weeds in the top of the compost.

Plants should be compact with fresh-looking foliage. Avoid any specimens with yellowing leaves, because this is a sign of starvation and check growing points and the undersides of leaves for pests. Also, make sure that the plants are well-established in their pots, but check that they don't have roots growing out of the drainage holes.

Trees, shrubs and climbers

Garden centres have permanent displays of hardy trees, shrubs, vines and other climbers, such as climbing roses, throughout the year. Some shrubs, particularly conifers, are grown in the ground and lifted with soil around their roots (known as *rootballed*) and a few, notably hedging shrubs, are sold during the dormant season bare-root.

Check that all container-grown trees, shrubs and climbers are well-established in their pots, but don't

buy any that have masses of roots circling the base of the pot. The foliage of all plants should look fresh and healthy. Make sure that variegated plants do not have any all-green shoots. Roots of bare-rooted plants should be moist while rootballed plants should have a large, firm rootball that is not breaking up.

Trees should have an upright leading shoot and a reasonably well-balanced canopy of branches. Many trees are propagated by joining them to the roots of another tree by a method called grafting. Most are grafted a few inches above the ground, but a few, such as weeping varieties, are grafted at the top of a straight stem to form a standard tree. Check that all grafts are well healed and the union is strong. Don't buy plants with shoots coming from below the graft.

Shrubs should be bushy with dense foliage and have a well-balanced shape. This is particularly important with evergreen shrubs.

essential tools and equipment

The number of gardening tools on the market is growing by the day. The best are based on designs that have stood the test of time. The only notable exceptions are the result of developing technology; a good example is the nylon-line trimmer that's useful for neatening the edges of a lawn (see page 27).

The basic tools

As a First-time Gardener, you need just ten essential tools to start gardening, less if you don't have a lawn. A variety of other tools are worth considering as they will save you time and labour; these include many powered versions that will tackle repetitive jobs quickly and easily (see pages 26–27). If your gardening gets more adventurous or you develop an interest in a specific area, then you may want to invest in a few specialist tools later on.

Pocket knife The most important tool of any gardener is a good general-purpose garden pocket knife **(1)** – ideal for cutting and trimming all around the garden. It can be used for light pruning tasks such as removing dead flower heads and for taking cuttings. It should have a straight blade of high-quality steel that folds away into the handle. Store it safely and sharpen regularly.

Spade A spade is used for digging, scooping soil and planting large plants. Choose a spade with a comfortable handle and a shaft that is long enough to prevent you from stooping – this can cause back problems. Long-handled versions are available for taller gardeners.

First-time Gardener's essential tools

10

Pocket knife
Spade
Trowel
Hoe
Leaf rake
Secateurs
Broom
Lawn mower
Edging shears
Hosepipe

2

1

Trowel This is a small hand tool used for light cultivation between plants and for planting bulbs, bedding plants and vegetables. Check that the handle is smooth and comfortable to hold in your hand.

Hoe Used for chopping off or uprooting annual weeds by cutting through just below the surface of the soil using a pull and push action. Choose one that is comfortable to use, with a handle of the right length for your height.

Wire rake This is used for clearing leaves **(2)**, raking gravel and scratching moss and dead grass clippings from the lawn. Check that its weight and balance is comfortable and choose one with closely spaced plastic or wire prongs.

Secateurs These are ideal for cutting back woody stems up to 1 cm thick, removing dead flowers and the general trimming of plants. Check that the handles are not too big for your hands when fully open and are comfortable to use. You will need to sharpen the blades occasionally.

3

Broom This is the best tool **(2)** for sweeping paved areas. Choose one with stiff bristles and make sure the head is securely fitted to the shaft.

Lawn mower For efficient mowing, choose a lawn mower that suits the size and style of your lawn. If you have a large lawn, select a mower with a wide blade; small lawns require narrower blades. There is a range of different models of lawn mower and each has its advantages and disadvantages, but the best all-rounder for the First-time Gardener is probably the wheeled rotary mower, which is versatile enough to tackle short and long grass. Check that the handle height is right for you and make sure you get a demonstration before you buy.

Edging shears Used for trimming the edge of a lawn **(3)**, clipping small hedges and other general trimming tasks around the garden. Long-handled versions take the backache out of lawn trimming, but are unsuitable for other jobs.

Hosepipe This is essential for delivering water to specific areas in your garden. Choose one that will reach all parts of your garden and doesn't kink when it is unravelled. Consider also buying a hose-reel for convenient storage and an adjustable nozzle to fit on the end so you can control the flow of water while you are using the hose. A hose lance is similar, but has a long spout that will effectively extend your reach, making easy work of watering hanging baskets and windowboxes.

FAQs – BUYING TOOLS

Q Where can I buy garden tools?

A To get the best selection, visit a large garden retailer during the spring when the store is well stocked. You also can buy tools by mail order or from commercial web sites on the Internet, but bear in mind that you will not be able to try them out before buying.

Q Do I need to buy new tools?

A No, second-hand tools that have been properly cared for are often as good and a lot cheaper than a new tool. The selection will be limited, so it is even more important to try them out to make sure they are comfortable. Check that tools are in good condition. Handles should be sturdy and blades straight for easy sharpening later. It is worth seeking expert advice before buying power tools second-hand.

Q What is the best way to care for garden tools?

A All tools need to be kept properly maintained if they are to work well. This means cleaning them immediately after they have been used. Scrape soil from cultivation tools, such as spades, rakes and hoes, and clean off plant material and sap from the blades of trimming tools such as the lawnmower, shears or secateurs.

Q How should I store tools?

A Any tools that are put away for long periods should be cleaned thoroughly, then all bare metal wiped with an oily rag to prevent rust. Sharpen dull blades before storage, so that the tool is ready to use when you need it, and have power equipment serviced. Store all tools in racks for convenience, in a dry, secure place, such as a locked garage or garden shed.

other useful equipment

As well as the ten basic tools (see pages 24–25), you may want to invest in or rent some other pieces of equipment. These are non-essential, but can make light work out of many tasks in your garden.

Digging, planting and weeding
To make these labour-intensive tasks easier, you could invest in the following gardening tools.

Garden fork Ideal for most digging tasks, especially in stony soil where a spade is less practical. A fork is very good for cultivating the soil between established plants because it will cause less root damage; it is also convenient for moving bulky materials such as garden compost.

Soil rake Used for spreading and levelling soil **(1)** before planting and sowing. Check that the prongs are evenly spaced and the rake head is securely fitted to the shaft.

Garden sieve Used for separating stones and other coarse debris from soil **(2)**. Those made from moulded plastic with a mesh size of 5 mm are perfectly adequate.

Cultivator Useful for cultivating large areas quickly, especially in neglected gardens. These are not worth buying unless you intend to dig large areas every year, such as a vegetable plot, but they can be hired by the day.

Watering and feeding
Ensuring that your plants are kept fed and watered can be an easy task if you have the right equipment.

Watering can If you have a very small garden or need to water just a few potted plants on a patio, a watering can may make more sense than a hosepipe. They are also useful for feeding container plants with liquid fertiliser. A separate clearly marked watering can should be used for applying diluted liquid weed killers.

Automatic watering If you have a lot of containers, consider installing a network of microbore tubing attached to the mains supply to make watering easier (see page 119). In warmer areas, a system of pop-up sprinklers could be laid to take the hard work out of watering elsewhere in the garden.

Hose-end sprinkler This small attachment fits on the end of a garden hosepipe and sprays water evenly over a large area. Static, rotating, pulse and oscillating types are available. Hose-end sprinklers can be left unattended, so you can do other things in the meantime.

Gardening gloves
Although not essential, gloves make gardening safer and more pleasant. You should buy at least two pairs: a pair of general-purpose, leather-palmed and fabric-backed gloves for weeding and working with soil, and a thick thorn-proof pair for pruning and cleaning up around the garden. Water-proof rubber gloves are also worth investing in for mixing chemical concentrates and for messy jobs, such as cleaning out a pond.

1

2

3

Hose-end feeder This is an attachment that fits to the end of your hosepipe, which contains concentrated fertiliser that is diluted as the water from the hose passes through it **(3)**. It is especially useful for applying a general fertiliser to large areas.

Cleaning up your garden

To keep your garden free of mess and clutter and looking its best all year, there is a huge range of tools and equipment available.

Compost bin This is used to recycle organic waste such as grass clippings, prunings and weeds into a useful soil improver. Choose one that contains about 1 cubic metre of compost and has a removable panel or slats so that you can access the compost easily. More compact, plastic rotating bins are worth considering in a small garden.

Ground sheets Use these for collecting and moving lightweight bulky materials, such as leaves and hedge prunings. Make sure it is made from tough fabric and has carrying handles. Baskets and trugs are useful.

Wheelbarrow This helps to move heavy, bulky materials. Choose a sturdy model with pneumatic tyre(s). It should be stable when full, and easy to manoeuvre when empty. You can buy an extension to increase the capacity, but these should be used only for carrying light materials, such as leaves. If you wish to move a large quantity of heavy materials, such as paving, hire a sack truck or trolley instead.

Loppers These are ideal for pruning woody stems between 1 and 3 cm thick. For stems over 3 cm thick use a **pruning saw**. Long-reach versions

on the end of a pole are designed for pruning high branches while still standing on the ground.

Shredder This is used to chop woody prunings and tough garden waste into small pieces that can be composted or used as a mulch. Shredders can be heavy to manoeuvre and noisy to use, so ask for a demonstration before you buy.

Sprayer Pump-up pressure sprayers can be useful for misting plants or applying chemicals.

Leaf sweepers and vacuums Both of these are useful for clearing up leaves in the autumn and litter at all times. Leaf sweepers are ideal for clearing large flat areas such as lawns, paving and drives, while vacuums **(4)** are more suitable for confined areas such as small courtyards and borders.

General lawncare

Green and lush lawns with neat edges can be easily achieved with the help of a couple of extra tools.

Nylon-line trimmer This is not an essential tool for the First-time Gardener, but it makes edging lawns and trimming long grass and weeds elsewhere in the garden easier. Make sure the model you buy has an automatic line-feed so you don't have to keep stopping to adjust the length of the cutting line.

Scarifyer A powered rake that makes light work of scratching accumulated dead grass clippings and debris from the lawn. Usually unnecessary, but can be rented if you desire.

4

instant improvements

There are many ways of making instant and dramatic improvements to your garden. Trimming and edging the lawn neatly, cleaning the patio, even weeding and covering the soil with an attractive mulch will make a difference. Adding a touch of coloured paint or stain to tired-looking fences and other garden structures is also quick and easy to do. If you want to go further, consider reshaping your lawn or adding one or two focal points such as a large terracotta pot or a statue. Both these changes will alter the way visitors view your garden, guiding gazes from one feature to the next.

Before making any changes, however, take into account the surroundings and scale of your garden. Large features should be sited with care because they can be imposing and dramatically alter the overall appearance and focus of your garden.

Creating an atmosphere

First impressions are very important in gardening. If you create an attractive gateway into your front garden and a welcoming path to the front door, your whole garden will be viewed in a new light by visitors. Use a combination of plants to provide year-round interest, so that regular visitors see something new with every visit. Position containers next to the front door and fill them with attractive displays to create a welcoming atmosphere. When planted with lush foliage, containers also can be used to soften areas of hard landscaping such as paving and walls. They can be used alone or in collections, or combined with another feature such as a set of steps or a garden seat **(1)**.

Buy colourful bedding or bulbs, such as tulips or lilies, in flower to dramatically improve your garden overnight **(2)**. Already planted hanging baskets and patio containers will also make an instant improvement.

Another way you can quickly transform the atmosphere in your garden is to buy plants that stimulate the senses. Add containers of scented plants along well-used paths and next to the patio or house where the aroma will be most appreciated. Also try including furry plants next to seating areas where they can be touched, and aromatic plants in between paving stones where they will be crushed underfoot and release their pungent scent (see page 56).

Adding focal points

By including one or two distinctive elements, such as an attractive container, ornament or dramatic-looking plant, you can instantly add points of focus in your garden.

Ornaments can be particularly useful for creating a sense of mystery, surprise or humour in your garden. A pair of rock towers **(3)**, for example, adds height and a sense of drama as well as the humour of knowing that such an unnatural stack should instantly collapse.

Containers can be used as a focal element in their own right or planted with eye-catching displays of flowers and placed anywhere in the garden. A trough placed in a raised stand and filled with potted lilies and chrysanthemums, for example, can add a splash of colour next to your house **(4).** The beauty of this arrangement is that when the flowers begin to fade they can

simply be removed and replaced with other potted plants or flowers which are just coming into bloom.

Make the most of small figurines by placing them on a plinth to raise them up or frame them in an arch to focus the eye. Larger human forms, such as busts or statues, tend to look most effective when partially hidden from view, among bamboos or grasses, for example. Animal figures usually look best positioned in a natural setting – a stork by water or a sleeping cat on a sunny wall are two good examples.

using colourful paints and stains

You can quickly turn drab features into something a bit special by using colourful paints and stains, which are widely available from DIY stores. They can be used all around the garden on wood, metal, stone or terracotta.

Choose a paint or stain that is suitable both for use out of doors and for the material you intend to cover. You must make sure that you prepare surfaces as directed, before applying the colour.

Using colours effectively

One of the most striking ways to use paints and stains is to choose a colour that already appears in your garden. This could be an existing paint or stain, the colour of paving or walls or the shade of flowers or foliage. A trellis at the back of a border, for example, will look all the more coordinated with its planting scheme if it's painted in the same colour as one of the main flowers within the border. Choose a flower that's in bloom for many weeks so that the effect is prolonged. Better still, add other plants with similar coloured blooms that flower at other times of year. On the other hand, you could choose a contrasting but complementary colour to make a feature out of a climber. If a wall painted bright yellow is used to support a purple clematis, for example, the effect could be quite startling. Again, it will last only as long as the climber stays in flower.

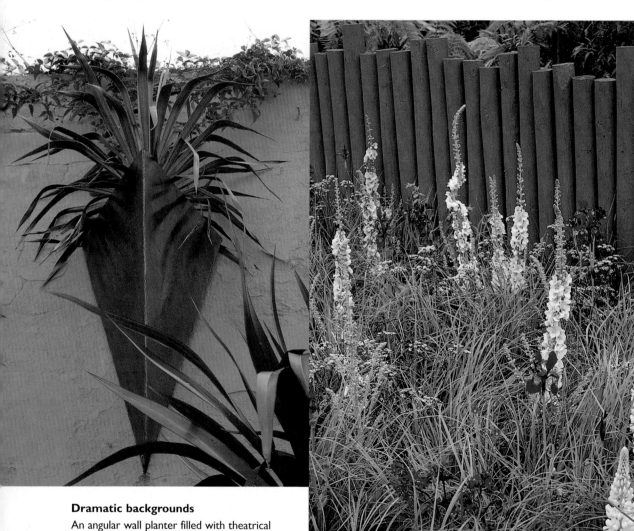

Dramatic backgrounds
An angular wall planter filled with theatrical foliage of yuccas contrasts with the deep orange-coloured wall (above); blue-stained poles provide a striking backdrop to a casual meadow garden (right).

As a rule, it is important not to have too many striking features in one garden. Otherwise they become counter-productive, effectively cancelling each other out. In areas where the summer sunshine is very strong and bleaches out subtle shades, however, you may need the dramatic contrast for the feature to be noticed at all.

Highlighting with colour

Paints and stains can be used to emphasise the existence of certain features such as ornate screens, arches or gates. Alternatively, you can use colours to turn eyesores into stylish and colourful features in themselves. A dilapidated shed, for example, can be transformed by adding finials to the roof and fancy fretwork along the eaves, and a windowbox or two at the side, before being painted with bright colours to look like a beach hut.

Paints or stains?

The range of coloured wood stains available is increasing all the time. Make sure you use water-based stains around plants and their supports, to prevent harming them, and the more effective solvent-based stains elsewhere.

Oil-based paints also can be used as long as you dilute them with turpentine (use 1 part paint to 2 parts turpentine). Specially mixed paints are best if you wish to create an exact shade.

Mix and match
A blue-stained pergola and matching trellis stand out against this garden's predominantly green planting scheme.

changing shapes and perspectives

Illusions play a part in most gardens, adding a sense of the unexpected. You can use various tricks to alter the perceptions of visitors and increase the sense of space. Most are easy to achieve and can be used in almost any garden.

Simple shapes

All garden designs are made up of a few simple shapes which have a considerable impact on the way the garden is viewed. Straight borders running down either side of a short garden, for example, would make it seem even shorter. One deep border that curves across the garden and into the bottom corner, however, would emphasise the longest dimension of the garden, making it seem larger than it really is.

Paths are also very directional elements – your eye is naturally led to where they end. If a path cuts right through a narrow garden, it can seem claustrophobic. You can prevent this by introducing changes in direction or obscuring the end of the path from view. Alternatively, try adding a focal point or an arch partway down the garden to form a visual break (see page 54).

Altering perspectives

Every view has natural lines of perspective. In the garden, you can redraw these lines to create an unreal sense of space. A garden fence that gets progressively shorter the further away it gets from the house, for example, will make the garden seem longer, as will a straight path that narrows as it goes down the garden. Emphasise the illusion by introducing a curve or two to make the path longer.

Colour and texture can be used to change the way we view a garden. Fine-textured plants, such as grasses and bamboos, or those with tiny leaves, such as box and berberis, tend to seem further away, while those with large leaves and strong outlines, such as a yucca, will appear closer than they really are. Similarly, bright whites and hot colours such as red, orange and yellow stand out in a border, while cool colours such as blue, gray, lilac and mauve have the opposite effect. Use this natural deception to your advantage to create the illusion of space where you need it. Any effect is most pronounced in the soft light at either end of the day.

1

Breaking up boundaries

Bare fences and walls not only look stark but they clearly mark the boundary line so that the garden can seem boxed-in. Disguising the boundaries or hiding them with plants can have the opposite effect. In a small garden, you can use climbers and wall shrubs as camouflage without taking up too much space. You don't need to clothe the whole boundary in foliage, but simply break up its strong outline. Further down the garden, a well-positioned specimen or two can do the trick. If your garden is larger, you can make the borders wider and include a range of trees and shrubs in your planting schemes.

When positioning plants, check they are having the desired effect from the places you are most likely to view the garden, such as from the patio or kitchen window. By varying the depth of borders and incorporating the tops of plants from neighbouring gardens or views, you can make any garden seem larger. Choose plants that blend in with those that can be seen outside to create a seamless transition.

Make the most of small spaces
Covering the high walls of this narrow passage with foliage and flowers **(1)** prevents it from feeling boxed-in, while the cool secluded seating area invites you to pause; climber-clad trellis **(2)** screens out the world without reducing the feeling of space in this roof garden; and tiers of hand-painted pots filled with clipped box and grape hyacinths **(3)** help break up this imposing boundary.

creating mystery and drama

All the best gardens have a distinct sense of drama and mystery that invites the visitor to explore. You can do this in your own garden by adding mirrors, creating concealed areas within the design or using garden dividers.

Rooms for improvement

Dividing a garden into small areas or 'rooms' using garden dividers is a good way of adding a sense of mystery. It also can make a small garden seem larger or a large garden more private.

Each 'room' can be used to showcase different styles or features, thereby creating a surprise around every corner as well as extending your gardening scope. One 'room', for example, could be a herb garden, another a vegetable garden and a third a wildlife area. Try to have a common theme linking all the areas – this could be the materials used to make the dividing screens, the paving materials, or the key plants within each 'room'.

In a small garden, a tranquil and secluded corner or 'room' can be created by adding a garden seat and a few plants, or a piece of trellis and a climber or two. To be effective, the corner needs to be in sun or shade (depending on your preference), and away from dripping trees or the noise of traffic. It also needs privacy and shelter, so you may have to increase the height of your boundary fence. You don't need a large screen to be effective, it just has to block or partially block the view of a feature or area beyond. A simple post covered in climbers strategically positioned can suffice. To ensure that you want to spend time in your secluded corner, add close-up interest, such as intricately marked flowers and foliage, and if possible an attractive view. Such areas also associate well with water features (see page 130).

In a large garden, you can divide the plot into roughly equal 'rooms' or have a main open area with hidden annexes slotted in around the edge. Where the garden is long and narrow, the area can be divided to form two or three roughly square compartments, with one leading onto the other. This is a good way of screening off unsightly utility areas used for storage – an ornamental garden with a lawn could lead onto a woodland garden which hides a shed or machinery at the end, for example.

Adding screens

Hedges, trellis and fences are the easiest way to divide a garden. Hedges can be neatly clipped for a formal garden or allowed to sprawl in an informal setting. Trellis and fences can be painted to stand out and as they take up little space, are ideal for small gardens. Trellis allows light to enter the garden, so it can be fairly tall without being imposing or claustrophobic.

Unexpected elements

Mirrors and perspective trellis (also called *trompe l'oeil*) can be used

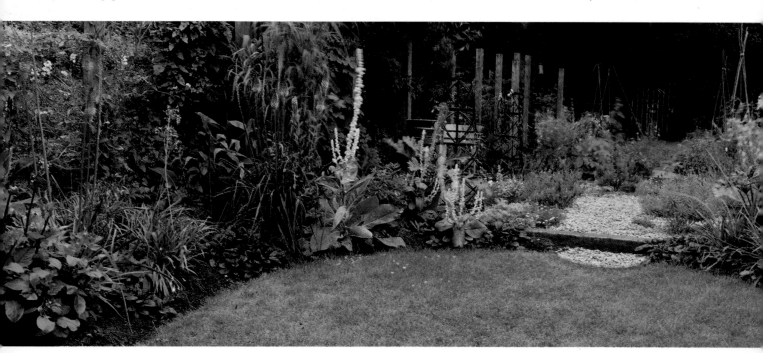

either separately or together in different parts of your garden to create drama and mystery.

A mirror adds light and a sense of space to the garden and so is especially effective in confined spaces. Position the mirror so that the reflection makes it seem like the garden continues beyond the wall. Angle it slightly so that you cannot see your own reflection and hide the edges to make it convincing. It doesn't have to be big: if framed to look like a small window, it can be very effective.

Secret corners

With a surprise around every corner, the different sections in this design (right) mimic the rooms of a house with a table and chairs in the 'dining room' and a bench in the 'lounge'. A gravel path or 'corridor' links the grassy lawn, bordered by colourful flowers, to two 'rooms' – a secluded seating area and a child's playground (below).

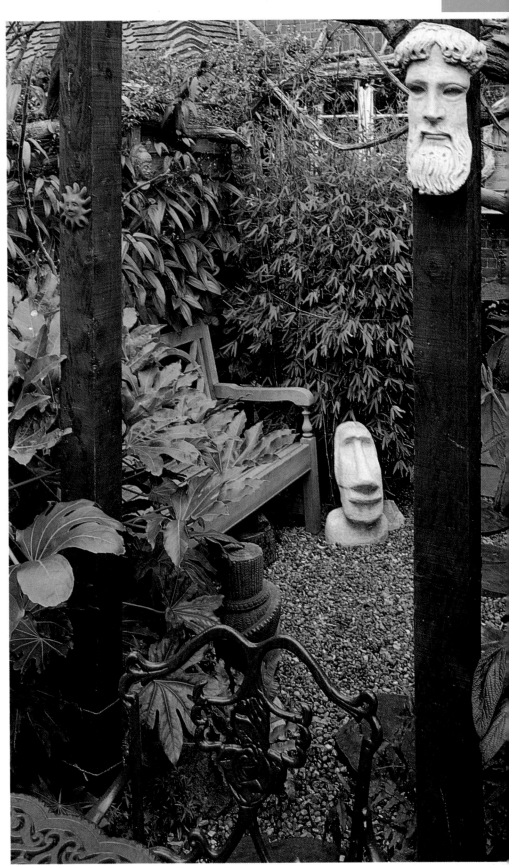

new approaches to garden design

Garden design has dramatically changed in recent years. The emphasis is no longer simply on the growing of plants, but on the expression of personality and the enjoyment of a convenient and pleasant outside space – a place to relax and reflect on our increasingly busy lives.

Rather than looking back to past glories for inspiration, most modern garden designers are pushing the boundaries of what we understand as gardening. They are using shapes, colours, textures, materials, proportion and, of course, plants, in challenging ways.

Getting inspiration

At gardening shows, many settings have become works of art, where the statement or concept lying behind the work is more important than the practicality. As snapshots they are thought-provoking and thoroughly enjoyable. But, in the real world, you cannot expect to maintain a garden of this type – real gardens evolve all the time, changing with every season and from one year to the next. Indeed, you probably wouldn't even want a very design-based garden, because such garden designs tend to be very personal expressions of their creators that are very unlikely to fit in with your particular needs or personality.

You can always learn from good design, however. Pick out individual elements that appeal, and build on those. Make a scrapbook of garden design ideas and features that you like. Cut out features from magazines and take photographs when visiting garden shows or friends' gardens. Visit famous gardens for inspiration, but most of all, experiment with your own ideas yourself. Don't be afraid to make mistakes – all the best gardeners and designers do.

1   2

Modern materials

Natural focal points, such as an upright conifer or a pond, are always popular for garden highlights. Wood, stone, and metal sculptures have been joined by lightweight cast-resin or plastic decorations, which look like natural materials but are usually much less expensive and easier to manoeuvre. For pathways and sitting areas, conventional flagstone, pebbles, and bricks have been joined by inexpensive wood chips and by pre-cast pavers that make installation a cinch. Adventurous gardeners can have fun incorporating unusual elements like seashells or flea-market finds. Glass chips can be used to great dramatic effect in a still pool of water – either forming sweeping curves or, as here, heaped into neat conical mounds which represent the piles of drying salt that were a vivid image from the creator's childhood in Vietnam **(1)**.

Sculptures imitating nature are nothing new, but there is something quite challenging about replacing plants with timeless sculptures **(2)**. The use of heaped stone chips in various colours along with the vertical cypress trees gives this garden a futuristic, even lunar look.

The combination of contrasting materials is a popular innovation. The galvanised planter **(3)** contains plants with dark foliage as a counterbalance. The deep purple phormium and the black grass-like *Ophiopogon planiscapus* 'Nigrescens' provides dramatic foliage. Pebbles create a sense of balance while the wooden decking provides changes in texture and colour.

New materials have enabled designers to challenge the thinking behind many traditional features, one of which is ponds. For example, in the courtyard garden design **(4)**, a curved water tank is used at the front of a raised bed. Water, pumped through the tank to flow like an endless river, creates a calming atmosphere. The bed behind the water tank is filled with sand and drought-tolerant plants, such as thrift, sedges and ornamental grasses, to provide a visual contrast to the running cool water alongside. The use of contrasting colours emphasises the overall effect.

2 essential features

Ground cover

Grass, plants or paving – however you choose to cover the ground will largely determine what you can use your garden for and how much time it will take to maintain.

The style and type of ground cover you use also will have a profound influence on the very nature and appearance of your garden's design. A well-planned and maintained area of lawn, for example, can improve the ambience of your entire garden. It even can become a key feature in its own right, helping to integrate all the different elements.

As a First-time Gardener, you have five basic ground cover options: a lawn or wildflower meadow; plants; loose gravel, stone, chippings or cobbles; wooden decking and various paving materials. Choosing one will produce a unified effect; combining them can create an exciting and modern design feature.

Before you make a final decision, it is important to consider what you want to use your garden for, how much time you are prepared to spend looking after it, and how much you can afford to spend on it. You also have to decide where your garden is sited. If it is in deep shade for much of the time, creating a lawn will be a struggle as the grass will become thin and patchy or be invaded by shade-tolerant weeds and mosses. Similarly, if your garden is on a steep slope, creating a lawn will be difficult and even dangerous to maintain – it would be better to create a ground covering of low-growing, well-behaved plants.

Bearing these things in mind, read on and use the design solutions outlined on the following pages to help you decide which material or materials will be most suitable for your garden floor.

plants or paving?

Though poets write of a garden as a green and pleasant place, and despite the obvious appeal and advantages of having a grassy outdoor patch, there are many other materials to choose from which are equally attractive and may be easier to maintain.

Lawns

Generally, lawns are easy to lay, require little gardening knowledge to maintain – as long as you have the right equipment (see page 24) – and offer a quick and attractive way of covering a large area of outdoor space for very little cost. Although it is possible to create a fine-quality, bowling-green-style lawn, it takes a great deal of effort and some skill to achieve. For the First-time Gardener, a far better bet is to opt for a hard-wearing, easily maintainable standard-quality lawn (often called a family or utility lawn).

To create a new lawn from scratch, you can either grow it from seed or lay turfs. Sowing seed is the cheapest and easiest option, but takes the longest to establish. If you want to create a lawn quickly, turfs can be ready for use in a matter of weeks, but they take more labour to lay and can be expensive.

Flowering lawns

If you have a large garden, covering the ground solely with grass may be impractical because this can take a lot of time to look after. If you really want a lawn, however, but do not have the time to maintain it, one option is to create a flowering lawn. To do this, either sow a special wildflower lawn mixture or plant native flowers and dwarf bulbs in groups in the existing lawn.

If you have very little spare time, try creating a wildflower lawn – one that you leave to grow naturally for most of the year. Filled with wildflowers, the grass needs cutting only twice: once during early spring and once after the flowers drop their seed (see page 44).

AT-A-GLANCE GROUND COVERING SELECTOR

TYPE	COST	WORK TO CREATE	WORK TO MAINTAIN	WEAR	GARDEN USES open areas	steep slopes	paths	patios & sitting areas
Family lawn	££	●●●	●●●●	●●●	✓	✗	✓	✗
Fine-quality lawn	£££	●●●●	●●●●●●	●	✓	✗	✗	✗
Wildflower meadow	£	●●●	●●●		✓	✗	✗	✗
Concrete	££	●●●●●	●	●●●●●	✓	✗	✓	✓
Paving slabs	££££	●●●●●	●	●●●●	✓	✗	✓	✓
Gravel	££	●●	●●●	●●●●	✓	✓	✓	✓
Bricks	£££	●●●●●	●●	●●●●●	✓	✗	✓	✓
Groundcover plants	££££	●●●	●●	●●●	✓	✓	✗	✓
Decking	££££	●●●	●●	●●●●	✓	✓	✓	✓
Bark or wood chips	£££	●●	●●	●●●	✓	✓	✓	✗

Successful partners
A combination of attractive paving materials with low-growing drought-tolerant plants help break up the appearance of this large area.

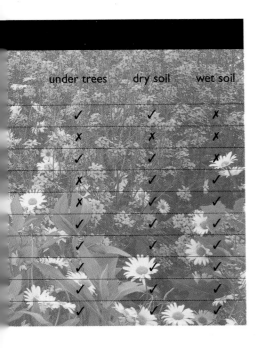

	under trees	dry soil	wet soil
	✓	✓	✗
	✗	✗	✗
	✓		✗
	✗	✓	✓
	✗	✓	✓
	✓		✓
	✓	✓	✓
	✓		✓
	✓	✓	✓

Groundcover plants

Low-growing plants are ideal for covering areas where a lawn is impractical, such as over a steep bank or in deep shade. They also are ideal for the novice because, apart from the occasional clean up in spring and after flowering, ground-cover plants require little mainten-ance. There are many types to choose from. Like lawn grass, it is important to buy a species that suits the location and climate in which you live (see page 160).

Some groundcover plants, like herbs, can be used to produce a 'virtual lawn'. Bear in mind, however, that even tough ground-cover plants cannot be used in areas that are constantly walked on. If you have a patch that gets only occa-sional use, try planting aromatic herbs such as thymes, which release their pungent scent when they are trodden underfoot.

Paving

The wonderful selection of materials available today can enhance the appearance of a garden and provide a practical, easy-care all-weather surface. It is ideal for heavily worn areas or for providing a flat, durable surface for garden furniture or a barbecue. Paving, however, can be fairly expensive as well as difficult and hard work to lay, especially if the area is sloping. Once it is laid, however, it is virtually maintenance free.

Loose materials

Gravel, stone chippings and cobbles are cheap, hard-wearing and easy to lay, so are ideal for areas where paving is impractical. Periodical weed control and raking may be necessary to keep them tidy. Loose materials are easier on the eye than great expanses of paving. They can be used to blanket the ground

Steps to success when covering the ground

- If you want a lawn or ground-cover plants, it is important to select species that suit the light levels and climate in your garden.

- Choose the surface that best fits your available maintenance time and how you plan to use your garden.

- If your budget and time is limited, you should start with a low-cost, low-maintenance option; change when time and money permit.

between plants helping to prevent weeds. They lessen evaporation from the soil surface, thus reducing the need for regular watering.

Wood chips or shredded bark are good options if you want to create a natural-looking area around any trees or shrubs.

For a highly modern design effect, try glass chips. This special glass is tumbled to remove any sharp edges and by using the many colours available you can create some exquisite designs.

Decking

If you want a natural look or to create a sitting area on a slope or a raised platform, decking is the material of choice. It doesn't need to be constructed on a flat surface and the wood is cut to fit, so it can be tailor-made for any situation. Construction is fairly easy, and the deck can be stained any colour you want. Decking tiles also can be laid directly on top of an existing flat surface such as an old patio or terrace.

creating a new lawn

There are several grades of lawn – each is made up of a different blend of several species of grasses. The one you choose should fit in with how much wear it will get and how much time you are willing to spend maintaining it. If you want a general-purpose lawn that is easy to look after and is reasonably hard-wearing, choose a standard-quality grade. Special mixtures for shade and wildflower meadows also are available. Make sure you check the information on the seed packets and ask your local supplier for advice if you are unsure which blend to choose.

Preparing the site

Whether you sow seed or lay turfs, thorough ground preparation is vital to prevent problems occurring later. The first task is to remove any perennial weeds, such as dandelion. Dig them out by hand, or if you prefer, apply an appropriate herbicide at least a month before turfs are delivered or seed is sown. When the weeds are dead, the soil needs to be dug to the depth of a full spade's blade (about 20 cm) and all large clods broken up. The soil should then be roughly levelled using a soil rake and any large stones removed.

Leave the site to settle for a week, then firm the soil by treading the whole area using shuffling small steps with the weight on your heels.

After that, the soil should be raked to even out any lumps or hollows. About a week before sowing the seed or laying sod, scatter some general-purpose granular fertiliser, a handful per square yard, over the soil and rake it into the surface.

Laying turf

The best time to lay turfs is when the grass is dormant from autumn through early spring, as long as the soil isn't frozen or so wet that it sticks to boots and tools. You can also lay a lawn successfully in summer, but regular watering is necessary until the grass is established. If the area to be covered is not clearly defined, use sand to mark it out. This will make it easier

Sowing grass seed evenly

To get a good-looking lawn, it is important to scatter the seed evenly over the surface. Use the following method to get best results. Choose a warm day when the surface of the soil is dry, but moist underneath.

- Use string and bamboo canes to divide the area into one-metre-square blocks. Measure a quarter of the amount of seed required for each square metre in a plastic cup. Mark this level on the cup and use it as a quick measure.

- Begin walking east to west and carefully scatter the seed in your cup evenly over the first block. Refill, and repeat for each block.

- Then turn around and repeat this process walking from west to east. When you get to the end, each square will have received half of its seed.

- Now, repeat the whole process walking north to south and then south to north. Each square metre will now have received four quarter measures of seed sown as evenly as possible.

- Rake the seed into the surface and cover the area with fine-mesh netting to keep the birds off. Water the whole area with a garden sprinkler and keep well watered until the grass has become established.

- When the grass is about 5 cm high, walk over the lawn and remove any stones that have come to the surface. Then roll the lawn using a garden roller, or the rear roller of a heavy lawnmower. Make the first cut when the grass is dry, the blades of the mower set high – at least 4 cm.

to estimate the number of turfs required. It is important to lay turfs as soon as possible after delivery, preferably the same day. If weather conditions make laying the turfs impossible, unroll each turf in a shady spot and give it a light watering to keep it moist, healthy and pliable.

Looking after a new lawn

Once laid, your lawn should be well watered using a garden sprinkler and kept moist until the turfs have knitted together. Keep the edges of the turfs especially moist because they are prone to drying out and can shrink to leave unsightly cracks. Don't walk on your new lawn for at least a month, except to trim the grass with the blades of the lawnmower set high (for details,

check your mower's instructions). During periods of drought, the new lawn should be watered thoroughly every few weeks during its first growing season.

Flowering lawns and ground cover plants

Add colour to the edge of your lawn by planting random groups of bulbs such as bluebells, crocuses, snake's head fritillaries, daffodils and snowdrops. Keep them in clumps to make them easier to mow around in spring. If you want the whole lawn to flower, either sow a wildflower and grass seed mixture, or add wildflower plants, such as bird's foot trefoils, sweet violets or celandines to an existing lawn. To create a spring-flowering meadow include cowslip, cow parsley, lesser

stitchworts, cuckoo flowers, lady's smocks, hawkbits, daffodils and summer snowflakes. For a summer-flowering meadow garden, use greater knapweed, field scabious, sorrel, speedwell and yarrow.

Good ornamental plants to choose as an alternative to a lawn include ajuga, bergenia, heaths and heathers, hosta, *Cotoneaster dammeri*, epimedium, heuchera, nepeta, groundcover roses, and periwinkle. Also try herbs, such as chamomile (choose the non-flowering variety 'Trenague') and creeping thymes.

Laying a new lawn with turfs

Before you lay your turfs, it is important to water the soil until it is thoroughly, but evenly, moist.

1 Roll out the first strip of turf along one side of your new lawn area using a straight edge, such as a plank, as a guide. Lay out the second strip of turf, butting it up closely to the first. Press each strip down using the back of a

spade. Continue to lay the strips, using two short planks to stand on the area of grass that you have already laid.

   To prevent the joints lining up together, stagger the turfs in alternate rows, like bricks in a wall. Use whole turf strips at the edges and place any filler pieces within the main area where they are less likely to dry out.

2 Use a mixture of equal-parts soil and sand to fill any cracks between the turf. Trim the turfs using a sharp spade guided by a plank along straight edges, and a stiff piece of hose around curves.

3 Flatten any lumps by jumping on the plank, working your way across the lawn.

maintaining a perfect lawn

Whether you've planted a new lawn or need to maintain an existing one, it doesn't take much effort to keep it looking good.

Trimming and mowing

Regular trimming and mowing are the secrets to a healthy lawn. These can be fun and satisfying pastimes provided your equipment is well maintained and you don't let the grass get too long (see FAQs, opposite). Installing a mowing strip (see page 49) can make mowing easier and cut down on trimming.

Keep it simple

Lawns with sweeping curves are easier to mow as you don't have to manoeuvre the mower around corners.

If you have a particularly dense, lush lawn it is worth removing the build-up of dead grass shoots (known as *thatch*) before it smothers and weakens the grass. Do this by giving your lawn a vigorous raking (known as *scarifying*). You can use a wire rake to tackle small areas but would be better off renting a powered scarifier for larger ones. If your lawn contains moss, treat this first (see opposite). If your grass is growing well and has good colour, ignore the thatch; it will naturally decompose and feed the lawn.

You also should clear your lawn of any fallen leaves because they can weaken the grass if left. If you have a small lawn, you can clear it using a wire rake or garden vacuum; larger areas are easier to clear using a leaf sweeper or a rotary mower with the blades set to the highest level (see operating instructions).

Weed control

Many gardeners prefer to tolerate or even learn to appreciate the diversity of weeds in their grass. However, if you want to improve the appearance of your lawn, remove isolated weeds by digging them out using an old kitchen knife, making sure you remove as much of the carrot-like, tap-rooted weeds as possible, or treat them using a dab-on weedkiller. If the weed problem is more widespread, treat the whole lawn with a special lawn weedkiller. Buy one that contains fertiliser, as

shape up your lawn

Lawns needn't be boring rectangles – you could jazz up your garden with a more interesting design. A lawn, however, should have a calming influence on a garden's structure and a simple shape will look best. Over-complicated designs are less easy on the eye, awkward to mow and have more edges, so they take longer to trim.

Fortunately, changing the shape of a lawn is very easy. Mark out your shape using a hosepipe for curved lines and bamboo canes for straight ones. Stand back and view how it looks from all angles, making the necessary adjustments until you are completely satisfied. To get a perfect right-angle, make a 3-4-5 triangle out of rough timber (see page 11). To create a perfect circle, mark out the circumference using sand dribbling through a hole in the bottom of a container, guiding your hand with string tied to a stake at the circle's centre.

this also will feed your lawn. You should apply weedkillers in early summer when the grass and weeds are growing strongly, but before the weeds flower and spread their seed.

Controlling moss

Moss can be a problem in a shady lawn or following a wet winter. Luckily, it is easy to eradicate using a chemical mosskiller; a combined feed and moss treatment can give your lawn a boost at the same time. If part or all of your lawn is regularly colonised by moss, adjust the cutting height of your mower, improve drainage (see below) and thin out any overhanging shrubs.

The cutting edge

A neat edge is the *pièce de résistance* of a perfect lawn. If your soil is light or sandy and crumbles easily, it may be necessary to recut your lawn edge every spring to keep it sharp. To do this, make a vertical cut around the edge of your lawn about 7.5 cm deep using a sharp spade or a special half-moon edging iron. Use a plank as a guide for straight lines or a hosepipe for curved lines. Ease the handle of the cutting tool toward you to create an even gully with a vertical edge. Discard the trimmed pieces of grass to prevent them from rooting in the border, causing a weed problem.

Improving drainage

If your lawn is used regularly during the summer months, the soil underfoot can become compacted, preventing surface drainage and restricting the amounts of air and water that are available at root level. To overcome these problems, aerate your lawn during early autumn using a garden fork for small areas or a powered aerator for large ones. Make sure the holes are at least 7.5 cm deep and spaced about 5 cm apart over the affected area. If you are using a garden fork, wiggle the handle around to enlarge the size of the hole. After aerating, apply a dressing of equal-parts sieved garden soil and sharp sand and brush into the holes.

FAQs – LAWNCARE

Q **When should I start cutting my new lawn?**
A Start mowing when the grass is about 6 cm long. Set the cutting height of the mower to 4 cm.

Q **How often do I need to cut my lawn?**
A During the growing season, cut the grass at least once a week if you have a family lawn, twice that for a fine quality lawn. Frequent mowing promotes thick and healthy grass that will be too dense to be colonised by weeds.

Q **How short should I cut my lawn?**
A Do not cut the grass too short because you will weaken it. After the first few cuts, aim to trim the grass by about one-third, cutting it no shorter than 2 cm for a family lawn and 1 cm for a fine-quality lawn. During a prolonged dry spell, raise the cutting height of your mower blades by 1 cm, to help the grass cope with drought. In the autumn, raise the cutting height to this level anyway and continue to mow as necessary until the grass stops growing. Do not mow if the lawn is waterlogged or frosted.

Q **Can I leave the clippings on the lawn?**
A Provided you mow regularly, the clippings can be left on the lawn to feed the grass as they decompose. If the clippings are longer than 2 cm, collect them and place on the compost heap (see page 168).

Q **How often should I trim the edges of a lawn?**
A Trim the edges at least once every other cut to keep it looking its best. Use long-handled edging shears to save strain on your back. If you have a large lawn you may want to invest in a powered edger or a nylon-line trimmer to make the job easier. The latter is particularly versatile and can be used to cut rough grass and weeds all around the garden.

improving your lawn

A neglected lawn often contains bare patches, caused by overgrown trees and shrubs, straggly edges and bumps and hollows due to tree roots. It also may make mowing more difficult.

Treating bare patches

Trees and shrubs overhanging the edges of a lawn starve the grass of sufficient light and so it is weakened and it eventually dies. When this occurs, ugly bare patches develop and shade-tolerant weeds start to take over. In order to overcome this problem, you can either reduce the size of your lawn by recutting the edge away from the overhanging shrub, or thin out the canopy of the overhanging plant to allow more light through and re-seed the area with a shade-tolerant mixture of grass seed (see page 44).

If one area of your lawn is used more than any other, such as around the barbecue or under a child's swing set, you could provide reinforcement. Replace the grass with a more durable material – gravel or bark chippings, for example – or protect the area with hard-wearing green plastic mesh. Buy this from your garden centre, then simply peg it into position over the precut area of lawn and allow the grass to grow up through the mesh to hide it. Then, re-sow any bare patches.

Tackling troublesome roots

Hills and troughs can make a lawn look poorly maintained, especially during the summer when lumps get scalped by the blades of the lawnmower and hollows show up as patches of lush, green grass. One of the main causes of a lawn's unevenness are tree roots growing just below the surface. Remove roots as described opposite ('Repairing lumps and hollows'), or raise the

Dealing with damaged edges

A carelessly placed foot while mowing or playing can damage the lawn edge. This can be repaired without recutting the outer shape.

1 Using a garden spade, cut a rectangle of grass that includes the damaged area.

2 Use the spade to cut under the grass evenly, so it is about 2 cm thick. Then, turn the grass patch around so the damaged area is within the lawn.

3 Now, fill the gap and any holes and cracks with good garden soil, and sow with a grass seed that matches the quality of your lawn (choose a shade-tolerant type for shady areas). Press the seed into the surface using the back of a soil rake.

Then water well using a watering can which produces a fine spray; take care not to wash away any seed. Finally, cover with garden fleece material or fine-mesh netting held down by stones. This protects the seeded area from the birds and keeps it moist. Remove the protective covering once germination begins.

level of your lawn over a period of time. To do this, you should mix equal-parts of sieved soil and sharp sand and sprinkle a thin layer evenly over the lawn every couple of months during the growing season. Do not add more than 1 cm at any one time, however, and never bury the grass completely.

Some trees also throw up shoots (known as *suckers*) from roots which can disfigure the appearance of a lawn. To remove these, you need to expose the root and point of origin of each sucker, and then pull off each sucker by giving it a sharp tug. Don't prune off the suckers at ground level, though, because this will simply encourage the roots to produce further, even more vigorous, suckers.

Making a mowing strip

Installing paving slabs or bricks around the edge of the grass can help to frame your lawn as well as provide all-weather access right around your garden. It will also mean you spend far less time trimming the edges and it makes mowing far easier.

To lay a mowing strip, dig a trench around the lawn, which is 7.5 cm deeper than your slabs or bricks. Fill the trench with a 7.5 cm layer of ready-mixed dry concrete. Place the slabs or bricks on top of the concrete, tapping them down to ensure that they are level with each other and the lawn. Now, brush dry mortar mix between the bricks or slabs, water well and allow to set. The strip is now ready.

Repairing lumps and hollows

Individual lumps and hollows can be tackled in the following way. If, however, a large area of your lawn is uneven, you would be better off raising the level of the lawn instead (see 'Tackling troublesome roots', left).

- For either a lump or hollow, make an H-shaped cut about 30 cm wide and 45 cm high. Use a sharp spade and centre the cut over the offending area.

- Carefully cut under the grass on both sides to produce two even flaps about 2 cm thick. Then, peel back the flaps making sure they do not tear or crack.

- Using a garden fork, loosen the surface under the grass flaps and remove any buried debris, such as rubble, that could be causing the problem.

- Add or remove soil as necessary to level the area, before firming and relaying the two flaps of grass. Check the area is level with a straight piece of timber.

- Finally, fill any cracks with an equal-parts mixture of sieved garden soil and sharp sand, then water thoroughly.

Using a mowing strip
A line of bricks or slabs can make mowing easier. Make sure you run the mower right over the brick strip to keep the edges trim.

easy-care garden surfaces

Joe and Marsha Fraser have two sons aged eight and ten and wanted to turn their dreary suburban garden into an attractive place for the entire family to relax yet provide enough space for the children to play. They are a busy family, so couldn't afford to spend too much time on routine maintenance. Marsha is interested in foliage plants and the whole family was keen to have a lawn. They were looking for a design that would incorporate a range of low-maintenance features, which are easy to keep looking good and well able to withstand the wear and tear that comes with two energetic children. The garden is south facing and slopes slightly towards a copse of mature trees which casts quite a lot of shade, especially in winter.

Somewhere to sit

The Frasers wanted a patio where they could sit and enjoy the garden, but didn't want an ordinary patio. They liked the idea of gravel, but this wasn't a practical option so close to the house because there was no doubt that with two lively children the small stones would find their way inside.

If you are in a similar situation, a good alternative that offers the look and feel of gravel but the convenience of paving is called bonded gravel. Rather than being loose, the gravel is bound together by a resin, which keeps it in place and forms a firm surface; ask your local garden centre or builders' merchant for details – you will have to get a professional contractor to lay it for you.

The Frasers needed quite a large area of paving, so to help break up the expanse they decided to create a patchwork effect using lines of frost-proof bricks to form borders between squares of paving. Marsha, who works as a film editor, particularly liked the idea of continuing the same design for the path across the lawn because it gives the impression of a strip of negatives. This paving not only helps to link the patio and lawn areas, but also forms an all-weather path to the woodland play area at the bottom of the garden. A couple of the squares near the edge of the paved area have been planted with a range of drought-tolerant plants, such as ornamental grasses, to help soften the impact of the regimented lines.

Making the patchwork

Laying a path is a relatively easy task and well within the scope of the confident First-time Gardener. Joe decided he would construct the paths himself, but hired a professional contractor to help him lay the paving patchwork.

To make the paths, Joe first needed to ensure that they were laid on strong foundations. To achieve this, he dug a 15 cm deep trench, slightly wider than the length of a brick, along each line of the patchwork pattern. Next he placed a 7.5 cm deep layer of dry concrete mix along each trench and then rammed it down firmly. Moisture from the soil was absorbed by the dry concrete mixture causing it to set firm. Once the concrete foundations had set, Joe laid the frost-proof bricks on a bed of mortar on top of the foundation layer, checking they were level and perfectly straight. He used spacers between the bricks to ensure that all the gaps were even. Lastly he filled the gaps with mortar, carefully smoothing the surface using a small piece of hose and clearing away any excess. The contractor firmed the base in each of the patchwork squares to leave the top 2 cm to be filled with the bonded gravel.

Low-maintenance lawn

To make cutting the grass easier, bricks have been laid around the edges of the lawn to form a mowing strip (see page 49) so that the lawnmower could pass straight over the top when mowing – practically eliminating the need for edge trimming. Although quite dramatic in appearance, the design of the lawn is in fact very simple, making it remarkably quick and easy to maintain.

The existing lawn was so patchy that the Frasers wanted to start again. They decided to lay a new lawn using turfs that contained a reasonably hard wearing blend of grasses. This type of lawn can cope with seasonal wear if you have children who enjoy playing in the garden, but still looks good. What's more, it doesn't need to be mown as often as a lawn containing finer grasses.

Long-lasting borders

The design contains two feature borders, one narrow and one deep, running down either side of the lawn. It is essential to cover all the bare soil with foliage so that weeds have less opportunity to become established. Before planting, the borders were thoroughly dug over and all the weeds, including the roots, were painstakingly removed. Marsha decided she wanted to grow a lot of foliage plants with some flowers providing seasonal variation and interest.

Instead of annual bedding plants that would need to be replaced every year, a combination of permanent edging plants are used in both borders. For foliage contrast, Marsha chose a variety of evergreen groundcover plants, including bergenia for its large rounded leaves, the variegated grass *Holcus mollis* 'Variegata' and the multicoloured *Ajuga reptans* 'Burgundy Glow'. In the narrow border, long-living trouble-free perennials including euphorbias, sedums and hardy

geraniums have been added. In the deep border, they have included shrubs, such as variegated dogwood, photinia and euonymus, which do not require regular pruning, are not susceptible to pest and disease attack and are tough enough to cope with the occasional football. All the beds are covered with a 7.5 cm layer of bark chips to keep the ground moist and to suppress weeds.

At the bottom of the garden a 7.5 cm layer of bark chips was also used to cover the soil between the trees and shrubs at the end of the garden to enhance the woodland effect and prevent weeds.

Blurring the edges
The different ground covers of paving, lawn and plants in this garden have been integrated successfully by allowing one element to run into the other.

Woodland floor
Between the mature trees at the end of the garden (above), a layer of bark chips was put down to create a natural looking, weed-suppressing ground cover.

a sun deck for all seasons

Jenny and Matthew Lawrence have a young daughter, Helen, age three, and have bought a house on the outskirts of town with superb views of the nearby hills. The garden faces southeast, so the Lawrences would like to take full advantage of all the sun it gets. They wanted an area outside the house where they could entertain friends, but would also provide some shade during the height of the summer. Paving would be too hot in their situation, so they decided on decking. As well as being quick and fairly easy to install, decking is also very versatile and can be adapted to fit any garden.

The first decisions

If you are adept at making home improvements, installing decking in your garden will be well within your capabilities. Otherwise, it is a quick (and therefore relatively inexpensive) job for a contractor. Before you commit yourself to anything, however, you must first consider exactly where you want the decking, its overall dimensions, and how much you are prepared to spend. Decking can be constructed from the naturally durable Western red cedar or pressure-treated softwood, both of which are available in kit form from decking suppliers. If your budget is tight, you can also build decking from rough-sawn softwood prepared for use outdoors, such as fence posts and gravel boards that are available from timber merchants and fencing suppliers. These will create a more rustic effect.

The Lawrences decided upon a cedar deck to run the full width of their garden, with a stepped front edge so that they wouldn't need a hand rail that would interfere with the view. To provide shade in summer, they opted to include a pergola covering about half of the deck, and added outdoor lighting so the deck could be used well into the evening.

Designing the deck

Planning is the key to a well-designed and constructed deck, so it is a good idea to make an accurate plan of your garden on graph paper before you go any further. Permanent features such as drain access covers and trees should be indicated. To help them visualise their design, the Lawrences marked out the area on the ground with pegs and string and used a second line to indicate the level of the final surface.

Once you are happy with the overall design, you should consider making a detailed plan of the decking construction if you are intending to build the deck yourself; this will make it easier to estimate the amount of timber you will need and, therefore, reduce waste later on. It is particularly important to get the overall width right, taking account of the width of each plank and the spacing between the planks to allow for drainage.

Building the base and top

The Lawrences hired a couple of specialist decking contractors to build their deck, who made quick work of the job. They first put together a frame for the decking and fixed this to sturdy posts concreted into the ground. Next they covered the ground with a special weed-proof

All hands on deck

A large area of decking was constructed so that dinner parties could be enjoyed on warm, summer evenings. Most of the garden was planted in lawn with feature plants adding structure and colourful flowers offering seasonal interest.

snowdrops and snowflakes appear in the soil around the tree, complemented beautifully by spring-flowering crocuses and daffodils which have been planted in the surrounding lawn. To help the different elements of the design to blend together, timber identical to the decking has been used to construct a garden seat and a series of frames down one side of the garden to support a variety of fruit crops. The shed at the end of the garden was converted into a playhouse for Helen and her friends. This has a small courtyard surrounded by a picket fence to keep them safe but still in view of her parents sitting on the deck at the other end of the garden.

landscape fabric to stop weeds growing underneath. The top of the deck was then clad with planks. The contractors fixed the two outermost planks in position first, and then laid the rest roughly in position, evenly spaced about 5 mm apart. The planks were then hammered into place and trimmed to leave about a 2 cm overhang on all sides. So that a drain inspection cover could be easily accessed, the planks over its top were cut and then secured with rust-resistant screws (pictured far left).

Seasonal features

Colour is provided in the form of potted plants. In the summer, the Lawrences used bedding plants such as coleus, marigolds, cineraria, and lobelia combined with spiky phormiums. In the spring and autumn, they added bright and cheerful potted bulbs. A variety of climbers have been encouraged to cover the pergola and other vertical surfaces. Up the posts in the middle of the deck, Jenny planted climbers that would eventually be trained right over the top to provide extra shade, and jasmine for its delicious scent. Passion flowers were also planted in tubs and trained up the walls of the house.

The majority of the rest of the garden is covered with lawn with a multi-stemmed silver birch as a focal point. The birch comes into its own in the spring when bulbs such as

A YEAR LATER. . . CLIMBING PLANTS

Once climbers have become established, they very quickly grow and cover their supports. Jenny used vertical wires attached to each post and along the overhead horizontal timbers of the pergola to make training the climbers as easy as possible. The scented jasmine (pictured) planted against one of the posts in the middle of the deck is a particular favourite with visitors because it fills the evening air with its fragrance from early summer until autumn.

Leading you
down the garden path

Paths are an important element of any garden design so should be given careful consideration. They not only provide access from one area to another, but their style will influence the rest of the garden.

Paths are very directional and suggest movement in the garden design. The straighter, narrower and flatter the path, the more it encourages us to move on. On the other hand, a gently curving path will invite the user to pause at every turn and appreciate his or her surroundings. In the picture opposite, two contrasting paving materials have been combined to create a spiral mosaic half way down the path. The effect is quite startling; not only does it add humour to the scene but an ingenious central focus is given to the path.

Selecting a style
The style of path should reflect the overall design of the garden. It is a good idea to repeat the paving theme used elsewhere in the garden to help the different features to gel. In a formal garden, for example, a straight path laid in a regular pattern will reinforce the geometric shapes used elsewhere. However, if you want the paths to be less obvious, try combining two or more flat paving materials in various sizes and colours.

In an informal cottage garden, a path can simply meander between features. Use loose materials, such as gravel or wood chips, which are easy to lay in curves, or put down small block pavers or bricks in an informal pattern. Allow plants to spill over to hide the edges and, on occasionally used sections, plant the cracks with tough aromatic plants (see page 56).

Creating illusions
A straight formal path laid directly down the garden can make a short garden seem smaller. To counteract this effect in a formal garden design, incorporate a change in direction such as a zigzag, or create the illusion of depth by tapering the path so that it gets narrower the further away it is from the house. Another design trick is to use diagonal paths that run across the garden, making the plot seem larger. Or you can let the path disappear from view behind a garden feature and when it reappears, make it visually different by changing the material it is made from or its width.

Choosing materials
The frequency and type of use a path gets should influence the materials and construction. If the path is to withstand heavy weight, the foundations will need to be deeper and the paving material stronger. Where a path gets only occasional foot traffic, simply laying slabs or other materials on firmed soil would suffice.

For a hard-wearing path that you can use in all weathers, choose bricks, blocks or concrete slabs; the latter are available in a range of sizes, shapes and finishes (see page 58). In an informal garden design, hard paving materials can be combined with loose gravel or pebbles, to soften their appearance. All-gravel paths are a practical option in many gardens because they are very easy to lay. Bear in mind, however, that pebbles on their own are uncomfortable to walk on, so suitable only for an occasional path. Another option for a rarely used path is grass.

Wood has natural appeal, too, and can be laid to create formal or informal effects. It is reasonably easy to construct and very versatile so can be adapted to fit any situation. Wood can also be stained to complement or contrast with its surroundings. Rough-sawn timber produces splinters and planed timber or wood blocks become slippery when wet or covered in frost, so it is a good idea to cover them with wire mesh to provide grip in shady areas. Alternatively, use specially prepared decking timber which is rot resistant and grooved to provide a non-slip surface.

Combining colours and textures
A spiral mosaic design using a variety of materials focuses the eye on the middle of the garden **(1)**; small-leaved ivies have been cleverly trained along the risers of a set of steps to soften the edges **(2)**; pieces of sawn timber make a natural edge to an informal path **(3)**; and a stained boardwalk adds colour contrast to a garden setting **(4)**.

paved patios

A flat, hard and strong surface is a useful one on which to place a barbecue or an outdoor table and chairs. Ideally, a patio should be positioned close to the house where it is convenient to use in an area that gets sun for much of the day. This is easiest to achieve in south-facing gardens. If the best view is from the side of your house, however, there is no reason why you shouldn't build a patio in this position. If you have a north-facing back garden, the best place for a patio may be away from your house where it catches the sun for most of the day.

Planning your patio

A patio needs to be sited on reasonably flat ground; otherwise you will have to invest a lot of time and labour building retaining walls, steps and terraces. You also need to consider how your patio will integrate into the rest of the garden's design, particularly in a small garden where the paved area will take up a higher proportion of the available space. Useful techniques, such as echoing the paving materials elsewhere in the garden or softening the edges of the paved area with plants (as described on the opposite page), both work well.

You can also use the paving stones to create interesting shapes – don't feel that you have to stick to square or rectangular paving stones. Another useful design idea to consider is to lay a path that curves away from the patio area and into the garden so that it disappears behind a border or another feature in the distance. This not only leads your eye away from the patio, but entices the casual observer to explore the rest of your garden.

If you decide that the best place for your patio is away from the house, make sure that you include a reasonably direct all-weather path between the two, so that your patio is easy to reach and will, therefore, be used on regular occasions (see page 54 for ideas).

Avoid positioning your patio under overhanging trees with large leaves that tend to drip for a long time after a rain shower or under lime and maple trees, which attract sap-sucking insects that will shower the area with sticky honeydew, making it unpleasant to use.

Once you have decided on the position and design of your patio, you could think about temporary or permanent screens, which can provide privacy from neighbours and shelter from cool breezes.

Concrete paver finishes

Brushed A finish that looks like broom brush marks in wet concrete.
Cobbled A multi-block finish to look like cobbles, bricks or other small unit paving.
Exposed aggregate The surface of the concrete slab is studded with exposed pieces of gravel.
Riven A weathered appearance that looks like natural flag stones.
Stippled The surface is covered by a series of raised lines or spots for a non-slip finish. This is ideal for shady areas where algae can make smooth paving slippery.

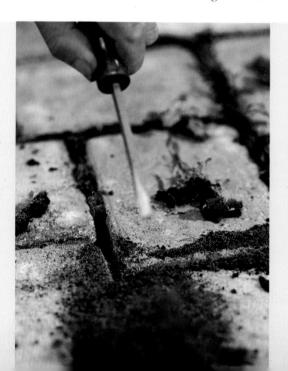

Adding texture to a paved area

Sow seeds of flowering plants such as aubrieta in the cracks between paving slabs to provide colour and interest. Wide crevices can be planted with small plug plants for a more instant effect.

- Use a screwdriver to remove the weeds, complete with their roots, then clear the soil and other debris from the crack to a depth of at least 7.5 cm (see picture, left), deeper if possible. Fill the crack with loam-based compost,

pushing it into place with a piece of wood or a bamboo cane.

- Level and firm the surface, then scatter seed thinly on the crack. Cover with sieved compost, then water using a watering can with a fine rose attached.

- When seedlings emerge, thin any overcrowded ones by removing the weakest. Once established, trickle a layer of fine gravel between the plants.

Choosing materials

A patio can be made of either a hard surface such as paving slabs or bricks, or a loose material such as gravel. Gravel also can be laid to form a solid surface if mixed with a bonding agent, such as resin. In general, hard surfaces require the most ground preparation and are hard work to lay, but are practically maintenance free. Loose materials tend to be less expensive and easy to install, but are less convenient to use and need seasonal maintenance such as weeding and raking.

When choosing a material, match it if you can to those already used in other parts of your house or garden. To make large expanses of paving appear less imposing, break them up with another type of material that contrasts in shape, texture and colour – gravel, lava rock or cobbles are ideal. Try to avoid using more than three materials in any one area; otherwise the effect will look too busy. To make the laying easier, make sure that the different materials are all of the same thickness.

There is a wide range of paving materials on the market. Concrete pavers are the most common and available in a wide range of sizes, shapes, colours and finishes to suit most situations (see the list above left). Some are available in several sizes which neatly fit together to form a more interesting paved pattern. Frost-proof bricks, glazed tiles and flagstone are other, more expensive options. They can be more difficult to lay evenly, however, so you may prefer to hire professional help.

Creating planting pockets

Add interest and a splash of colour to your patio by using a variety of low-growing plants within the patio area. Plants can soften and break up large areas of stark concrete and prevent your patio appearing bleak and bare.

The best plants are those which are drought-tolerant such as acaena, alchemilla, dianthus, diascia, sempervivums, smaller sedums and ornamental grasses. Around the edge, use mat-forming, aromatic plants such as camomile and creeping thymes, which can stand up to occasional foot traffic.

1 Using a spade, ease up the slab and set to one side. Push a strip of old carpet under the spade to prevent it from damaging the surrounding paving.

2 Remove any gravel under the slab and then loosen the soil underneath. Dig out the soil to a depth of 30 cm and replace it with fresh soil. While the plants are still in their pots, water them and allow to drain. Place the plants, while still in their pots, on the planting area and adjust the arrangement until you achieve a pleasing result.

3 Plant the largest specimens first, then fill in the gaps with the smaller plants. (If you are using bulbs, see page 60 for instructions on planting.)

4 Water the plants thoroughly and then mulch with gravel, stone chippings or pebbles that either contrast with or complement the colours of the paving.

Flower borders

No garden is complete without a generous selection of flowers. They herald the changes from one month to the next, providing seasonal variation in hue, form and texture. Some, such as early spring bulbs, produce wonderful blooms for a few short weeks; while others, such as reliable summer bedding, last for several months, creating an unbroken succession of colour and interest.

Flowers can be classified according to how long they live and the way they grow. The annuals and biennial types bloom for one season only, but perennial flowers and bulbs can last for many years. Flowers come in all shapes and sizes, too, from the most delicate alpines that eke out their existence in cracks between paving stones, to monster border plants that throw up rocket-like flower spikes or produce flamboyant blooms the size of a saucer.

The selection on offer is huge and constantly growing, with even an average garden centre offering several hundred varieties as seed, seedlings, small plants and flowering specimens in spring and early summer. For the First-time Gardener, however, such an unlimited choice may seem overwhelming. Your choice of flowers should depend on whether you want them to last for one season or more, the time of the year you want them to bloom, what the growing conditions are like in your garden, and how they will blend into your colour scheme.

Although there are many flowering gems to be found, there also are quite a few duds that you should avoid. Use the guide on the following pages to help you make the right choice.

spring flowers

Spring bulbs herald the coming of the growing season and are an easy and reliable way of adding much needed colour at the beginning of the year. Bedding plants follow soon after, while certain perennials are in flower even earlier than this.

Making use of bulbs

Bulbs can be used all around the garden: in beds and borders, naturalised in grass, planted under deciduous trees and shrubs, and even in containers (see page 114).

Plant spring-flowering bulbs as soon as they become available (see FAQs, opposite).

To get the best results, you need to plant the right bulb in the right place – taking into account the bulb's soil and sunlight requirements as well as its flowering height and colour. Spring bulbs offer many different, often bright, colours that when used effectively can make eye-catching features in their own right. However, a poor combination of heights and colours can be disappointing or even garish. To help you combine different types effectively, use the colour photographs and heights detailed on the packets of pre-packed bulbs as a useful reference.

To achieve a natural appearance, bulbs should be planted in irregular shaped groups or drifts (see FAQs, opposite). Plant odd numbers of bulbs to avoid creating unnatural-looking symmetrical plantings. Large bulbs, such as tulips, can be planted in small groups of five or so, but smaller bulbs, such as crocuses and anemones, need to be planted in larger drifts of twenty or more to have an impact. Perhaps the easiest and most reliable bulb for the First-time Gardener to start with is the daffodil. Given a sunny site, it will flower reliably, producing its bright yellow trumpets year after year.

If you have problems with squirrels digging up the bulbs for food in winter, try burying a piece of chicken wire over the bulbs at planting time.

After flowering, the plants should be allowed to die naturally, so that they can build up enough reserves to flower the following year. For this reason, it is important not to remove foliage until at least six weeks after flowering; for the same reason, don't tie the plant into bundles as is often recommended.

Spring bedding displays

Plants such as forget-me-nots and pansies combine well with spring

Spring carpet of flowers
Tulip 'China Pink' and the spring bedding double daisy 'Red Pomponette' combine to form a brilliant spring ground covering in a mixed border.

PLANTING DEPTHS FOR BULBS

BULB TYPE	PLANTING DEPTH	BULB TYPE	PLANTING DEPTH	BULB TYPE	PLANTING DEPTH
Anemone	2.5–5 cm	Fritillary, snake's–head	5 cm	Lily, enchantment	13–18 cm
Cyclamen	1 cm	Large daffodil	13–20 cm	Ranunculus	7.5–10 cm
Crocus	5–7.5 cm	Gladiolus	10–13 cm	Snowdrop	5–7.5 cm
Chionodoxa	5–7.5 cm	Grape hyacinth	7.5 cm	Species tulip	10–13 cm
Dwarf daffodil	10–13 cm	Hyacinth	10–15 cm	Squill	7.5–10 cm
Freesia	7.5 cm	Iris (bulb)	7.5–13 cm	Tulip	15–20 cm

flowering bulbs to create bold splashes of early colour, and help extend the flowering period right through to summer.

Bedding plants come in a wide range of bright colours as well as pastel shades. Most will grow in sun or shade and will tolerate all types of soil, although they will perform better if given the ideal conditions (see plant label). Spring annuals should be planted during early spring. Space them between 15 and 30 cm apart, depending on the type of plant.

Colour choice is largely a matter of personal taste, but combinations of pastel colours always work well, as does planting compatible colours such as blues and pinks, or yellows and reds in the same scheme. Another reliable pairing worth a try is to plant a single colour bulb, such as yellow tulips, with a planting of single-colour bedding plants, such as blue forget-me-nots.

Early perennial interest

Evergreen perennials such as elephant's ears (*Bergenia*), hellebores and lungworts (*Pulmonaria*) provide the flowering link between winter and early spring. The saucer-shaped flowers of the Lenten rose (*Helleborus orientalis*) are borne in shades from white to deep maroon, while the stinking hellebore (*H. foetidus*) offers both attractive foliage and flowers, so is double value in early spring. Another good foliage plant is lords and ladies (*Arum italicum*), which produces arrow-shaped dark green leaves marbled with cream.

Although most herbaceous perennials don't come into leaf until early summer, a few useful plants provide attractive foliage in mid- to late spring. The new growth of some hostas, for example, is particularly attractive as they unfurl in mid- to late spring. Euphorbias, such as *Euphorbia amygdaloides* 'Purpurea', produce striking foliage. Ferns supply delicate greenery.

FAQs – BULBS

Q What kind of soil conditions do bulbs need?

A In general, most bulbs prefer a well-drained but moisture-retentive soil in full sun. Several bulbs, such as glory-of-the-snow (*Chionodoxa*), autumn crocus, lily-of-the-valley (*Convallaria*), hardy cyclamen, winter aconite, dog's-tooth violet (*Erythronium*), snowdrops and squills, however, thrive in areas of dappled shade.

Q When should I plant spring-flowering bulbs?

A The best advice is to plant them as soon as they are available, provided the soil conditions allow. This means late summer for daffodils and early to mid-autumn for the rest. Tulips can be planted as late as early winter in milder areas without affecting the following season's flowering display.

Q What's the best way to plant bulbs?

A Bulbs can be planted individually using a trowel or special cylindrical bulb planter, but for larger drifts they are easier to plant in a trench scooped out using a spade. Space bulbs out in an irregular pattern for the most natural effect.

Q Which way up should a bulb be planted?

A If there are no roots showing around the flat bottom of a bulb, plant it with the pointed side facing upward. Crown imperials (*Fritillaria imperialis*), however, should be planted on their sides to prevent the hollow bulb from filling with water and rotting.

Q How deep should I plant them?

A As a general rule, a bulb should be planted in a hole about three times as deep as the bulb is high. So, a 5 cm high bulb should be planted in a 15 cm deep hole. Use the chart opposite as a guide.

colourful summer flowers

Although a temporary addition, summer bedding plants, commonly called annuals, can provide wonderful colour displays during the summer months. They can be used all around the garden, as individual specimens in small groups or in massed displays.

Creating displays

There is a huge range of summer bedding varieties, but for reliable long-lasting displays look no further than ageratum, alyssum, begonia, pot marigold (*calendula*), dahlia, dianthus, busy Lizzie, lobelia, French marigold, petunia, pansy, pelargonium, salvia tagetes and verbena, which will all flower continuously from early summer. Bachelor's-buttons, cleome, cosmos, sunflowers and zinnias are easy annuals to grow from seed planted directly in the garden. Most will flower best if planted in full sun and kept well watered, but some can also tolerate shade and drought (see opposite).

Summer bedding plants are tender and usually raised in a heated environment indoors, so they cannot be planted out before the threat of frosts has passed in frost-prone areas, otherwise they will be killed. You must make sure that any summer bedding plants have been acclimatised to the harsher weather conditions outside before you buy them (ask the garden centre for advice). This process is known as hardening off (see page 114). The exceptions to this rule, however, are antirrhinum and alyssum which can tolerate a light frost, so they can be planted a week or so before the other plants – useful if you have a lot to plant. If frost threatens after planting, cover the displays with a protective double layer of garden fleece. If disaster strikes and plants do get a light frost, cover them with sheets of newspaper early in the morning to slow the rate of thawing, as this is when most of the damage is caused. Don't allow the soil to dry out before planting.

If you want massed displays of annuals, use the chart below to calculate how many plants you will need. Combine plants with complementary colours and a range of heights to create attractive displays.

HOW MANY PLANTS

BEDDING PLANTS	NUMBER OF PLANTS (per square metre)	PLANTING DISTANCE	BEDDING PLANTS	NUMBER OF PLANTS (per square metre)	PLANTING DISTANCE
African marigold	25	20 cm	Heuchera	10	30 cm
Ageratum	15	25 cm	Impatiens	25	20 cm
Alyssum	45	15 cm	Lobelia	45	15 cm
Antirrhinum	20	23 cm	Mesembryanthemum	45	15 cm
Begonia (fibrous-rooted)	45	15 cm	Nasturtium	10	30 cm
Calendula	45	15 cm	Nemesia	25	20 cm
Carnation	45	15 cm	Ornamental tobacco	10	30 cm
Cineraria	25	20 cm	Pansy	25	20 cm
Coleus	45	15 cm	Pelargonium	10	30 cm
Dahlia (dwarf)	10	30 cm	Petunia	15	25 cm
Dianthus	25	20 cm	Phlox	45	15 cm
Echeveria	45	15 cm	Salvia	25	20 cm
Echium	10	30 cm	Stocks	25	20 cm
French marigold	25	20 cm	Tagetes	25	20 cm
Gazania	25	20 cm	Verbena	15	25 cm
Helichrysum (dwarf)	25	20 cm	Zinnia	15	25 cm

Puddling in for a perfect start
If the soil is dry, fill the planting hole with water before planting so that the roots get plenty of water.

Place taller plants in the centre and smaller ones toward the edge of the scheme, so that all the plants can be seen. Also try to include individual plants which contrast in height, form and colour to the annuals. Foliage plants such as phormiums or dusty miller work particularly well, as do tall flowers such as amaranthus, canna, nicotiana or fuchsias.

Reliable perennials

There is a wide variety of garden perennials. Some are saints and some are sinners, so it is vital you choose the right varieties (see First-time Gardener's Best Bets, right).

Several perennials, such as achillea, lambs' ears, golden rod and comfrey are invasive, and so need digging up and dividing every few years to keep them under control.

A few perennials (such as purple loosestrife, lady's mantle, bronze fennel, borage and *Centaurea montana*) invade by dropping seeds, which germinate to form new plants. These can become a weed problem unless you root out young seedlings as soon as you see them.

Some taller perennials, such as peonies and tall asters, tend to flop over at the stem as soon as the flowers start to open. To avoid the need to stake plants, use tall perennials that can stand on their own, such as foxglove, rudbeckia and red-hot poker.

Perennials should be considered permanent additions to your garden. Plant them in spring or autumn into weed-free soil that has been improved with well-rotted organic matter. Try to plant taller varieties among shrubs to give them natural support. If this is not possible, push bamboo canes into the soil next to the plants and link them together with string or use special linking stakes. The plants will grow up through the support so that it cannot be seen by the time the plant is in flower.

Exotic summer bulbs

You can add an exotic touch to your summer displays by planting certain summer flowering bulbs. Agapanthus, allium, alstroemeria, iris and lilies are hardy in all but the coldest regions. Others such as acidanthera, gladioli, ixia, saraxis and tigridia are tender and so will not survive outdoors over winter in frost-prone areas. All summer bulbs require a sunny, sheltered site and well-drained soil. Plant them in mid-spring after the threat of frost has passed. Stake individual flower stalks with a bamboo cane to prevent them from flopping in bloom.

FIRST-TIME GARDENER'S BEST BETS

 Bedding for shade
Ageratum, antirrhinum, begonia, busy Lizzie, lobelia, pansy, pelargonium and pot marigold (*Calendula*).

 Trouble-free perennials
Agapanthus, 'Bressingham Blue', *Artemisia* 'Powis Castle', bear's breeches (*Acanthus*), bugle (*Ajuga reptans* 'Atropurpurea'), *Centranthus ruber*, crambe, day-lily (*Hemerocallis*), delphinium Belladonna hybrids, *Diascia rigescens*, *Dianthus* 'Doris', *Eryngium alpinum* (pictured right), *Hosta sieboldiana*, Japanese anemone, *Lamium maculatum* 'White Nancy', Michaelmas daisies 'Monch' and 'Violet Queen', *Paeonia mlokosewitschii*, penstemon, *Salvia superba*, sea holly and *Verbena bonariensis*.

 Drought-tolerant bedding
Dianthus, marigolds, pelargonium, petunia, pot marigold (*Calendula*), tagetes and verbena.

 Weather-resistant bedding
Alyssum, antirrhinum, dianthus, French marigold, lobelia, pansy, pelargonium, petunia, salvia, tagetes and verbena.

autumn and winter blooms

Many gardens suffer from a lack of flower power during early autumn as the summer displays wane. Often the only colour is provided by seasonal leaf tints, bark and eye-catching crops of berries. Yet there are a number of reliable autumn-blooming flowers that can add colour to your garden even at this late date.

Bulbs in the autumn

A few bulbs, including tender nerine, the hardier colchicums and *Sternbergia lutea*, will add a splash of colour to the garden during the autumn. The spidery pink blooms of nerines are, perhaps, the most distinctive of these flowers and like a warm sheltered spot, such as the base of a sunny wall. The pink- or white-flowering colchicums, which have large crocus-like flowers, and hardy cyclamens both do well in sun or partial shade found under leafless deciduous trees at this time of the year. Like other colchicums, the double variety 'Waterlily' **(1)** produces its flowers before the leaves, making them particularly striking when set against the bare earth. However, the flowers can be ruined by splashing mud in heavy rain. The strap-shaped foliage also has to be left until early summer when it dies down. The autumn daffodil, *Sternbergia lutea*, produces lots of bright yellow flowers and dark green strap-shaped leaves. It flourishes in sunny parts of the garden with well-drained soil.

Autumn and winter colours

You can create wonderful autumn and winter colours by encouraging several early and mid-summer flowers to give repeat performances later in the year (see page 66).

For the best displays, however, it is worth planting a few flowers that naturally bloom at this time. Fill your borders with fantastic blocks of purple by planting Michaelmas daisies. Don't choose the true Michaelmas daisy, *Aster novi-belgii*, however, because it is prone to flopping over and falling victim to mildew disease. Instead, search out the more compact and trouble-free *Aster x frikartii* 'Monch' or *A. amellus* 'Violet Queen', which will give you a blockbuster show that can last for up to three months. These plants grow happily in sun to light shade in most soils.

Many red-hot pokers (*Kniphofia*) flower towards the end of the summer, but it is the smaller more sought after types such as the pale yellow 'Ice Queen' and 'Little Maid' that will be in bloom during early to mid-autumn. If you want the traditional fiery orange-red flowers look for the variety *K. rooperi*. Position red-hot pokers where they will get a lot of sun and in soil that does not remain waterlogged for long periods in winter.

Iceplant (*Sedum*) is another popular garden plant that flowers late, bearing its distinctive flat red or pink flowerheads that are so attractive to bees and butterflies. The variety 'Autumn Joy' is perhaps the best and longest lasting, but 'Brilliant' is a similar plant worth looking out for. Iceplants are drought-tolerant and prefer full sun and well-drained soil.

Perhaps the best loved border flower in autumn is the chrysanthemum. Unfortunately, in frost-prone areas you need to dig up the

---

FIRST-TIME GARDENER'S BEST BETS

 Flowers in the autumn
Ceratostigma willmottianum, Chinese lantern (*Physalis*), *Chrysanthemum rubellum*, *Cimicifuga*, *Colchicum autumnale*, corydalis, *Cyclamen herderifolium*, *Fuchsia magellanica*, iceplant (*Sedum*), Japanese anemone, *Lirope muscari*, Michaelmas daisies, *Nerine bowdenii*, *Phygelius*, red-hot poker (pictured left), *Schizostylis* and *Sternbergia lutea*.

 Winter interest
Christmas rose (*Helleborus niger*), dwarf bamboos, elephant's ears (*Bergenia x schmidtii*), hardy ferns, *Helleborus lividus*, *Iris foetidissima* 'Variegata', *Iris unguicularis* and ornamental grasses.

 Good frosted flowers
Agapanthus, bear's breeches (*Acanthus*), cardoon (*Cynara*), Chinese lantern (*Physalis*), crocosmia, fennel, honesty (*Lunaria*), iceplant (*Sedum*), ornamental grasses, Penstemon, *Phlomis fruiticosa* and sea holly (*Eryngium*).

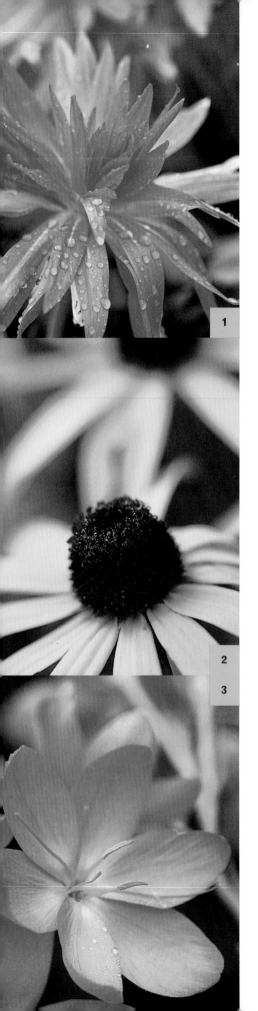

roots and keep them somewhere frost-free over the winter. The relatively hardy *C. rubellum* varieties, however, will survive outside in most areas. Chrysanthemums like a sunny position and well-manured soil to flower at their best.

Rudbeckia fulgida 'Goldsturm' **(2)** is a superb late summer and early autumn flower for the border. It is very easy to grow and bears an abundance of large yellow daisy-like blooms with a pronounced brown central cone. It forms a compact 60 cm high plant with glossy green foliage. For a taller version at the back of a border, try 'Autumn Sun' which can reach 1.8 metres high. Both like any fertile soil and full sun, although the former will flower pretty well in light shade.

The Kaffir lily, *Schizostylis*, is an excellent choice because it is fantastic looking and easy to grow. The different varieties flower at slightly different times, producing blooms of various shades of red, pink and white. So, by growing two or three varieties you could get a succession of blooms from late summer to mid-winter in mild areas. Good varieties include 'Major' (deep red), 'Viscountess Byng' (pink) and 'Sunrise' **(3)**.

Flowers for frosty weather

A few hardy evergreen perennials are able to brave the winter weather and can add pools of light to brighten otherwise dreary winter border scenes. You can choose from a variety of plants. One of the earliest flowering is *Helleborus lividus* which can be in bloom from mid-winter, bearing its pink-tinted white flowers until mid-spring. The better known Christmas rose flowers a little earlier, but it can be temperamental unless you can give it a shady spot with a rich alkaline soil. These should be planted close

to the house so they can be appreciated from the warmth and comfort of indoors.

A couple of irises are also worth including in your winter borders. *Iris foetidissima* is usually grown for its seedpods that split to display bright orange seeds over the winter months, while the variegated form offers bright evergreen cream-striped foliage. The Algerian iris (*I. unguicularis*) can be a battered looking plant by the time winter arrives, but this is more than made up for by its wonderfully robust winter blooms – the deep lilac shade of its flowers really warms the heart.

The earliest elephant's ears to flower is *Bergenia* x *schmidtii*, producing contorted sprays of pink flowers at the turn of the year. Other varieties, such as *B. purpurascens*, offer rich, red, purple or bronze foliage that cloaks the ground all winter long. All elephant's ears are tough plants that can survive in sun or shade, but can be prone to frost damage in especially cold regions.

leave flowers to frost

Don't be in a hurry to clear herbaceous borders when the flowers fade, since many dead blooms have an architectural quality that will provide interest throughout the winter months, especially after a heavy frost. Ornamental grasses look wonderful all winter so should be kept in the garden, but other plants such as a spiky sea holly, cardoons, the papery seedheads of honesty and bright orange Chinese lantern, as well as the distinctive flowerspikes of bear's breeches and iceplant, are also worth saving.

bigger and better displays

Many garden flowers can be encouraged to bloom longer or produce a second flush later in the season. The trick is to make sure that the plants put all their energy into producing more flowers rather than seedpods and seed. To achieve this, remove the seedpods regularly so they don't have a chance to develop. With some flowers the effect this has can be significant. Sweet peas, for example, stop flowering once they have lots of seedpods forming on their stems. By picking the plants over regularly you will stop this from happening, making the plant go on producing flowers longer.

Getting more flowers
Pinch off faded blooms from roses between finger and thumb to improve the overall display and encourage them to flower longer.

Pruning and deadheading
The best time to remove old flowers, known as deadheading, is as soon as the flowers start to fade. Not only does this prevent the plant from wasting its energy producing seed, but the seedpods are easier to spot if the petals are still attached. Indeed, with some plants, such as petunias and pansies, the seedpods can be a bit difficult to find because they tend to hide among the foliage.

Deadheading should be carried out regularly, perhaps once a week if you have the time. For plants with soft stems, old flowers can be pinched out between finger and thumb, but with others you might find it easier to use an old pair of scissors or secateurs. The only practical way to deadhead plants that produce a lot of tiny flowers, such as alyssum, is to use scissors.

A few garden flowering plants, such as foxgloves and delphiniums, produce their blooms on tall spikes. Once the last flower is over, these too can be removed to encourage a second flush later in the season. Use a pair of secateurs to cut the old flower spike back to the first sideshoot, which will bare the flowers later in the season.

Even foliage bedding plants such as coleus and senecio, which are grown for their attractive leaves benefit from having their flower buds, if any, removed. In this case, the buds should be cut off before they open so the leaves stay healthy and vigorous for longer.

Many perennial plants can look a bit the worse for wear by the middle of summer as the old foliage gets attacked by disease or is scorched in the sun. A few plants, notably hardy geraniums and violas, will respond to being trimmed back hard by producing a bright new mound of foliage and sometimes a second flush of flowers. This can be traumatic for the plant, so keep it well watered and give it a boost of fertiliser. Use a pair of shears to trim off the old foliage. Other perennials, such as aquilegias, pulmonarias and alstroemerias, can be cut back hard after flowering in early summer;

Longer-lasting displays
You can get a second flush of blooms from many popular flowers by cutting them back after flowering.

FIRST-TIME GARDENER'S BEST BETS

Flowerspikes to remove
Antirrhinum, delphinium, foxglove, hollyhock, lupin, monkshood (*Aconitum*), penstemon, *Salvia* x *superba*.

Flowers to cut right back
Catmint (*Nepeta*), *Centaurea montana*, geum, hardy geraniums, lamium and violas.

Flowers to deadhead
African marigold, ageratum, alyssum, anchusa, arctotis, California poppy (*Eschscholzia*), China aster (*Callistephus*), cornflower (*Centaurea*), cosmos, dahlia, dianthus, fleabane (*Erigeron*), French marigold, gaillardia, Livingstone daisy (*Mesembryanthemum*), marguerite, mimulus, osteospermum, pansy, pelargonium, petunia, poppy (*pictured right*), pot marigold (*Calendula*), scabious, and sweet pea.

they won't flower again, but will produce attractive new foliage, adding to the overall display.

Self-seeding flowers

Some garden flowers, including allium, aquilegia, feverfew, foxglove, poppy, forget-me-not, lady's mantle (*Alchemilla mollis*) and pot marigold, (*Calendula*) will scatter their seed all over the place if they are not deadheaded after flowering. Do this as a matter of priority to stop them becoming a serious weed problem.

The First-time Gardener can turn this habit to good advantage, by allowing self-seeders to colonise areas such as the cracks and crevices between paving and any bare earth along sunny passageways that would otherwise remain bare. Or

you could create a low-maintenance prairie-style area filled with a perpetual supply of colourful flowers and grasses.

Watering and feeding

Water plants well after cutting back and give them a high-potash liquid feed such as tomato fertiliser to encourage a second flush of blooms in late summer. Plants that have been deadheaded are also worth feeding during early summer. Flowers that like poor soil conditions, such as nasturtiums, canary creeper and godetias, however, should not be fertilised because this will encourage leafy growth at the expense of flowers.

---

expert tips   **Delayed flowering**

If you have large clumps of plants, such as coreopsis, helenium, phlox and Michaelmas daisies, you can extend the overall period of the display by selective trimming. Simply cut back about one-third of the stems before the flower buds appear. New branched growth will be produced from further down the plant on the trimmed stems, and the flowerbuds carried on this new growth will appear later than the flowers borne on the stems that were not cut back, thereby spreading the flowering display over a longer period.

a shady perennial paradise

Judy and Chris Barnes bought a dilapidated house in the city which needed a lot of restoration work. The garden, too, was full of challenges. It was a narrow garden that was kept in deep shade for most of the day because of a large tree in a neighbour's garden. The soil appeared dry and impoverished. Despite being an enthusiastic gardener, Judy found it very difficult to get anything established. The Barnes would like their garden to be an oasis full of flowers and lush foliage, with plenty of space for sitting out on warm days. However, they didn't want to spend all their available time on garden maintenance.

Ground raising

Restoring this garden was not going to be easy. The neighbour's tree had spread its roots just below the surface of the soil, right across the garden, removing most of the available moisture and nutrients. Its branches stretched just as far overhead, cutting out most of the sunlight during the day. Clearly some drastic measures were needed. The Barnes' decided to raise the level of their garden to create a root-free environment for their new garden plants. They opted to create a series of planting beds between areas of decking at various levels.

Steps and decking

The garden is accessible from both the first floor and the kitchen on the second floor. It was from the latter that Judy and Chris would view and access their garden, so the design needed to look good from this point. The existing series of steps from the kitchen door were rotten and unsafe so needed replacing. Judy and Chris decided to base their garden design around a combination of small decks made from pressure-treated timber with a wood preservative. Planting would be confined to perimeter beds and pots. They employed a professional team to build the deck structure with linking walkways and a new set of steps to the most elevated area outside the kitchen door. This was the only deck to receive a lot of direct sunlight.

Bamboo boundaries

The existing boundary wall around the garden was in a rather poor shape, and needed to be brushed down and re-pointed. To create the jungle effect that Judy wanted, and to raise the height of the boundary without blocking out too much sunlight, Chris attached 1.8 m high split bamboo screens along each wall.

Creating the beds

Most shade-tolerant plants with lush foliage prefer a moist soil, so the quality of their remaining soil between and around the decks needed to be improved. To do this, Chris used good quality topsoil enriched with heaps of well-rotted organic matter. This helps to increase the soil's water-holding capacity. Over 600 bags of soil and manure had to be carried through the house to the back garden to fill all of the beds.

Lush planting

A range of foliage perennials were used to create a jungle effect in their garden. Judy bought a huge *Gunnera manicata* which has huge rhubarb-like leaves. This she placed at centre stage and then surrounded it with a variety of hostas, angelica, euphorbia, rogersia and dragon arum (*Dracunculus vulgaris*). For foliage contrast, many ornamental grasses were added, including white and cream-variegated species.

At the back of the borders, trees such as the maidenhair tree (*Ginkgo*) and a Japanese maple variety 'Vitifolium' were planted, the former for its unusual fan-shaped leaves and the latter for its deep red autumn foliage. To complete the jungle atmosphere, a mature evergreen *Ensete*, with its long paddle-shaped leaves reminiscent of a banana plant, was placed in the deepest border at the bottom of the garden. If you decide to plant an *Ensete* in your garden, you should be aware that it is not a very hardy plant, so it requires protection during the winter in frost-prone areas.

Flowering interest

To add seasonal focal points in any garden, it is a good idea to plant flowers. Judy used flowers to edge many of the borders. Dramatic spikes of foxglove, ligularia and lilies are used to good effect with ground-cover flowers, such as bugle (*Ajuga*), lysimachia, and lilyturf (*Liriope*).

She also used other perennials including the red masterwort (*Astrantia*) and toadlily (*Tricytris*) to help fill the gaps, and combined them with seasonal additions of potted shade-tolerant summer bedding plants, such as impatiens and ornamental tobacco. Around the seating area, tender palms completed the exotic scene.

Jungle atmosphere

Rustic furniture and bamboo screens add the finishing touches to this jungle of lush foliage plants under the canopy of a large tree. The summer display is supplemented by beautiful pots of colourful shade-tolerant annuals (below). From the raised deck outside the kitchen, the garden can be seen in all its glory (right).

revitalising old flower borders

After ten years of wonderful summer displays, the herbaceous borders in Anna and Steven Donovan's leafy suburban garden have lost their appeal. This is a common problem in well-established gardens. The plants produce fewer flowers, and the blooms that do appear tend to be smaller and don't last as long as they once did. Many of the Donovan's favourite varieties disappeared altogether. They want to revamp the borders and recapture the glories of past years without starting all over again and buying new plants.

Problem borders

Long-established herbaceous borders are prone to several problems. The more vigorous plants tend to spread out and swamp their less vigorous neighbours, and the centre of large clumps die out as they spread. The soil also becomes depleted of nutrients. In addition, older plants are more prone to pest and disease attacks, which spoil their displays, and perennial weeds can become established throughout the bed, ruining the overall appearance of the borders. Fortunately, all of these problems can be overcome by digging up the whole border, enriching the soil and reinvigorating the displays.

Anna and Steven's first job was to decide which plants they wanted to keep and which they were happy to dispose of. The best time to do this is in the summer when the plants are in flower; you should clearly tag with a label all the plants you have chosen to keep.

Digging up the border

Anna and Steven chose a fine mild day in the autumn to dig up the border. Before you start removing any of the plants from the soil, the first job is to cut off any old foliage which has started to die down for the winter. This will make access easier and you will be able to clearly see what you are doing. It took Anna just half an hour to trim back all the selected plants.

The next step is carefully to remove the selected plants from the soil. Anna and Steve used a spade to cut around each plant to loosen the solid rootball. They then cut through the roots under each plant and levered the rootball carefully from the soil using a spade or garden fork. Very large clumps of roots had to be cut into sections with a spade before they could be moved.

Steven laid out a black plastic sheet on the ground in a shady spot to hold all the selected perennials, and folded one end of the sheet over the top to prevent the roots from drying out. Finally, they dug up all the old plants they didn't wish to keep.

Improving the soil

Anna and Steve then set about clearing the weeds from the soil and digging in lots of well-rotted organic matter. This helps to improve the structure and water-holding capacity of the impoverished soil. A general-purpose fertiliser was also scattered on the surface and forked into the soil at the rate of 50 g per square metre.

Preparing the plants

As they grow, many perennials develop into larger and larger clumps, each with many growth buds. By separating a clump into smaller sections, each with several healthy buds and plenty of roots, you can invigorate an old plant. This easy technique is known as division. The sections taken from around the edge of an old clump will provide the most vigorous new plants. These will establish quickly, produce the best flowers and be able to shrug off pest and disease

---

expert tips   Dealing with weeds

The roots of many troublesome perennial weeds, such as bindweed, can become tightly enmeshed with flowers' roots. This not only means that they are competing for soil moisture and nutrients, but also makes them impossible to clear from the beds by pulling them out by hand, since any small piece of the weed's root left in the ground will resprout and start colonising the bed all over again. The only way to deal with this problem for good is to dig up the affected plants and painstakingly pull out all the weed roots from the roots of the flowers. This may seem laborious, but it will save a lot of time in the long run.

attacks more effectively. The old woody central sections of each rootball should be discarded.

To begin the process of dividing their selected plants, Steven placed another sheet of plastic on the wide path to give them plenty of room to move around. All clump-forming perennials are divided in the same way. The best tools for the job will depend on the size of plants being dealt with. For the large solid rootballs, such as the rudbeckia, Steven used a sharp spade to slice through the dense and woody core. To separate smaller clumps, such as the sedum, he used a sharp knife and a pair of old secateurs.

Many of the flowers he and Anna saved, including asters, formed loose clumps that were easy to divide by hand, simply by gently teasing the roots apart. Those clumps that were tangled tightly together were pulled apart using a pair of garden forks held back to back. Anna found that herbaceous plants, including the bergenias, which had loose fleshy underground stems (called rhizomes), were easy to chop up using long-handled secateurs. Finally, the Donovans checked over all the sections they intended to replant to remove any weed roots (see the expert tip, on the page opposite).

A few herbaceous plants flower better when the roots are congested, so should not be divided unless they have outgrown their allotted space. In the Donovan's garden, clumps of *Agapanthus* and peony, which were still flowering well, were not divided.

Replanting the new bed

The new sections were planted carefully at the same depth as before. The soil around the plants was pressed down gently to firm it and watered thoroughly. All bare soil was covered with a 5 cm layer of well-rotted manure to keep the ground weed-free. The new herbaceous border was then kept well watered throughout the following season until all the plants were well established.

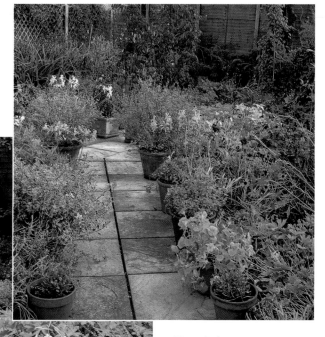

Drastic improvement
The fiery displays in this herbaceous border have been transformed by a thorough overhaul. Summer displays of penstemon, crocosmia and *Echinops* are complemented by nasturtiums and potted geraniums (pictured left). The addition of *Schizostylis* and *Rudbeckia* with *Nerines* extend the colour theme into the autumn (picture above).

When the going gets tough
Shade-tolerant hostas, ferns and foxgloves cover the ground in this shady corner **(1)**; under a high pine canopy, tough shrubs such as hebe and eucalyptus thrive **(2)**; dianthus and other drought-tolerant plants have found their niche **(3)**; seaside plantings of lavender and crocosmia brave the bright sunlight and the salt-laden winds **(4)**.

Tough customers
for difficult situations

Every garden contains at least one border where plants are reluctant to grow.

Fortunately, there are flowers to suit every situation, even dry soil under trees,

provided you give them a helping hand to get established.

Some plants are well adapted for growing in difficult conditions where other plants would fail to thrive. The key to success is to choose the right plants for the particular conditions, but you must also prepare the soil thoroughly before planting (see page 166). If all else fails, you can always grow plants in containers (see page 110).

Windy tunnels and exposed gardens
Long, straight passages between buildings are usually heavily shaded and dry. The buildings also can act as a wind-tunnel, producing buffeting currents of air even on quite still days. To cope with these conditions, a plant needs to be very resilient. To maximise the conditions, paint the walls a pale colour to increase the chances of growth in these light levels and use bamboos and tough shrubs, such as aucuba, to act as a windbreak at both ends of the passage. Suitable flowers for windy, shady spots include hellebores, *Heuchera*, hosta, *Pulmonaria*, annual lobelia and polyanthus.

In coastal gardens, the exposure is made worse by salt-laden winds – scorching the foliage of all but the toughest plants. In this situation try perennials such as *Eryngium*, crocosmia, *Senecio* and yucca or bedding plants such as antirrhinum, *Arctotis* and *Dimorphotheca*.

Dry soil under trees
The soil under established trees and alongside hedges is usually filled with roots that draw out all the available moisture and nutrients. This makes the ground difficult to cultivate and prevents new plants from becoming established. To make matters worse, the area will be in shade for much of the year. To add a splash of colour under the shade of deciduous trees, such as silver birch and rowans, try planting foxgloves, busy Lizzies, honesty, forget-me-nots, tobacco plants or pansies, or bulbs such as dwarf daffodils.

For a permanent underplanting of perennial flowers, try barrenwort (*Epimedium*), euphorbias, hardy geraniums, *Helleborus foetidus* and *Heuchera*. If the trees produce a dense canopy of foliage but don't come into leaf until mid-spring, you could underplant them with drifts of bulbs that are in flower earlier in the year – try snowdrops and bluebells or carpet the floor with *Cyclamen coum* or *C. hederifolium*.

Damp and shady areas
Soil that remains constantly moist causes many plants to rot, particularly over the winter months. This usually occurs where the water table is high and the soil is heavy, containing a lot of clay. If your soil remains waterlogged for long periods, choose moisture-loving flowers such as astilbe, Japanese primrose or arum lily. If your soil drains but remains moist after rain, you could create a woodland effect of perennial flowers such as primroses, hostas, pearl everlasting (*Anaphalis*), Solomon's seal or dicentra. If you have problems with slugs and snails in damp, shady areas, try growing plants such as pulmonia and hardy ferns, which such pests tend to leave alone.

Exposed dry borders
Borders in full sun require plants that can take bright light and often high temperatures. Your local garden centre will stock many suitable sun-lovers such as sweet peas. Sunny borders at the base of a wall are particularly tough because the wall may absorb soil moisture and also radiate heat, making it a real hot spot. Here, turn to plants with silvery, hairy, or waxy leaves – adaptations that prevent moisture loss through the foliage. Try perennials such as bergenia, euphorbia, hardy generanium, or verbascum.

Climbing plants

Climbers are an asset to the First-time Gardener as they can be used to enhance the appearance of every garden. They are easy to grow and most require little maintenance provided you choose the right plant for the position.

Climbing plants can be used all around the garden to provide vertical interest to flat borders, create screens to cover eyesores and break up the stark appearance of walls and fences, as well as provide shade when trained over arches and pergolas. Many climbers, notably evergreen ivies, can also be used to cover the ground, providing a foliage carpet that decorates the floor and helps keep weeds at bay. Climbers are of particular value in small gardens that have high walls or fences because they can be used to add living colour and interest without taking up a lot of ground area. Every vertical surface can be covered, because there are climbers suited to growing in sun or shade and types that will tolerate most soils. They even can be grown successfully in containers on a patio or balcony.

Every style of garden suits climbing plants. Most climbers can be trained easily into any shape or form to suit a formal setting. When tied against the bars of trellis or along wires attached to a wall or fence, for example, a perfectly symmetrical design can be achieved. Climbing plants look wonderful in informal gardens, too, where they can be left to their own devices – new growth can cascade from a support or fence to produce a billowing froth of flowers and foliage.

Many climbers, such as clematis, are grown for their spectacular flowers, which are produced in abundance for many months. A few, such as jasmines, have a delicious fragrance, while others, such as ivies and vines, can be grown for their attractive and bold foliage, which is often strikingly variegated and takes on dramatic tints and hues in the autumn. There are also climbers that produce attractive seedheads and colourful berries, which can decorate your garden during the winter.

adding interest using climbers

An essential element of any garden, climbing plants can be used to cover fences and other structures to hide eyesores or provide a colourful backdrop to other plants. If you choose the right plant for the position and plant it correctly, a climber will look after itself and need less maintenance than most other garden plants.

Many climbers originate from the tropical rainforests so are not hardy in temperate areas, but there are still plenty of hardy types to choose from if your garden is prone to frost.

In nature, climbers use other plants as a means of support; growing quickly up towards the sun and spreading out over the supporting plant's canopy. For this reason, many climbers are so vigorous they can be used to quickly cover large or unsightly areas – an expanse of stark wall or a dilapidated shed, for example. On the other hand, climbers quickly outgrow small spaces, so it is important to match the vigour of your climber to the growing space available; otherwise you will spend a lot of time keeping it in check.

Choosing a good plant

There are climbers to suit both sun and shade as well as most types of soil from light, sandy soil to heavy clay. Climbers also can be grown successfully in containers. Small pots can be used to grow annual climbing plants such as sweet peas and black-eyed Susan (*Thunbergia alata*), whereas large tubs placed against a wall or other sturdy support can accommodate the largest of climbing specimens. Small evergreen climbers such as ivies or vinca are also useful for planting around the edge of a container to trail over the edge. (See page 110 for details about growing plants in containers.)

Although most climbing plants flower in the summer, there also are excellent varieties that put on their

Natural support
This majestic scented rambling rose has been trained to scramble through the canopy of an old apple tree to give it another season of interest.

Steps to success with climbers

3

- Decide the size of structure you want to cover.

- Choose an appropriate climbing plant to cover the area involved.

- Construct supports and tie the climbers to them securely.

display at other times. If you choose carefully you can combine different climbers to create a year-round display of fabulous foliage and berries. Use the plant lists on the following pages to help you choose.

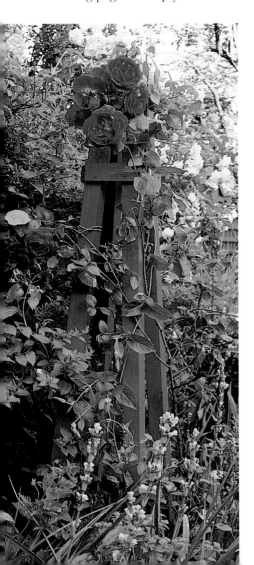

Buying tips

Look for healthy specimens with well-balanced frameworks of stems and no physical damage or signs of pests and diseases.

Avoid plants with rootballs covered in weeds or tightly coiled roots around their bases. Some plants, particularly roses, are sold as bare-rooted plants, and these should have moist, fibrous root systems.

Container-grown climbing plants should be bought in the spring. The soil is moist and the weather is becoming warmer at this time of year, so the plants are easier to establish. You will also find the best selection of plants during spring.

The natural climbers

Many climbing plants are self-clinging, which means once they are established they can hold on to the support without the need for tying in shoots as they grow.

Clematis and honeysuckle, for example, produce twining stems or leaf stalks that tangle themselves into the support; while sweet peas and passion flowers produce coiling tendrils that spiral around the support and hold on tight. Some plants, such as Virginia creeper, produce tiny suckers that stick fast onto any surface, and ivy produces a fringe of aerial roots from its stem that provide a firm anchor.

Other climbers, such as roses, are not self-clinging; they need to be tied onto the support (see page 78).

Colour contrasts
A cerise-pink climbing rose makes the most of a bright blue obelisk support to stand out from the crowd in this informal border display.

FAQs – CLIMBERS

Q **Are climbers difficult to prune?**

A Most require little or no pruning. Simply trim once a year to keep them within bounds. Some flowering climbers, particularly clematis, wisteria and roses, however, require special pruning if you want them to bloom to their full potential (see page 184 for details).

Q **Will climbers damage my house?**

A While it is true that some climbers can speed the deterioration of unsound walls with crumbling mortar, sound brick walls will not be damaged. If you allow a climber to scramble over guttering and a tiled roof, it will grow under the tiles and the foliage can block gutters. By giving the plant a trim at the end of the growing season you can prevent this from happening.

Q **Do you have to have a wall or fence to support climbers?**

A No, but it is essential that you match the growing vigour of the climbing plant to the size and strength of the support. A solid wall can support a vigorous vine that produces lots of heavy growth, while trellises, bamboo canes or even a string wigwam can support a slow-growing or more delicate climber.

Q **How do you cover a bare fence quickly ?**

A Climbers naturally grow towards the light, so if you spread out the stems horizontally, they will produce shoots from each leaf joint to produce more upward growth that will quickly clothe the support.

Q **Are all climbers tender?**

A No, although many originate from the tropical regions of the world and are not hardy enough for growing outdoors in colder regions. Others are perfectly hardy or are at least hardy enough to survive when trained against a sheltered, south-facing wall.

planting and supporting

All climbers need support. You can use wires or trellis fixed to a sturdy wall or fence, or provide them with their own free-standing support such as an obelisk, arch or screen. Many garden structures, such as arches and pergolas, are available in kit form from garden centres (see page 92).

All climbing plants enhance the appearance of your garden, but you can extend the flowering period of your climbers and create some eye-catching displays by combining two or three climbing plants onto one support using the methods described below. Choose varieties that have the same cultural requirements so that pruning and other maintenance tasks can be carried out at the same time.

Attaching climbers to walls and fences

Before planting your climber, fix the trellis or wires onto the wall or fence about 30 cm above the ground, making sure they are strong and firmly attached.

Using trellis Choose sturdy well-made trellis that will last many years. Avoid the cheap expanding-style trellis for all but the lightest of climbing plants.

Mark out the position of the trellis on the wall or fence. Then, screw the spacing battens onto the vertical surface to help maintain the airflow between the climber and its support – this helps to prevent disease and damp problems. Screw the trellis directly to the battens to form a permanent feature.

Alternatively, hinge the trellis to the bottom batten and then attach it to the top one using a hook and eye mechanism. This allows easy access to the supporting fence or wall to carry out periodical maintenance. A section of wire fence, attached to wooden supports or a wall, makes a quick trellis for annual climbers.

Using wires Strong, plastic-coated or galvanised wire is attached to a wall or fence using special hooks called vine-eyes (available from garden centres). These can be screwed directly into wooden fences. On walls, however, you need to use a different method. About 30–45 cm above the ground, mark out holes 1 metre apart across the wall. Drill these holes in sound mortar using a 5 mm bit, then push in the wall plugs and screw in the vine-eyes. Attach the wire to the end vine eye using a pair of pliers. Then thread the wire through the intermediate vine eyes. Once through the

Putting up trellis

Securely fix the trellis to the wall using corrosion-resistant screws. Use spacers between the wall and the trellis to increase air flow and reduce the incidence of disease.

final vine-eye, pull the wire taut before securing with pliers. Repeat this process with the other parallel wires, spacing them 30–45 cm apart up the wall.

Double-value climbers

Climbers that naturally clamber through other plants are an ideal way of brightening up dull shrubs or hedges, or providing a second season of interest to a large flowering shrub. Bear in mind, however, that the climbing plant will be

Planting a climber near a wall

The soil alongside walls is often dry and lacking in nutrients, so good soil preparation is essential before planting. To do this, dig the soil to a full spade's depth and remove any weeds, large stones and other debris. Incorporate plenty of well-rotted garden compost or planting mixture to improve moisture retention. If you have heavy soil, add a bucketful of grit to improve drainage. Then, fork in a slow-release general fertiliser before planting.

Dig a large hole at least twice the size of the plant's rootball 45 cm away from the wall or fence. Add some more planting mixture into the base of the hole.

1 Position the plant in the hole at a 45 degree angle to the wall so that it leans toward the wall and reaches the bottom of the trellis or wire support (which should be at a height of 30–45 cm up the wall or fence). Use a cane placed across the hole to check that the top of the rootball is level with the surrounding soil.

Clematis are susceptible to wilt disease so are best planted deeper than other climbers. Position the top of the rootball 7.5 cm below the soil surface so that if the top-growth is killed by wilt there are plenty of buds underground to regrow the following year. After planting, take care not to damage stems when cultivating or hoeing the soil.

competing with the supporting plant for food and moisture. The climber should be planted in a spot level with the edge of the supporting plant's foliage. This area is known as the drip zone because it is where rainwater runs off the shrub's canopy. Prepare the planting area by digging a hole and removing roots, weeds and other debris. Add some manure and a slow-release general fertiliser. Line the sides of the hole with old timber to prevent root invasion from the supporting plant. Place more planting mixture into the hole, then attach one end of a rope to the shrub and lay the other end underneath the rootball of the climber in its planting hole. Check that the top of the rootball is level with the surrounding soil and fill the hole. Firm and water well and apply a layer of well-rotted manure or bark chips as a mulch to reduce moisture loss and prevent weed competition. Tie the climber to the rope and entwine any long stems into the shrub support.

2 Fill in the hole with soil, firming it down periodically with the heel of your foot to remove any air pockets. Water well and cover the surrounding soil with a 5–7.5 cm layer of well-rotted manure or bark chips to reduce water loss and prevent weed competition. Keep the mulch clear of the climbers' stems to prevent rotting.

3 Now, tie the plant's support cane (this comes with the climber when bought) to the bottom of the trellis using string or a wire tie so that it is firmly anchored.

4 Finally, train a few of the longer climber stems onto the bottom of the trellis, tying them to the support if necessary.

spring climbers

When the frosts end and the weather becomes warmer, you can add instant interest, scent and colour to your garden using a range of climbing plants.

Early-flowering clematis

Producing their blooms on growth created during the previous season, early-flowering clematis are some of the best spring-flowering climbers.

Clematis cirrhosa are the first to appear in early spring, and their bell-shaped creamy blooms stand out well against the plant's evergreen foliage. Look out for 'Freckles' and 'Balearica', both of which bear blooms that are spotted dark red inside. Reaching about 3 m, these climbers are worth growing near a doorway or over an arch near a path where their decorative flowers can be appreciated.

Another early-flowering clematis is *C. armandii* **(1)**, which produces scented white blooms during mid-spring. Two of the best varieties are the pale pink 'Apple blossom' and the white 'Snowdrift'. All grow in sun or light shade but, like *C. cirrhosa* and its varieties, these plants need winter protection in cold areas.

Continuous spring colour can be achieved by planting varieties of *Clematis alpina*, such as 'Frances Rivis' **(2)**, or *C. macropetala*. They all bloom from mid-spring to early summer and produce attractive seedheads in autumn. *Clematis alpina* bears dainty nodding flowers against attractive ferny foliage and can grow successfully in sun or shade. 'Columbine' (pale blue), 'Constance' (red), 'Frances Rivis' (blue) and 'Willy' (pink), are all worth searching for. The best *C. macropetala* varieties include 'Maidwell Hall' (purple) and 'Markham's Pink', which produce attractive semi-double blooms.

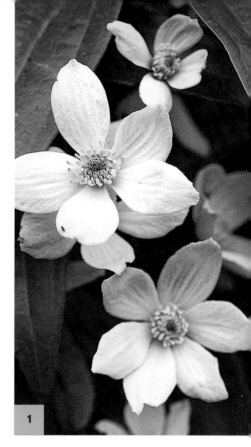

1

To cover a fence or pergola with colour in late spring, opt for one of the excellent *Clematis montana* varieties. They are all hardy and can be grown in sun or shade. The best varieties are 'Elizabeth' (pale pink), 'Grandiflora' (white), 'Rubens', 'Tetrarose' and 'Pink Perfection' (pink). All but 'Grandiflora' have attractive purplish leaves as well.

Climbers for extra colour

The earliest wisterias, *W. sinensis* and its varieties 'Blue Sapphire' (violet) and 'Amethyst' (mauve), appear in late spring and early summer. All are vigorous, reaching 7 m high and wide, so need plenty of space as well as lots of sun.

For something different, the chocolate vine, *Akebia quinata*, produces small, scented chocolate-coloured flowers in mid-spring, which can be followed by purple fruits later in the year. It is semi-evergreen with twining stems and attractive five-lobed leaves, which quickly cover fences and screens. It prefers sun and well-drained soil, but will tolerate some shade.

FIRST-TIME GARDENER'S BEST BETS

Climbers for shade
Clematis alpina, *C. alpina* 'Frances Rivis' or 'Pamela Jackman', *C.* 'Asaso', 'Ascotiensis', 'Carnaby', 'Charissima', 'Countess of Lovelace', 'Dawn', *C. x durandii*, *C.* 'Edith', 'Fireworks', *C. flammula*, *C.* 'Gipsy Queen', 'Hagley Hybrid', 'Jackmanii Superba', 'Lasurstern', 'Marie Boisselot' or 'Miss Bateman', 'Nelly Moser', *C. macropetala*, *Hydrangea petiolaris*, ivies especially 'Goldheart', 'Green Ripple' and 'Hibernica', *Parthenocissus henryana* and 'Purpurea'.

Climbers for sun
Akebia quinata, *Clematis* 'Lord Nevill', *Lonicera periclymenum* 'Belgica' or 'Serotina', *Parthenocissus quinquefolia*, climbing and rambler roses, *Solanum crispum* 'Glasnevin', *S. jasminoides* 'Album', *Vitis vinifera* 'Purpurea', *Wisteria floribunda* 'Alba' or 'Macrobotrys', *W. sinensis*, *W. sinensis* 'Alba' or Black Dragon'.

Climbers for light shade
Actinidia chinensis, *A. kolomikta*, *Clematis alpina*, *C. alpina* 'Frances Rivis', *C.* 'Bees' Jubilee', 'Comtesse de Bouchaud', 'Doctor Ruppel', 'Earnest Markham', 'Gipsy Queen', 'Hagley Hybrid', 'Jackmanii Superba', 'Lady Betty Balfour', 'Mrs Cholmondeley', 'Nelly Moser', 'Rouge Cardinal', 'The President' or 'Etoile Violette', *C. montana* 'Elizabeth', 'Grandiflora', 'Pink Perfection', 'Tetrarose', 'Rubens', 'Ville de Lyon', 'Vyvyan Pennell', *C. tangutica*, ivies *Hedera canariensis* 'Gloire de Marengo', *H. colchica* 'Dentata' or 'Sulphur Heart', *H. helix* 'Buttercup' 'Cristata' and 'Glacier', *Lonicera japonica* 'Aureoreticulata', *L. japonica* 'Halliana', *L x brownii* 'Dropmore Scarlet', *Parthenocissus henryana*, *P. tricuspidata* 'Veitchii', *Pyracantha* 'Mohave'.

2

Evergreen climbers

Most evergreen climbers, including passion flower, a few clematis and jasmine, are grown mainly for their flowers and wonderful scent (see relevant flowering times). Ivies, on the other hand, are grown purely for their attractive foliage. They have earned their popularity because they are tough, trouble-free and offer year-round interest.

Ivies can be used all around the garden in virtually any soil; some thrive in full sun while others cope well even in deep shade. Most, however, do best in dappled shade in moisture-retentive soil. Nearly all are hardy with the exception of *Hedera canariensis* and its varieties.

When choosing ivy you need to match its rate of growth to the area it has to cover; it can become invasive so choose carefully. As a general rule, the larger the distance between the leaves on the stem, the more vigorous the ivy.

If you want to cover the ground with ivy (3), choose varieties such as 'Hibernica', 'Ivalace', and 'Manda's Crested', which have exaggerated ivy-shaped leaves that look very attractive. If you want to add light and interest to an area – under a tree, for example – choose the variegated cream-coloured 'Glacier' or the yellow-variegated 'Dentata Variegata' instead. In a sunny location, cover the ground with the large-leafed variety 'Dentata' or the pale green 'Parsley Crested', both of which are vigorous enough to out-compete any weeds.

North-facing walls are unusually difficult to cover, but this is an ideal location for several variegated ivies such as the aptly named 'Goldheart' and the bright yellow-leafed 'Buttercup', which will cloak the surface with its coloured foliage.

For south-facing walls or fences, the *H. canariensis* variety 'Gloire de Marengo' is a good choice. It is particularly tolerant of drought, so perfect for such sunny spots, but it does need protection in winter in colder areas.

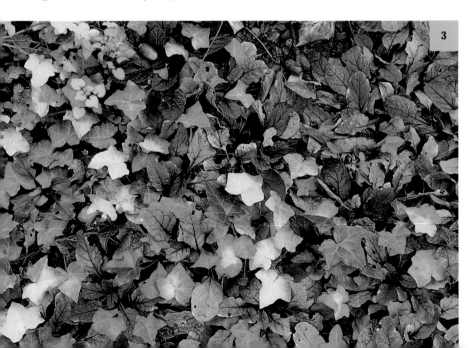

3

covering tree stumps

Evergreen climbers, including ivy, are ideal for disguising tree stumps. Choose a vigorous variety with attractive leaves to get the best cover. Combine it with a clematis or honeysuckle for flowering interest, especially during the summer. All these climbers are resistant to honey fungus, a serious disease that infects decaying tree stumps.

summer scent and colour

Hot summer weather gives the First-time Gardener a chance to grow some wonderfully aromatic roses, honeysuckles and clematis.

Climbing and rambler roses

There is a huge range of climber and rambler roses. Some are small enough to be trained against a single post, whereas others can reach well over 7 m tall and wide, requiring a large pergola to support them. The flowering times also vary; many produce a burst of colour over a few weeks in early summer, while others offer an intermittent display over several months – often described as repeat or recurrent-flowering.

Before you decide to buy a specific variety, it is important that you find out how susceptible it is to the three main rose diseases of blackspot, mildew and rust.

Many of the modern varieties have been bred to be more disease resistant and less vigorous than their older counterparts. For large flowers on a reasonable-sized plant try 'Aloha', which has rose and salmon-pink blooms, or the popular 'Summer Showers', which has canary yellow flowers. Both are repeat-flowering so add interest on and off all summer long. If you are looking to cover a fence panel or the side of a shed try the larger 'New Dawn' **(1)**, which has pink blooms. For even larger areas, try 'Wedding Day' and 'Kiftsgate', both of which produce cream flowers.

Heavenly honeysuckles

Climbing honeysuckles are easy to grow, require little pruning and offer attractive foliage, as well as distinctive and colourful flowers many of which are scented. A few varieties also bear showy berries.

Honeysuckles grow wild in different parts of the world including North America, Europe and China, which means they require quite different growing conditions in the garden to do well. The First-time Gardener can take full advantage of this as it means that there is a honeysuckle to suit almost every position in the garden.

When positioning honeysuckles, bear in mind that they are prone to blackfly, which exude a sticky substance called honeydew that falls to cover leaf surfaces and anything else that lies below the climber. Avoid planting them over pergolas and around windows where the sticky excretions could become a considerable nuisance.

For a small support in a sunny spot, choose one of the *Lonicera etrusca* varieties, such as 'Donald Waterer', which bears wonderful red and cream flowers or 'Michael Rosse' and 'Superba', both of which produce cream and yellow blooms. In semi-shade try the periclymenum varieties 'Belgica' (purple and cream), 'Graham Thomas' (yellow and cream) or alternatively, 'Florida' (purple and white).

To cover an arch or larger support try japonica varieties such as 'Repens' or 'Hall's Prolific' which grow to 7 m tall. Both bear white blooms that turn buff then cream with age, and attractive purple-flushed foliage.

Scented double act

Combine climbers with contrasting or complementary colours if they flower at about the same time. Here a scented honeysuckle and a rambling rose create the perfect partnership against a sunny wall.

Summer clematis

Clematis montana and its varieties bloom for up to 10 weeks so can be used to add colour to walls and fences well into the summer. Later-flowering varieties bloom on new growth produced during the current season. One of the best is the versatile *C. tangutica*, which yields nodding yellow flowers and should cover a small support in any given position from full sun to deep shade. Similar in size and nearly as adaptable is *C. viticella* and its varieties, which perform well in sun or partial shade. There are many good forms, but perhaps the best is 'Etoile Violette' which bears purple flowers with yellow stamens.

As the summer progresses many of the showy large-flowered hybrids come into their own. Among the stars are 'Bees Jubilee' (pink), 'Comtesse de Bouchaud' (mauve), 'Doctor Ruppel' (deep pink, pale edges), 'Gipsy Queen' (deep purple), 'Hagley Hybrid' (mauve), 'Marie Boisselot' (white), 'Nelly Moser' (pink and deep pink stripes) and 'The President' (purple).

Scented climbers

Many garden climbers are scented, and choosing one is very much a matter of personal preference.

Fragrant honeysuckles include *Lonicera* x *americana* and the varieties 'Halliana', 'Belgica' and 'Florida', all of which produce that familiar sweet honeysuckle aroma. A few of the early-flowering clematis are noted for their sweet, honey-like scent too. The evergreen *C. armandii* fills the air with its delicate aroma during mid-spring, while the deciduous *C. montana's* perfume is slightly stronger and slightly later. Even more pungent at this time year is the wisteria 'Macrobotrys' with its sweet vanilla fragrance – be careful where you plant this, however, as the fragrance can be overpowering.

During early summer, many climbing and rambling roses are highly scented. For example 'Paul's Himalayan Musk', 'Treasure Trove' and *R. helenae* have a fruity smell, while 'Zéphirine Drouhin' and 'Mermaid' **(2)** have a sweet floral fragrance. For something different, try 'Gloire de Dijon' for its rich tea-like perfume. All are ideal for covering open structures such as pergolas, allowing the breeze to pick up the delightful fragrances.

If you are looking for a sweet intoxicating perfume, the common jasmine (*Jasminum officinale*) is hard to beat. Plant it near a patio where its rich perfume will pervade the whole garden.

Quick-growing annual sweet peas **(3)** (*Lathyrus odoratus*) are ideal to add sweet scent to a new garden or seating area. Good mixtures to try include the aptly named 'Fragrantissima' and 'Bouquet Mixed'.

Exotic climbers

The passion flower (*Passiflora caerulea*), grown for its striking white and blue flowers during summer, sometimes produces edible orange fruit. Another exotic summer climber is the trumpet vine (*Campsis radicans*), which sparkles with orange flowers and has a backdrop of feathery foliage. The related and similar looking variety 'Madame Galen' is more reliable, so ideal for the First-time Gardener. Both need good soil and warm sunny walls in a sheltered spot.

autumn and winter climbers

When the cold weather sets in, there is no need to say goodbye to colour and interest in your garden. Many climbers continue to produce wonderful blooms and foliage right through the autumn and into winter.

Ornamental climbers

These have no equal in terms of their spectacular foliage displays in the autumn. The rich green leaves transform into fiery hues of vivid orange and red, setting the whole garden ablaze with colour. Even when the foliage falls from ornamental climbers, an attractive branching network of slender stems are revealed that can decorate a wall or fence support. There are two principal groups of ornamental climbers: the creepers and the decorative vitis.

The Virginia creeper *Parthenocissus quinquefolia*, has distinctive palm-shaped foliage and needs a large sunny wall or fence; though it will tolerate any soil type. Even though not quite so vigorous, *P. henryana* has similar foliage except the veins on each leaf are highlighted in white. If anything, the foliage is even more fiery come the autumn and is ideal for cloaking a stark wall or fence. It grows well in sun or shade, even dense shade. Both varieties produce a crop full of berries in the autumn.

For a medium-sized support in semi-shade, the related Boston ivy (*P. tricuspidata* 'Veitchii') is a good choice. It is clothed in glossy, three-lobed maple-like leaves that turn brilliant shades of orange and scarlet. These creepers are self-clinging so need no training, other than cutting back wayward shoots. You will need to use secure wires on the walls or fences to get them started in the right direction. They can also be trained into a tree or over a large hedge (see page 78–79).

The best ornamental vine is perhaps *Vitis vinifera* 'Brant', which produces stunning tints in the autumn, turning copper, yellow, orange, red and purple.

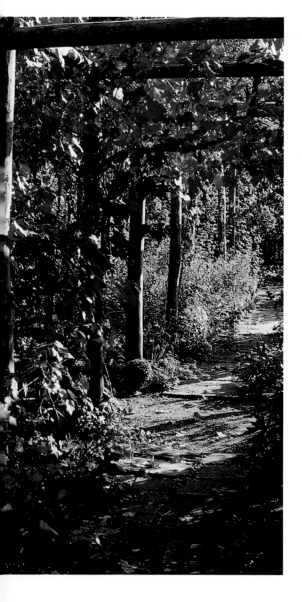

Tunnel of purple foliage

Climbing over a pergola, an ornamental vine, such as *Vitis vinifera* 'Purpurea', transforms the garden as it changes to a deep shade of purple in the autumn.

After a warm summer both climbers produce fruit suitable for wine-making. They are fairly vigorous and so are ideal for covering large structures, such as a pergola, or for disguising eyesores such as an old shed. Their stems will also sprawl, making attractive ground-covering under shrubs and trees.

Consider the crimson glory vine (*V. coignetiae*) if you want to obscure a serious eyesore that is in the sun or partial shade. It can grow to monstrous proportions when it is planted in a sheltered site, covering an area up to 27 m across with its huge heart-shaped leaves, each of which can reach 30 cm across. Like the other vines, the crimson glory vine takes on attractive autumn colours of red, orange and yellow.

Late-flowering climbers

Several varieties of clematis continue to flower well into autumn and a few will brave the winter months. A second flush of bloom is often produced by popular hybrids in late summer and autumn. These blooms are often smaller varieties and are produced on new growth that formed earlier in the year.

Among the best of the naturally late-flowering hybrids are 'Lady Betty Balfour' (purple) and 'Madame Baron Veillard' (pink). There are also some late-flowering species including *Clematis flammula*, which produces masses of tiny star-shaped white blooms in early autumn followed by berries, and *C. rehedriana* which bears small bell-like flowers. *C. tangutica* and *C. viticella* are also worth growing for their nodding yellow and purple blooms, respectively.

Other flowering climbers that continue to bloom into the autumn include the perennial nasturtium

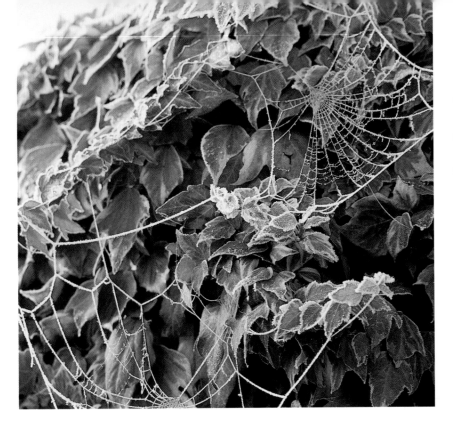

Frosty reception
Evergreen variegated ivy covered in spiders' webs make a striking point of interest in the early morning sunlight after a heavy frost.

Although it is treated as a climber, winter jasmine is really a deciduous shrub that needs tying to a support.

In mild areas, the wonga wonga climber, *Pandorea pandorana*, is also worth considering. Plant it near to the house so you can admire and smell its fragrant creamy and red trumpets which are held above attractive glossy leaves during the winter months.

Tropaeolum speciosum, which grows to 3 m or more in sun or light shade and is covered in scarlet blooms held above attractively lobed leaves. Its near relation, *T. tuberosum*, bears yellow and scarlet flowers against leaves that have a bluish tinge. Both are herbaceous so will die down to ground level after the first frost. Lift tubers in colder areas and store them over the winter somewhere cool but frost-free, such as a garage.

Passion flowers usually finish in late summer but one variety 'Lavender Lady', keeps producing purple blooms into the autumn even though it doesn't produce fruit. Like other passion flowers it needs a sunny spot and well-drained soil. In similar soil, but in a lightly shaded spot, try the Chilean bell flower, *Lapageria rosea,* for its waxy red bells that last until autumn.

Over the winter months and into the spring, *Clematis cirrhosa* and its varieties 'Balearica' and 'Freckles' will bear their creamy flowers in shady areas during mild spells. The red-splashed petal varieties are particularly attractive. The blooms are not terribly frost hardy, however, so

often die in extreme weather. The winter jasmine *Jasminum nudiflorum*, on the other hand is reasonably hardy, except in really cold conditions, and bears its distinctive bright yellow blooms through until early spring on bright green stems.

FIRST-TIME GARDENER'S BEST BETS

 Flowers
Campsis, *Clematis akebiodes*, *C. x durandii*, *C. flammula*, *C. rehderiana*, *C. tangutica*, *C. terniflora*, *C. viticella*, *C.* 'Abundance', 'Arabella', 'Betty Corning', 'Blue Angel', 'Blue Bell', 'Dorothy Walton', 'Duchess of Albany', 'Etoile Rose', 'Golden Tiara', 'Gravetye Beauty', 'Jackmanii Superba', 'Lady Betty Balfour', 'Lady Northcliffe', 'Little Nell', 'Marie Boisselot', 'Mrs Cholmondeley', *C. orientalis* and varieties, 'Sir Trevor Lawrence', 'Star of India', 'Sunset', 'The Vagabond'; *Jasminum polyanthum*, *Lapageria rosea*, *Mandevilla laxa*, *Plumbago capensis*, *Solanum jasminoides* and *Tropaeolum*.

 Foliage
Actinidia chinensis, *Ampelopsis aconitifolia*, *Clematis cirrhosa*, 'Wisley Cream', ivy varieties such as 'Adam', 'Atropurpurea', 'Aureovariegata', 'Glymii', 'Ivalace', 'Parsley Crested' and 'Silver Queen'; *Hydrangea petiolaris*, *Parthenocissus*, *Trachelospermum jasminoides*, ornamental climbers and wisteria.

 Seedheads or berries
Actinidia chinensis, (male and female varieties needed) *Ampelopsis aconitifolia*, *Billadiera longiflora*, *Celastrus scandens*, *Clematis alpina* and varieties, *C. orientalis* and varieties, *Humulus lupulus* and varieties, *Lonicera etrusca* and varieties, *L. japonica* and varieties, *L. periclymenum* and varieties, *Parthenocissus*, *Passiflora caerulea*, *P. edulis* and ornamental climbers.

vertical gardening with climbers

Roger and Jill Sherman bought a converted brick-built schoolhouse with a courtyard that is a sun-trap in summer. The yard was heavily dominated by old brick walls that, although attractive, made the garden seem very confined. They wanted to make maximum use of all the vertical growing space as well as the changes in level the garden provided. They particularly liked the idea of dividing the garden into different 'rooms'.

Improving the soil

The main problem the Shermans faced was the very poor free-draining soil, which needed improving before they could start planting. The soil at the base of the walls was very dry and little rain reached these areas. To improve the situation, the existing soil was dug out to a depth of 45 cm and replaced with a good quality topsoil enriched with plenty of well-rotted farmyard manure.

When deciding on plants for this sort of position, it is not worth planting clematis because it needs a soil that remains moist with its top-growth in the sun. Instead, choose drought-tolerant, sun-loving climbers. Jill planted passion flower (*Passiflora caerulea*) and *Solanum crispum*, which appreciate a warm, sheltered position. After planting, the soil was covered with a thick layer of well-rotted organic matter to help reduce moisture loss. However, a 15-cm-wide space was left around each climber to prevent the organic matter from touching the plants' stems.

Clearing the walls

Like most old walls, these were in need of repair before they could be used to support climbers, especially the self-clinging types such as Virginia creeper and ivies. All loose material was cleared from the walls using a wire brush. The loose mortar was picked from the cracks and then the walls were re-pointed. Jill didn't want to spoil the appearance of the walls with wooden trellis, so she opted to use long galvanised screw-in vine-eyes to attach parallel heavy-duty galvanised wires 30 cm apart up the wall. The vine-eyes were spaced every metre along the wall for vigorous climbers and at intervals of 1.5 m elsewhere. The advantage of wires and vine-eyes is that they are virtually invisible even on areas where there are no climbers.

Dividing the garden

A good way to split a garden into pretty and secluded 'rooms' without cutting down on the sense of space is to install a series of plastic-coated metal arches. These are available in kit form, and slot and bolt together incredibly easily. In Roger and Jill's garden, the end sections of the arches were concreted into the ground and, where possible, bolted to an upright wall using expansion bolts. This made the structure very secure and stable, and suitable for long-term vigorous climbers. Roger and Jill decided to plant several wisterias that would cover the frame quickly and eventually merge to look like one plant.

To the north side of the garden, a pair of climbing roses were planted against the metal arch. They chose two good varieties: 'Albertine', which bears pink flowers during early summer, and 'Madame Alfred Carrière', which blooms until early autumn – both are reliable and free-flowering.

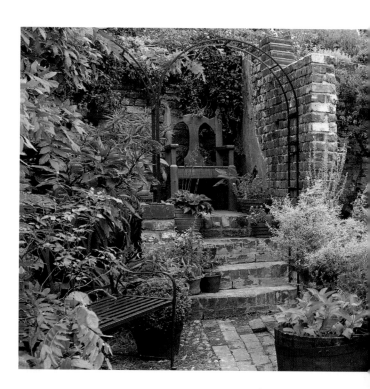

Quick cover

To help camouflage the large expanse of brick building to one side of the courtyard, Roger and Jill decided to plant a quick-growing honeysuckle and a jasmine. These needed to be planted in well-prepared soil and trained up a series of wires, as before. If you wish to create a delightfully natural effect, you should allow the plants to sprawl at will in some areas. Quick-growing annual climbers, such as morning glory, black-eyed Susan and canary creeper, were also planted to ensure a mixture of colourful climbers throughout the first year.

Climbers in trees

To brighten up the evergreen foliage of the tree in the centre of the middle courtyard, the climbing *Bomarea caldasii* has been added. Distinctive, bright-orange blooms stand out against the evergreen backdrop and will be borne more or less continually from late spring to autumn. The wiry growth of this climber makes it particularly suitable for this purpose because it will not swamp the growth of the tree.

Plants for all seasons

To ensure that you have plenty of colourful interest throughout the year, it is important to select a range of different climbers. The following would provide a display in all seasons. In spring the Virgin's bower (*Clematis cirrhosa* 'Balearica') and the scented chocolate vine (*Akebia quinata*) would be good choices, followed by *Clematis montana* and *Actinidia kolomikta* in early summer. Mid-summer favourites, such as scented summer jasmine and the Chilean potato vine (*Solanum*), are also good, as well as *Clematis tangutica* and ornamental vine. To fill the winter gap, winter-flowering jasmine and evergreen variegated ivies are always welcome.

Climbing out of adversity

A range of climbers were chosen to cope with the difficult conditions. Sun-loving passion flower and *Solanum* were used in the sunny courtyard, while shade-tolerant ivies and hoya covered some of the north-facing walls.

reviving old climbers

Oliver owns a property on the outskirts of a small town. Over the past year, he has lovingly restored it, which has taken up most of his free time. Now that he has finished the house, he wants to spend time restoring the garden and wishes to create an outside area filled with summer colour. The old garden contained a number of interesting climbers that Oliver would like to incorporate into his new garden design. Most of the existing climbing plants, however, are overgrown and in need of serious renovation. His aim is to use the climbers to hide or disguise as much of the boundary fence as possible in his long, narrow plot, to make the garden seem larger than it really is.

Time for drastic pruning

All the climbers in Oliver's garden have been left unpruned for many years. When this happens, climbers tend to turn woody at their bases and produce very few flowers. Any blooms that do appear often grow out of sight on new growth, which is produced at the top of the plant. Most climbers respond well to heavy pruning, although you may lose the flowering display for a year or two until the plant produces new growth. The best time to carry out drastic pruning of climbers is while they are dormant between autumn and early spring. It is also an ideal time to make repairs or replace supports while they are easily accessible.

Reinvigorating clematis

One of the attractions of Oliver's garden was the variety of clematis used to clothe the fences on both sides, but they were very overgrown and in need of a drastic trim. Before you can prune clematis, you need to know whether they produce their flowers on growth produced the previous year (early-flowering), during the current year (late-

flowering) or both. To find this out, Oliver had carefully kept a record of each climber's flowering habit the previous year, to make sure he used the correct pruning method (see page 184). However, with the help of reference books and a neighbourly experienced gardener who lived down the road, he was able to identify all but one of his clematis. He did, however, know that this mystery clematis flowered on new growth so needed to be cut back in early spring.

He pruned back the spring-flowering *Clematis montana* 'Elizabeth' after it had flowered. The other two clematis in his garden were 'Lasurstern' and 'The President', which are mid-summer flowering. Both varieties produce their blooms on old and new wood, so Oliver pruned them by cutting selected shoots back to a pair of plump buds close to ground level. Other stems were simply trimmed to fit the support. He then securely tied all unpruned stems on the clematis to their supports (1).

1

Chopping back honeysuckles

There were two honeysuckles in Oliver's garden. The first covered part of a panel fence near to his house. This plant was so top heavy that it practically doubled over with the weight of its stems that had grown beyond the support. Before any detailed pruning could be done, Oliver used a pair of shears to cut back the massed tangled growth to reveal the main stems. When most of the tangle had been removed, he changed to a pair of secateurs to selectively remove or shorten alternate sideshoots to create a basic structure of evenly spaced shoots. He then tied these onto their supports. The second honeysuckle, further down the garden, still had new shoots growing from its base, so this climber didn't need to be cut back so drastically. Oliver removed all the top-heavy growth as before, but only pruned the stems back to a new shoot low on the plant. He then thinned out congested stems by removing the largest and oldest first and leaving the newest growth.

Ornamental climbers

Vigorous *Vitis* respond well to cutting back hard, which is just as well because the pair of climbers at the end of Oliver's garden were starting to take over. It is important to prune ornamental vines before the end of winter; otherwise the cuts can bleed badly as the sap starts to rise in spring. Oliver started regaining control of his monster vine by tracing the wayward stems back to the main stem while still attached to the support. He then cut back the stems cleanly, using a pair of loppers for the large stems and secateurs for smaller ones. Once he identified a framework of main stems, Oliver tied-in those stems in the best position and removed the rest completely, using a special pruning saw. New shoots produced from the base were also tied to the support during the following year.

Curbing rambler and climbing roses

A thicket of overgrown rambler rose stems battled with the ornamental vines and dominated a bottom corner of Oliver's garden. To tackle this beast, Oliver kitted himself out with thick leather gloves, goggles and a thick coat. He also found a piece of old carpet to act as a thorn-proof shield when gaining access to the middle of the thicket. His aim was to cut out all the oldest shoots back to ground level, but this was easier said than done as the thicket was incredibly overgrown. With a little perseverance, however, he managed to cut back all but a handful of vigorous new shoots, which were gingerly tied to the new support.

Unlike rambler roses, climbing roses don't respond well to drastic pruning. There was one gnarled old specimen that was prone to diseases, however, which Oliver wanted to keep because it produced a constant trickle of pretty flowers all summer. So, he decided to give it the kill-or-cure treatment by cutting it back hard with a pruning saw to leave just a couple of shoots near ground level. This he hoped would help reduce the disease problem and encourage the plant to regrow healthily.

Good company
Revitalised climbers filled the new garden design with colour. Next to the house, Oliver added a new climbing rose to partner the clematis 'Lasurstern'. This rose neatly filled the colour gap between the clematis' early and late blooms.

A YEAR LATER... NEW FLOWERS FROM OLD

Nearly all the climbers responded well to the cull of unproductive growth, producing vigorous new stems near the base, and many added a splash of colour to the new garden with a display of flowers in the first year. All the new growth was trained onto the supports and used to replace older stems that were pruned out. Unfortunately, the old climbing rose didn't survive, so Oliver decided to replace it with a new plant the following year.

Adding interest
to borders with climbers

Arches, pergolas, trellis and posts are ideal ways of adding height to your garden quickly. Such garden structures also offer the opportunities to grow climbers if you do not have a suitable wall or fence.

Climber-clad structures not only look great but are easy to construct (see page 92). They can be used to draw the eye to certain parts of the garden or create the illusion of depth and provide a tempting glimpse of the partially hidden areas beyond.

Providing a backdrop
Use painted trellis or posts linked by stout coloured rope to create an elevated support at the back of a large border. Alternatively, try rustic poles and posts to make a series of A-frames on legs that will provide an attractive geometric pattern at the back of the border that can be clothed in a curtain of flowers and foliage. A vigorous clematis, climbing rose or the perennial golden hop would make effective seasonal backdrops, as would the fiery autumn hues of the ornamental vine, *Vitis vinifera* 'Purpurea'.

Framing a view
An arch or pergola, made from a simple DIY kit or constructed out of rustic poles, is an ideal way of framing a point of focus, such as a birdbath, or drawing the eye to a distant feature, such as a statue at the end of a path. In the picture opposite **(4)**, for example, the shady arch covered by the delicately fragrant 'Iceberg' rose effectively brings the garden beyond into focus.

An arch can be placed over a path to allow close scrutiny of foliage and flowers, or positioned mid-border where it can be viewed from a distance. To ensure that the arch doesn't fight for attention, its size should be in proportion with the rest of the garden and the vigour of the climber to complement its surroundings. A broad path, for example, would look best if bridged by a heavy-weight arch and covered with a variety of colourful climbers that provide interest through the seasons, while a simple statue would be complemented by an elegant metal arch clad

in a colourful small-leaved ivy that framed the focal point all year round. Be prepared to experiment with colour for an eye-catching feature. For instance, try growing a climber that bears contrasting bright-yellow flowers over a blue painted arch.

Secluded seating
Arches are also an effective way of creating a secluded seating area in a small garden. Again it is important to maintain a sense of proportion and choose a seat that fits within the arch comfortably. Also make sure that the position you choose has an attractive outlook; otherwise you'll be less tempted to stop and rest each time you pass by. You can then cover the arch with perfumed rambling roses such as 'Albéric Barbier', 'Albertine', 'Emily Gray', 'Sander's White Rambler' and 'Seagull'. Alternatively, make a cool and shady retreat by covering the arch with an ornamental vine or the ferny foliage of summer jasmine. On a large arch or pergola, combine several climbers including clematis and honeysuckles for a succession of colour and scent throughout the summer. For example, in the picture opposite **(1)**, the two scented climbing roses have been planted alongside wisteria and jasmine to form a striking feature and fragrant pergola.

Adding a focal point
A simple climber-clad post can make an attractive focal point in its own right. A formal atmosphere is easy to create using metal obelisks, which look especially effective when used in pairs either side of a path. Less formal structures can look just as good in the right setting and cost next to nothing to make. A tripod of bamboo canes or a handful of long twiggy prunings, bundled together at one end with string and stuck in the ground, can be covered in annual climbers, such as sweet peas, morning glories or canary creeper.

Floral frames
Scented roses, jasmine and wisteria cover a white-painted trellis pergola **(1)**; clematis partners a wall-trained ceanothus **(2)**; a rose-clad arch focuses the eye ahead **(3)**; and golden hop covers a rustic arch **(4)**.

constructing arches and pergolas

The design and material from which an arch or pergola is made should complement the style of the rest of the garden. Wooden structures, for example, are chunky and can have an angular feel, so they look most effective in a traditional garden design. This is particularly the case with rustic poles, which look best when covered in billowing scented climbers in a cottage-garden setting. Arches and pergolas made from slim timbers and coloured with wood stain or coated in paint, however, can look effective in a contemporary garden, especially when covered in a climber with a contrasting flower colour. In a larger garden, pergolas with brick or stone piers and a timber overhead frame are worth considering.

Metal-framed pergolas or arches offer a sleek and clean appearance that complements most modern garden designs. If you have enough space, you could try to incorporate attractive circular structures or shady arbors. These look decorative and can be used to create a cool place to eat. You should also remember that arches and pergolas must be strong enough to take the weight of the climber you have in mind, as well as being sufficiently well anchored so that they don't collapse in high winds.

Kits or special orders

Many easy-to-assemble, flat-packed kits in wood and metal are now available and the range of designs is growing. To help you choose which style to opt for, many of the larger garden retailers and DIY stores have a selection of assembled kits on display. (Manufacturers of the various kits may also be able to tell you where you can go locally to see one of their structures assembled.)

Local fencing specialists often produce designs of their own, so it's worth checking out what outlets there are in your area before you

---

FIRST-TIME GARDENER'S BEST BETS

Climbers for scent
Clematis armandii, C. montana, everlasting pea (*Lathyrus latifolius*), honeysuckle, jasmine, roses 'Aloha', 'Compassion', 'Madame Grégoire Staechelin', 'Maigold', 'Rambling Rector', 'Sander's White Rambler', 'Seagull' and 'Veilchenblau'.

Climbers for arches
Less vigorous clematis, honeysuckles, jasmine and the thornless roses 'Kathleen Harrop' and 'Zéphirine Drouhin'.

Climbers for pergolas
Actinidia kolomikta, clematis, honeysuckle, jasmine and roses such as 'Adélaide d'Orléans', 'Albéric Barbier', 'Albertine', 'Crimson Shower', 'Dorothy Perkins', 'Emily Gray', 'Félicité Perpétue', 'Phyllis Bide', 'Pink Perpétue', 'Sander's White Rambler', 'Seagull', 'Swan Lake' and 'The Garland'.

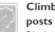

Climbers for pillars and posts
Black-eyed Susan (*Thunbergia alata*), Canary creeper (*Tropaeolum*), clematis, Chilean glory flower (*Eccremocarpus*), Cup-and-saucer vine (*Cobaea scandens*), morning glories (*Ipomoea*), sweet pea, variegated ivies and roses such as 'Aloha', 'Compassion', 'Dortmund', 'Golden Showers', 'Handel' and 'New Dawn'.

buy. Make sure that wooden frames are made from pressure-treated wood or wood with natural durability, such as western red cedar, larch or Douglas fir.

If you want a structure to fit a specific space in your garden, you may have to have one specially designed and built by a contractor; alternatively, you could make it yourself from the component parts. You should ask for advice at your local builders' merchant or fencing specialist if you want a wooden structure, or contact manufacturers of metal ones to get a catalogue and price list. Metal structures should have a thick plastic coating without cracks or chips. Also, check that the frame slots together easily and the pre-drilled holes for bolts line up to make the kit easy to assemble.

Putting them together

Well-made metal structures are probably the easiest and quickest to put together – expect to spend about half a day for a pergola and half an hour for an arch. The sections simply slot together and, once constructed, the whole structure is rigid and quite lightweight so it can be easily moved around.

Wooden structures require more do-it-yourself skill to build, though are still well within the scope of a First-time Gardener. Wood arches are usually supplied with extra-long vertical posts so they can be concreted into the ground.

When building a wooden pergola, it is very important to get the posts in the right position at the outset, so measure the position accurately and mark it out with pegs and string or with spray paint **(1)**. You then need to dig holes for the main post anchors. Use a spirit level to check that the posts are upright before adding concrete to the holes **(2)**. You should be aware that the wood may rot if concreted directly into the ground, so you may prefer to trim each of the posts and bolt them to metal fence-post spikes that are driven into the ground with a sledgehammer.

Choose a suitable climber for the site and size of the structure (see box, opposite). At the base of each upright post, plant single specimens or pairs of climbers with complementary flowering times **(3)**. Wooden pergolas are quite heavy once assembled, so make sure you have at least one extra pair of hands available during the final stages of construction.

Shrubs and trees

Perhaps the most important plants in the garden, shrubs and trees are the backbone that brings a permanent sense of structure to the design as a whole as well as to individual borders. Many change dramatically throughout the year, giving a variety of seasonal interest. In short, shrubs and trees represent a wealth of colour and diversity that no garden should be without.

Shrubs are woody perennial plants, smaller than trees, usually with several stems or trunks. Some varieties, such as camellia, produce spectacular displays of flowers that rival the floral shows of summer bedding, while others, such as maple trees, offer a stunning array of coloured leaves in the autumn. Many shrubs and trees bear berries in the winter while others fill the air with heady fragrance all summer.

Shrubs and trees need the right growing conditions to thrive, so check the plant label before you buy. Many are adaptable to a variety of conditions, while some will thrive in heavy clay soil or other difficult areas. They will even grow in exposed seaside gardens and alongside heavily polluted roads. Although most shrubs prefer a sunny site, there are some that will do well even in heavy shade. Use the lists of recommended shrubs and trees to help you make the right choice.

Deciduous plants drop their leaves at the end of the growing season, while evergreens hold onto their leaves. The latter can provide year-round structure, but if you have too many, the garden will seem static, changing little throughout the year. The secret to success is to have a balance: one evergreen to every two deciduous plants. You also need to decide how big you want the specimen to grow and how quickly. This can vary a great deal between seemingly close relatives. The dwarf pine, for example, grows to less than 1 m, whereas the Scots pine can reach well over 30 m. Finally, consider what function you want the shrub or tree to perform, so you can decide upon its shape (see also page 16).

spring selection

Spring-flowering shrubs and trees herald the new season with a burst of bloom **(3)**. No matter where you live, the garden centre will be loaded with flowering shrubs at this time. Always ensure your soil and light conditions match the plant's requirements.

Classic choices

Camellias offer stunning flowers that look best against dark glossy foliage **(1)**. For a reliable display, choose one of the *C.* x *williamsii* varieties such as 'Anticipation' with its peony-flower shaped crimson blooms, 'Debbie' (deep pink) or the semi-double 'Donation' (pale pink). Camellias grow best in acid soil areas, but also grow well in containers filled with special acidic soil. They also need to be protected from cold winds and early morning sun, which can ruin the blooms.

Magnolias are another spring favourite. If you have the space, the tulip magnolia (*M.* x *soulangeana*) varieties such as 'Alexandria', which bears fragrant, white, flushed purple blooms, or the fast-growing and free-flowering pink 'Lennei' **(2)** are ideal. In a smaller garden, the star magnolia (*M. stellata*) varieties such as 'Rosea', 'Royal Star' and 'Waterlily' may be a better bet.

Another spring favourite is forsythia. The orangey 'Beatrix Farrand' is a good choice for a large border because it has the bonus of attractive purple leaves in the autumn, but for a smaller-sized garden go for the floriferous bright yellow 'Lynnwood' or 'Spectabilis'. An alternative to forsythia would be broom: varieties such as *Cytisus* x *praecox* 'Allgold' or 'Warminster', both of which have long arching stems bejeweled with flowers in spring. Or try the yellow-flowered

Kerria japonica varieties 'Golden Guinea' and 'Pleniflora', both are good options for the First-time Gardener. If you want a reliable evergreen shrub with bright yellow spring flowers search out *Berberis* x *stenophylla*. It is good in shade and can be grown as an informal hedge.

For something a little out of the ordinary, consider the purple broom *Cytisus purpureus* or the wire-netting bush (*Corokia cotoneaster*), which bears starry yellow flowers towards the end of spring. You may have to contact a shrub specialist for these plants, however.

Spring aromas

Fragrance is a welcome attribute alongside a well-used path in spring – *Choisya ternata* is a good choice as it has citrus-scented flowers and foliage and it produces further flushes of blooms later in the year. The variety 'Sundance' is tempting to buy because of its bright yellow foliage, but it is liable to scorch in strong sunlight and it produces few flowers. Towards the end of spring, lilacs make a brief, but welcome entrance. Although they have a short flowering season, their scent is so divine that they are worth it. Keep an eye out for *Syringa microphylla* 'Superba' because it will produce a second flush of blooms in late summer.

Foliage interest

Many trees and shrubs have colourful spring leaves that can be used to add interest to the back of a border, as a backdrop to bright displays of spring bulbs or even as a striking focal point. Perhaps the best shrub for this purpose is *Pieris* 'Forest Flame' because it is a dark-leafed evergreen that produces strings of tiny white, bell-shaped, scented flowers and bright red new growth that slowly darkens as it matures. *Pieris* prefers semi-shade and an acidic soil. Equally appealing for sun or shade is *Photinia* x *fraseri* 'Red Robin', which produces bright red new foliage in spring.

To add brightness to a shaded corner try *Philadelphus coronarius* 'Aureus', which glows when it produces its bright yellow new leaves. They age to a mellow yellow during the summer months, only to brighten again in the autumn. Another yellow-leafed shrub for a difficult spot is *Ribes alpinum*, which does well on poor soils in shade – on the north side of a wall, for example.

Trees with bright spring foliage need to be viewed from both a distance and close up to be appreciated to the full, so plant them at the end of a path or near the boundary in your front garden. This way they are easily accessible, but you can still view them from the house. In a small garden try *Acer pseudoplatanus* 'Brilliantissimum' or *A. negundo* 'Flamingo', both of which grow to only 5 m or so when mature. They both bear pink foliage in spring and yellow hues in the autumn, with the latter having the added attraction of variegated foliage all summer. Other varieties of acer, such as 'Aureum' and 'Rubrum', have equally attractive spring growth but reach about twice the size.

FIRST-TIME GARDENER'S BEST BETS

For shade`
Aucuba, box, camellia, elaeagnus, euonymus, fatsia, mahonia, osmanthus, *Prunus laurocerasus*, *P. lusitanica*, privet, rubus, skimmia, viburnum and vinca.

For polluted air
Berberis, camellia, chaenomeles, cistus, cotinus, cotoneaster, cytisus, deutzia, elaeagnus, escallonia, forsythia, genista, holly, hypericum, lilac, mahonia, philadelphus, potentilla, privet, pyracantha, rhododendron, skimmia, spiraea, symphoricarpos, viburnum and weigela.

For clay soil
Aucuba, berberis, chaenomeles, cornus, corylus, cotoneaster, forsythia, hypericum, mahonia, philadelphus, potentilla, pyracantha, spiraea, viburnum, vinca and weigelia.

For coastal areas
Arbutus, arundinaria, castanea, choisya, cordyline, cotoneaster, crataegus, cytisus, elaeagnus, escallonia, euonymus, fraxinus, fuchsia (*pictured right*) garrya, genista, hebe, helianthemum, hippophae, ilex, lavender, olearia, pittosporum, poplar, pyracantha, rosemary, salix, santolina, senecio, sorbus, spiraea, tamarix, ulex, viburnum and yucca.

For chalky soil
Arbutus, aucuba, berberis, buddleia, box, ceanothus, choisya, cistus, cotoneaster, deutzia, elaeagnus, escallonia, euonymus, forsythia, fuchsia, garrya, hebe, holly, hypericum, kerria, kolkwitzia, lavender, lilac, mahonia, olearia, peony, philadelphus, photinia, pittosporum, potentilla, privet, pyracantha, rhus, rosemary, sambucus, santolina, senecio, tamarix, vinca, weigela and yucca.

best summer choices

Several of the best garden shrubs not only produce spectacular displays during the summer but also scent the air with their delightful perfume. Roses are perhaps the best example, but there are other shrubs that will also help perfume your garden display.

Aromatic plants

Lavender is one of the most widely grown shrubs, preferring well-drained soil in a sunny spot. If your soil is heavy, grow lavender on a mound filled with a mixture of rubble and sand, covered with a 15 cm layer of topsoil mixed with grit to improve drainage in the winter months. Taller varieties worth growing in the middle of a border include 'Alba' (white) and 'Folate' (purple), but to really appreciate the scent, grow lavender next to a path as a low hedge or edging plant. For this situation choose dwarf varieties such as 'Hidcote' (purple), 'Hidcote Pink' (pink) or 'Munstead' (purple).

French lavender (*L. stoechas*) has distinctive 'wings' that protrude from the top of each flower, making it particularly decorative and worth giving a prominent position. The best variety is the purple 'Papillon'.

For a sweet honeysuckle-like scent, try growing the moderately tender *Abelia chinensis*, which bears its pale pink blooms in mid- to late summer. It grows in most soils but likes the sun and shelter from the wind, so would be ideal at the base of a south-facing wall or fence. It's not very hardy, so in colder areas it will need protecting in winter. Alternatively, it could be grown in a container and moved indoors during the coldest months.

The butterfly bush, *Buddleja davidii*, will grow almost anywhere provided the soil drains freely. Its musk-scented, conical flowers act like a magnet to pollinating insects and butterflies. Look for a named variety to get the best floral display: 'Black Knight' (deep purple), 'Royal Red' (purple-red), 'White Profusion'

(white) and 'Lochinch' (lilac-blue). Oddities include the variegated leaves of 'Harlequin' (purple-red) and the dwarf 'Nanho Blue' (deep blue). These all need hard pruning in the spring (see pages 182–185).

If you like soap scents, then the Californian tree poppy, *Romneya coulteri*, is a must. It is one of the most spectacular summer-flowering shrubs, producing yellow-centred, white poppy-like flowers up to 12 cm across. These are set off to perfection against their feathery bluish-grey foliage. It takes several years to get established, however, and in cold areas should be treated as a herbaceous perennial because the above-ground shoots will be killed in winter. Cut back all growth to ground level in spring, in any case, to maintain a neat habit.

Foliage for colour and texture

Many good garden shrubs offer interesting and colourful foliage. A good all-rounder is the evergreen hebes, which will grow almost

---

FIRST-TIME GARDENER'S BEST BETS

 For bees and butterflies
Berberis, buddleia, ceanothus, chaenomeles, cistus, cotoneaster, cytisus, daphne, elaeagnus, escallonia, fuchsia, hebe, lavender, lilac, olearia, perovskia, potentilla, privet, pyracantha, rhus, skimmia, spiraea, ulex, viburnum and weigelia.

 For birds
Aucuba, berberis, buddleia, callicarpa, chaenomeles, clerodendrum, cotoneaster, daphne, flowering currant, hebe, hippophäe, hypericum, ilex, lilac, mahonia, pernettya, pyracantha, rhus, skimmia and viburnum.

 For scent
Abelia chinensis, *Berberis stenophylla*, *Buddleja davidii*, *Cytisus battandieri*, daphne, flowering currant, hamamelis, lavender, lilac, *Lonicera fragrantissima*, magnolia, myrtle, osmanthus, roses and *Viburnum fragans*.

 Disease-resistant roses
'Alexander', 'Amber Queen', 'Anne Harkness', 'Arthur Bell', 'Bright Smile', 'Canary Bird', 'Cheshire Life', 'Congratulations', 'Dutch Gold', 'Fragrant Delight', 'Frau Dagmar Hartopp', 'Grandpa Dickson', 'Just Joey', 'Lover's Meeting', 'Matangi', 'Mountbatten', 'Peace', 'Roseraie de l'Haÿ', 'Royal William', 'Silver Jubilee', 'Southampton', 'Sunblest', 'Queen Elizabeth' and 'Trumpeter'.

anywhere – in wind-swept seaside gardens, in heavy or light soil, in the sun or the shade (although this will reduce flowering). For attractive foliage choose variegated varieties such as *Hebe* x *andersonii* 'Variegata' or *H.* x *franciscana* 'Variegata'. Other distinctive hebes include the low-growing 'Pagei', which has grey foliage, and 'Red Edge', which has red-edged grey leaves. The larger 'James Sterling' is particularly striking because it has wonderful burnished-gold foliage.

The hairy leaves of the evergreen *Convolvulus cneorum* give it a silky grey appearance, which creates the perfect background for its pink flower buds that open to white trumpet-shaped blooms in early summer. It needs a sunny spot with well-drained soil and benefits from winter protection in colder regions.

Ferny foliage is a particularly attractive feature of some shrubs. The bottlebrush tree, (*Callistemon citrinus*), is a sun-loving plant that does best in the shelter of a south-facing wall or fence. It is particularly worth growing in the milder conditions often found near a coast. For the best bottlebrush flowers, look for 'Splendens', but in colder areas, the hardier but less showy *C. rigidus* is a better bet. Another shrub with decorative ferny foliage is *Sorbaria*. It is an attractive large shrub with frothy white flowers up to 20 cm long. To get the best displays of leaves and flowers, cut back the stems after flowering.

Trouble-free roses

Roses have a lot to offer the First-time Gardener – for sheer flower power they can't be beaten. There are literally thousands of varieties so you won't be short of choice, and many offer a delicious scent, too. Roses are, however, renowned for their susceptibility to the diseases of blackspot, mildew and rust, so it is important that you choose with care to be sure of buying disease-resistant varieties (see First-time Gardener's best bets, opposite).

If you want scented roses, search out the yellow 'Arthur Bell' or 'Mountbatten', the salmon-pink 'Fragrant Delight' or 'Silver Jubilee', orange-red 'Lovers Meeting' or 'Matangi', or the deep red 'Royal William' – if your local garden centre doesn't sell them, try contacting a rose specialist.

Sensual planting
Colourful roses, aromatic French lavender and furry lamb's ears (*Stachys*) are combined with other sun-loving plants such as red valerian (*Centranthus*), catmint (*Nepeta*) and hardy geranium in this sunny border.

colour into winter

When nearly all other garden interest is winding down for the winter, certain shrubs and trees can provide brilliant colour. Because most new trees and shrubs can be planted in the autumn, this is a good time to plan an autumn display. But the danger for the First-time Gardener is to be tempted by bright scarlets, oranges and yellows only to find the plant is lacklustre for the rest of the year. Fortunately, there are plenty of examples that have more to offer than just a rainbow of shades in the autumn.

Autumn favourites

Valued for their striking autumn foliage colours, maples **(1)** are a common sight in many gardens. Where space is limited, the Japanese maple (*Acer palmatum* 'Dissectum') is ideal for a sheltered position in light shade. Forming a neat mound of ferny leaves, the intricately divided foliage is bright green as it unfurls in spring, but still looks great all summer. In the autumn, the leaves turn brilliant shades of pink, red and orange. For extra summer colour, try one of the named varieties such as 'Dissectum Apro-purpureum', 'Dissectum Garnet' and 'Dissectum Crimson Queen', all of which have wonderful purple leaves. If your soil is heavy, it is best to grow these plants in containers.

Another purple-leafed shrub that has added value in winter is the deciduous berberis, *B. thunbergii* 'Atropurpurea'. Its richly coloured foliage takes on vivid red hues in the autumn before dropping from the plant to reveal a hidden treasure of red berries in the winter. Although a really versatile shrub that can cope with almost any soil in sun or shade, it produces its best leaf colours in full sun. For a really tight corner you could try the dwarf variety 'Atropurpurea Nana', which grows to just 60 cm tall.

In a woodland setting, consider *Fothergilla major* for its eye-catching autumn foliage in shades of orange, red and scarlet. It has the bonus of scented flowers in late spring before the leaves unfurl. Another option is the winged euonymus or spindle bush (*Euonymus alatus*) which is slow growing, reaching the height of about 2 m in ten years. Leaves turn an attractive pink shade in autumn and drop to reveal the decorative corky ridged bark on the stems. At other times, use the uninspiring foliage as a foil for summer flowers. Avoid this shrub if your garden is plagued by blackfly because it is a favourite over-wintering site for this pest.

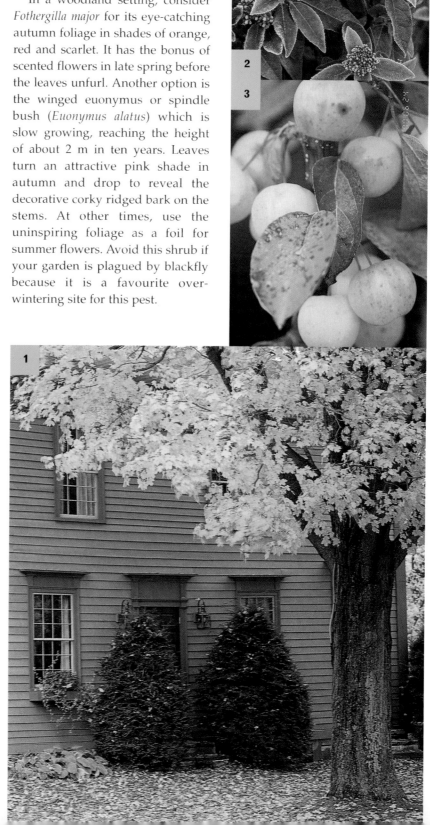

If you have space, the smoke tree, *Cotinus coggygria*, is worth planting as a focal point in the middle of a lawn, for example. Apart from its bright autumn tints of orange and yellow, in summer it is covered in a haze of pinkish flowers that turn to a smoky grey. The variety 'Flame' offers the best leaf colour in autumn, but purple leaf forms, such as 'Royal Purple' and 'Notcutt's Variety', are also good.

A reliable performer in any garden, the hardy *Viburnum tinus* (3) is an evergreen shrub with a neat bushy habit, which bears flattened flowerheads of pinkish white blooms. The attractive buds first appear in mid-autumn and open over a period of time from mid-winter followed by blackish fruits.

Berries for winter wonder
A bonus in any garden, berry-producing plants can be included to give added interest to the coldest months. The decorative value of berries tends to be short-lived, however, because they are usually eaten by birds and other wildlife, but the following shrubs and trees produce an abundant harvest that will last at least until the coldest weather sets in.

Rose hips, pyracantha and skimmia berries and fruiting trees such as ornamental malus (2) and sorbus are the usual fruit-laden plants on offer at garden centres, but there are others worth seeking out. *Mahonia japonica,* for example, has so much to offer as a plant that its eye-catching strings of blue berries are almost forgotten. The plant's upright architectural shape and distinctive horizontal holly-like foliage are reasons enough to include it in your garden. Before the berries appear, they also produce attractive, scented flowers. There are many good varieties, but

FIRST-TIME GARDENER'S BEST BETS

For autumn colour
Acer, berberis, betula, *Carpinus betulus, Crataegus prunifolia,* cotinus, fagus, fothergilla, *Liquidambar styraciflua, Liriodendron tulipifera, Nothofagus antarctica, Nyssa sylvatica,* poplar, *Robinia pseudoacacia* and sorbus.

For great bark
Acer capillipes, A. davidii, A. griseum, A. grosseri 'Hersii', A. pensylvanicum, A. palmatum, Arbutus × andrachnoides, A. menziesii, Betula albosinensis 'Septentrionalis', B. ermanii, B. nigra 'Heritage', B. papyrifera, B. utilis 'Jacquemontii', Corylus colurna, Eucalyptus dalrympleana, E. pauciflora 'Niphophila', E. perriniana, Parrotia persica, Prunus serrula, Stuartia pseudocamillia and S. sinensis.

For winter berries
Berberis, euonymus, hippophäe, holly, (*pictured below*), mahonia, malus, pernettya, pyracantha, skimmia, sorbus and stranvaesia.

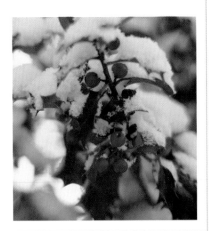

'Charity' has the best flowers and 'Lionel Fortescue' displays the most impressive foliage. In especially cold areas choose the hardier *M. aquifolium.*

The silvery willow-like foliage of the sea buckthorn, *Hippophäe rhamnoides,* is one of the most striking berried plants, because the large bright orange fruit are produced in abundance. You will need to buy both male and female plants to get a good crop of berries. It is ideally suited to exposed gardens, such as by the sea, and will grow in any well-drained soil. The stems are armed with sharp spines so it makes a good boundary plant. Its underground runners, however, can be invasive.

Year-round colour
Evergreen conifers are the stalwart of winter displays. They range from ground-hugging prostrate types, for covering the ground, to narrow vertical columns that can be used like exclamation marks at the end of

a border planting. Most provide a static display of constant colour throughout the year, with different varieties offering subtly different colours – from bright yellow to deep bronze, from the palest green through steely blues to almost blackish-green shades. The variety you choose should depend on the function you want it to perform; for example, choose a prostrate variety for weed-smothering ground cover. Growth rates and ultimate sizes vary enormously, however, from miniature plants that grow less than 2 cm a year, to giant specimens that reach well over 30 m tall. They also vary in their hardiness, so check before you buy.

Two good garden varieties worth highlighting are *Thuja occidentalis* 'Rheingold' and *Cryptomeria japonica* 'Elegans'. Both remain small enough for most gardens but gain an attractive bronze tint in the autumn.

planting trees and shrubs

It is important to plant trees at the correct spacing if they are going to fulfil their potential. If you plant them too close to one another, either you will have to move them later on, which is hard work and not always successful, or you will have to prune them regularly to keep them in check. With the exception of very slow-growing species, don't be tempted to buy semi-mature plants to create an instant border. These are not only expensive but also take far longer to get established than smaller, less mature plants.

If you do buy small plants, however, your planting scheme can look somewhat barren for the first few years. There are two ways of overcoming this. First, you could plant quick-growing but short-lived 'filler' shrubs in between your main shrubs. Many inexpensive shrubs such as forsythia, butterfly bush, mock orange and rose-of-Sharon can be used. These establish quickly and provide a good display during the early years, but they will need to be removed once the main shrubs grow and need more space. The second option is to fill the gaps between the main shrubs with a mixture of bulbs, ground-covering perennials and hardy annuals. These give instant colour to the border and will slowly die out over the years as the main shrubs shade them out and use up the moisture and nutrients.

Getting the best from new shrubs and trees

It is essential that new shrubs and trees don't run short of moisture around their roots or suffer from competition from weeds and other plants. The easiest way to achieve this is to water thoroughly after planting and to cover the soil with a

Correct planting distances

There is a very simple formula you can use for calculating the planting distances between shrubs or trees. First, you will need to find out the mature height of the shrubs or trees you are buying. This information is often given on the label but it is also worth looking up the varieties in a good plant encyclopaedia. Once you have found out this information, add together the mature height of the two specimens you are planting adjacent to one another. Now, divide this number by either three, to get the correct planting distance for shrubs, or divide it by two to get the correct planting distance for trees.

7.5-cm deep layer of organic matter, such as bark chips, or a 1-m diameter sheet of mulch matting.

In drought-prone areas, make watering easier by ridging up the soil about 30 cm from the tree to form a small reservoir around the base. Any water will remain in the reservoir until it has soaked into the soil **(1)**. Alternatively, hammer a

plastic pipe into the ground near the plant and fill it with gravel, then pour the water down the pipe **(2)**. The gravel holds the water, while the pipe directs it to the roots.

To keep weeds at bay, turn to mulch. A generous layer of wood chips, chopped leaves or other organic material smothers weeds and makes it easier to hand-pull

Planting shrubs and trees

To ensure that shrubs and trees establish quickly, they should be planted carefully. Container-grown plants can be planted at any time of the year but establish far quicker if planted in the spring or autumn. Specimens sold with no soil around the roots, known as bare-root, should be planted while dormant. Evergreens and conifers are best planted in the spring. Always water the plants well before you plant them.

1 Dig the soil thoroughly and remove any weeds and large stones. Now, dig a large planting hole, about twice as wide as the rootball and a little deeper. Prick over the bottom and sides of the hole with a fork to allow the roots to spread out easily – this

any that do sprout later. Renew the layer of mulch as necessary as it decomposes.

Most shrubs benefit from the occasional pruning (see page 182), but a few can be left to their own devices – *Aucuba japonica* varieties, *Acer palmatum* 'Dissectum', *Berberis thunbergii* varieties and *Yucca filamentosa*. It is usually impractical to remove the dead flower heads from garden shrubs and trees, but a few will benefit. Roses, azaleas, camellias, lilacs and rhododendrons are all worth deadheading as their flowers fade. But, leave the old flowers on hydrangeas until spring as they provide winter interest and help protect the new flower buds.

Some popular shrubs are prone to producing vigorous shoots from the roots, known as suckers. These need to be removed by excavating the soil from around the root and tearing the sucker from the root. Don't just cut off the sucker because this will encourage more to be produced. Some variegated shrubs also produce vigorous and less decorative all-green shoots, which should be removed using secateurs.

Several shrubs, such as bay, choisya, *Jasminum officinale*, myrtle and ceanothus, need winter protection in colder areas. Wrap up evergreen shrubs, such as bay and myrtle, with an insulating double layer of garden fleece or a quilt made from a double layer of netting stuffed with straw or dry leaves. Protect any conifers and choisya from cold winds by wrapping them in windbreak netting. To protect the roots of semi-tender plants, cover the soil with a thick layer of evergreen prunings, bark chips or dead leaves held down by netting.

is particularly important in heavy clay soil. Then, incorporate some well-rotted manure or proprietary planting mixture into the bottom of the planting hole.

2 Place the plant in the hole and lay a bamboo cane across it to check that the hole is deep enough. Adjust the depth, if needed, so that the plant is at the same depth as it was in the pot (look for a change in bark colour to indicate the soil depth for bare-root trees and shrubs). Check over the rootball and remove any weeds and loose soil, then gently tease out the roots using your fingers. Place the plant in the hole then add about 15 cm of soil around the edge, before firming with your heel. Repeat this process until the hole is filled. Water thoroughly (see opposite).

3 Knock a sturdy wooden stake into the soil at a 45-degree angle to the tree trunk so that it avoids the rootball. To keep the tree stable, tie the trunk to the stake using a special tree tie with a spacer (available from garden centres) to stop the tree rubbing against the stake as it grows. Cover the surface of the soil with a 7.5-cm deep layer of an organic mulch, such as bark chips or cocoa shells, to suppress weeds and help retain soil moisture.

planning a year-round border

Debbie and Tom had neglected their garden while renovating their house. Apart from a formal walled area nearest the house, they wanted to create a formal structure to the rest of their garden design, but were also keen to include lots of informal borders full of fragrant flowers. Although they wanted the planting scheme to peak during the summer months, they also liked the idea of including several plants that offered lots of interest at other times of the year, too.

Formal structure

If you want your garden to have year-round appeal, you need to include both deciduous and evergreen plants. Too many evergreens may make your garden uninteresting for much of the year; too few and your garden will lack continuity and look bleak in winter. As a rule of thumb, it is best to aim for about one evergreen for every two deciduous plants.

Debbie and Tom's garden design was based around a symmetrical series of beds separated by simple straight grass paths. A wider paved walkway ran down the middle of the area forming a natural focal point out of an arched gateway that leads to the walled garden nearest the house. They wanted to add height and colour to this formal design that would last all-year round. They opted to use a series of semi-mature upright conifers rescued from elsewhere in the garden to form an evergreen parade. Standing like sentinels down each main border, the junipers' columnar shapes added a real sense of drama to the scene.

Several other evergreens, including osmanthus, viburnum and myrtle, were incorporated into the border's planting plan to provide a backbone structure throughout the year. Tom wanted to include a series of box trees clipped into

spheres and conical shapes. As an unusual finishing touch, he added a bird-bath water feature that became the envy of all his friends. He made it from a salvaged feeding trough that he bought at the local flea market. He positioned it in the centre of the main walkway and raised it up on bricks to give it more height and presence.

Flowering informality

To contrast with the formal plantings of static evergreens, Debbie wanted to fill the borders with a combination of deciduous shrubs and perennials with airy or relaxed habit and plenty of summer flowers. Her aim was to transform the formal borders by overwhelming them with informal growth during the summer months.

She decided to give the polyantha rose, 'Little White Pet', centre stage because she liked its huge trusses of mini pompom-like flowers that last all summer long. Grown in groups of threes and fives along the main borders, the plants spilled out onto the paths so that passers-by could fully appreciate the fragrant white blooms, giving the whole garden a fairy-tale atmosphere. These roses are not large or vigorous; they grow to a height and width of between 70 cm and 1 m, so they would suit even a small garden.

At the back of the borders, Debbie planted the taller pink-flowering rugosa rose 'Frau Dagmar Hartopp', for its highly fragrant blooms and repeat flowering performance. As an added bonus, it produces a crop of tomato-shaped deep red hips in the autumn.

Spring interest

Most people buy plants for their garden in spring and this can lead to gardens looking great at that time of year, but rather lackluster at other times. A well-designed planting scheme has lots of colour and interest throughout the year. To achieve this, Debbie and Tom chose plants that bloom at different times to offer more than one season of interest as well as plants that produced berries, autumn leaves or coloured winter bark.

Under the roses they planted shade-tolerant snowdrops and winter aconites, which brightened up the borders before the roses came into leaf. The dainty white snowdrops are the first to emerge, followed by the bright yellow blooms of the winter aconites. Elsewhere, other bulbs, including crocus, scillas, chionodoxas and muscari, plus later-flowering dwarf tulips, were planted in irregular blocks to give a succession of colour during the spring months.

Summer scenes

Apart from the roses, which bloom more or less all summer long, Debbie and Tom added a range of herbaceous perennials to boost the light and airy feel of the summer border. At the back of the border, large frothy plants, such as *Crambe cordifolia* and baby's breath, were included for their clouds of summer flowers. Tall spires of foxgloves, hollyhocks and mullein as well as the attractive globes of alliums were also added. Toward the front, they chose lady's mantle (*Alchemilla mollis*), catmint (*Nepeta* x *faassenii*) and hardy geranium, *G. sanguineum* and its variety *G. sanguineum* 'Striatum'. A few hardy annuals were scattered here and there to fill any unsightly gaps. Plants such as love-in-a-mist (*Nigella*), night-scented stock and candytuft were particular favourites.

Flowers in the autumn

Many of the summer blooms lasted well into the autumn, but to add more interest to the border at this time of the year, Tom planted late-flowering herbaceous perennials including aster, sedum and rudbeckia. He chose A. x *frikartii* 'Mönch' for the back of the border – a clump-forming plant that bears lavender-blue flowers from mid-summer to mid-autumn on 90-cm stems; *Sedum* 'Autumn Joy' toward the front for its flattened pink flowerheads in late summer that darken to bronze by the end of the autumn; and *Rudbeckia fulgida* 'Goldsturm' for a mid-border position where it bears a succession of brilliant yellow brown-eyed daisies from mid-summer to mid-autumn.

Winter wonderland

The clearing of borders and any pruning was left until after the worst of the winter weather. This meant the old stems provided some protection to the crowns of less-hardy plants in the border during the coldest months and helped decorate the scene, creating an interesting winter landscape, especially after a heavy frost.

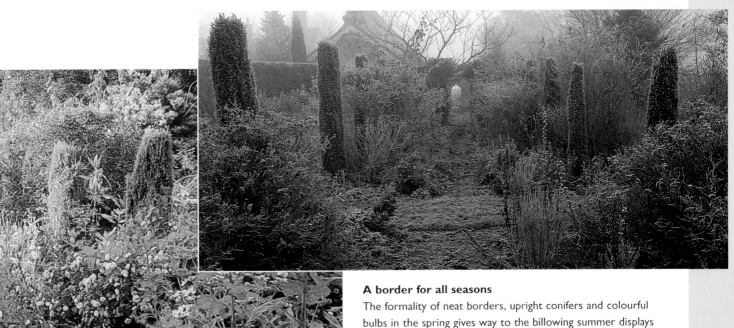

A border for all seasons
The formality of neat borders, upright conifers and colourful bulbs in the spring gives way to the billowing summer displays of roses and herbaceous plants (left); in the eerie light of winter, the skeletal remains of the herbaceous flowers (above) reveal the ghostly dark shadows of the evergreen shrubs as the sun rises on a frosty morning.

controlling overgrown shrubs

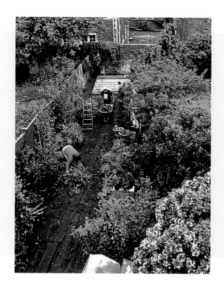

A garden can seem extremely small when it becomes overgrown after it has been neglected over a period of time. Meg and Paul realised this when they bought their first home – a detached house in the suburbs. Although the house was less than 20 years old, its previous owners, a retired couple who were dedicated gardeners, had planted a range of interesting but vigorous shrubs that had filled all the available space in the garden. Meg and Paul wanted their garden to have a more structured look, but hoped to use as many of the existing shrubs as possible. They were also keen to add a sitting area that would not detract from the rest of the garden's design.

Treasure hunt

When you renovate a neglected garden, preserve existing plants particularly if they are healthy and flowering, because it is expensive to replace them with mature specimens. With this in mind, Meg and Paul decided to research the plants in their garden for a year before clearing out the old and bringing in the new. During this period they kept a record of what plants were in their garden and when they flowered, and tried to identify as many species as possible. In the meantime, they drew up plans for a garden overhaul.

Regaining control

If you know when a shrub flowers, you can be sure to prune it correctly without losing all the blooms during the following year. The records that Meg and Paul had collected enabled them to decide the best time to prune most of the shrubs in their garden. For those shrubs they couldn't identify, they opted to prune using the one-stem-in-three method during early spring. This is where one-third of the shrub's oldest and largest stems are cut back hard to within a 5–10 cm of ground level each year (see page 182).

Dieback and disease

Meg's priority was to remove dead and diseased stems or branches from the existing plants. She sterilised the cutting blades of her pruning tools with a garden disinfectant after removing every diseased branch, to prevent disease from spreading to healthy branches and shrubs.

Lopsided growth

Some of the shrubs had been heavily shaded and developed a lopsided shape, with weak growth on one side and vigorous growth on the other. These shrubs required a different pruning treatment. Paul used the one-stem-in-three method for the majority of each shrub, but cut back the weak sides very hard – pruning each stem back to a plump bud near to the ground. The vigorous growth, on the other side of the shrub, he simply trimmed lightly. This is because the more you prune off a plant, the greater the response you will get from the plant when it puts out new shoots. So, by pruning weak shoots heavily you encourage new vigorous growth, whereas the light pruning of the vigorous side has the opposite effect.

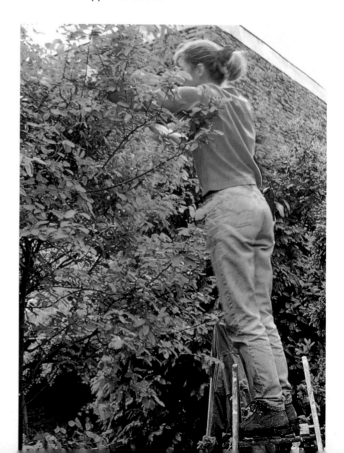

All-green shoots

Several of Meg and Paul's variegated shrubs had developed all-green shoots that were more vigorous than their desired ornamental form, spoiling the appearance of the shrub. Meg checked each shrub over and pruned the all-green shoots she found back to the main stem. The resulting new growth was all variegated.

Hard pruning

Shrubs that flower in summer bear their flowers on new growth produced during the current season. This means they can be cut back hard without losing flowering display the following year. These shrubs are best pruned in early spring before new growth starts. Using a pair of long-handled loppers and a pruning saw, Meg tackled the large butterfly bush and lavatera, cutting all stems back to within 5–10 cm of the ground. They also discovered several dogwoods that produce brightly coloured winter stems and a mock orange (*Philadelphus coronarius* 'Aureus') normally grown for its colourful golden foliage. To improve the performance of these shrubs, Meg cut all the stems back hard to near ground level during early spring.

Evergreen shrubs

During late spring, after the threat of frost had passed, Paul pruned back the evergreens, which included overgrown *Elaeagnus*, *Photinia*, and *Viburnum tinus*, to remove leggy growth. He made sure that any vigorous shoots were cut back to another shoot lower down, rather than leaving a bare stub. This is because evergreens are generally less likely to produce new shoots from old woody stumps.

Light and space

One bonus of cutting back all the shrubs hard was all the extra light and space this created. Meg took the opportunity to underplant these areas with colourful geraniums, iris and euphorbias in sunny spots, and dwarf bamboos, hostas and hardy ferns in the shady corners. In the largest open space, near to the house, they had an area of decking installed.

A shrub-filled haven

The area of decking located in a sunny spot by the house was an ideal vantage point for Meg and Paul to relax and appreciate their new colourful, plant-filled garden.

Good boundaries
for a modern garden

A boundary wall or fence can have a huge impact on the atmosphere of a garden. It is important to select a style that will reinforce the overall look and feel of your garden design, but also bear in mind its practical function when choosing the type.

A boundary wall, fence or hedge can perform several functions in a garden, depending on its size and the type of materials you choose. At its most basic, a boundary simply denotes the borderline between one garden and another. This can be a line marked out on the ground with paving stones, for example, or a simple hedge reaching just knee high. This form of boundary is often used in front gardens where privacy is not a major issue. White-painted picket fences are another popular option at the front of a house, as is ranch-style post-and-rail fencing in rural areas.

Walls, fences and hedges also provide shelter in exposed gardens, a backdrop for planting schemes, and privacy and security if this is desired. Solid, high boundaries offer more security and privacy and are often favoured for the back garden. In a small garden, however, high boundaries tend to be overwhelming.

Permanent walls
Walls last a lifetime if well built but are expensive and take a lot of skill and labour to erect. They can be made from a wide range of materials, including bricks, natural stone and concrete blocks, and can be adapted in design to suit any style of garden or effectively combined with other materials such as wooden trellis. The appearance of old walls can be improved easily by first rendering and then painting them to add light or a splash of colour to the garden.

Feature fences
By far the most popular type of boundary, fences are relatively quick and easy to erect. On the other hand, fences do need good foundations for the supporting posts and require occasional maintenance to keep in good order. Since they can be made from an enormous range of materials, including various woods, metals and even plastic in almost any style, there is a fence to

suit every garden design. The materials can be combined to good effect, too. In the Japanese-style garden (pictured right), for example, there is a solid wood barrier on the outside providing security that looks imposing. But on the inside, the simple split-bamboo screen erected against it has a much softer appearance and suits the Eastern style of the garden. In a situation where a high boundary is needed but light and a feeling of space are important, a see-through boundary such as trellis can be effective. Add height for privacy and make the fence solid if security is your priority. It is often best to compromise, combining both solid and see-through sections.

Living boundaries

Hedges have a soft natural appearance that can be changed to something more formal when kept neatly trimmed. They are cheap, too, but take a long time to grow. Even quick-growing hedges such as Lawson's cypress can take many years to provide a dense cover. They also need to be trimmed regularly and take up more space than fences or walls.

You must take into account your local climate and soil when selecting hedge plants. Dense-growing compact shrubs such as box and lavender make perfect small hedges; evergreen shrubs and conifers are best for larger ones. If you live in a windy seaside location, escallonia and griselinia are good sturdy choices.

On the border line

Blue-stained poles provide support and a stylish backdrop to the foreground plants **(1)**; wood and split bamboo join forces to create a sympathetic yet secure boundary **(2)**; a metal fence is softened by covering it with trellis **(3)**; brick and wrought-iron work well together **(4)**.

Potted plants

Growing plants in containers offers many exciting opportunities for the First-time Gardener, however big or small your garden. Scent and vibrancy can be added to paved areas, doorways can be brightened and inhospitable corners can be given a seasonal boost of colour.

Containers produce better displays by raising the plants off the ground, making them easier to view. Plants with intricate flowers or foliage can be brought closer to the eye, and those that fill the air with a heady scent can be grown in areas where they will be most appreciated. Common pests, such as slugs and snails, also are less of a problem.

A further advantage of growing plants in pots is that you are not reliant on the quality of the soil in your garden. Indeed, you can grow plants that require a totally different type of soil – acid-loving plants such as camellias or rhododendrons, for example, can be grown successfully in tubs even if your garden soil is alkaline. Pots and tubs also allow you to correct gardening mistakes more easily. If you inadvertently combine two incompatible plants in the same pot, one or both can be removed and replaced very quickly.

Finally, plants in containers can be moved. This means that they can provide instant solutions to problem areas in and around your garden or be shifted to sheltered spots during the winter where they will be better protected from harsh elements.

choosing pots and plants

Anything that can hold a reasonable amount of compost can be used as a container for plants. Old sinks can be successful; in fact even leaky containers, such as baskets, can be lined with perforated black plastic beforehand to produce unusual and stylish planters.

Your choice should complement the look of your garden and be suitable for the plants you wish to grow. For example, you will need large sturdy frost-proof pots for permanently planted trees or shrubs.

Terracotta pots

These are perhaps the most versatile of all containers because they can be used in almost any garden. They are widely available and you can choose from a variety of designs. If you live in a cold area, make sure you buy pots that are guaranteed frost-proof if you intend to leave them out during the winter.

Urn-shaped terracotta pots that narrow at the neck may look appealing, but you will find them difficult to plant and maintain.

Terracotta is a porous material, which means water is lost through the sides of a pot via evaporation. You can help to prevent evaporation, however, by lining the inside of the pot with plastic before adding compost and plants (see page 114).

Good combinations

Galvanised pails set off the natural tones of terracotta pots as they ascend a series of steps (pictured top). Each pot holds a contrasting spring-flowering display of daffodils or hyacinths. In a hot spot in summer (right), a variety of containers, filled with strikingly different drought-tolerant plants, are grouped.

You can also buy specially glazed, non-porous pots that come in many attractive styles and designs. Make sure all pots have drainage holes.

Wooden containers

Half-barrels and other tubs have a rustic appeal and are large enough to plant permanently with a shrub or small tree. Their wide bases make them very stable. Genuine half-barrels, used for wine- or beer-making, are handmade and self-sealing. But, mock barrels and square and rectangular planters may need lining with plastic to prevent water leaking out.

Square or rectangular planters are popular for entrances and formal settings. The most durable ones are made of a strong wood, pressure-treated with preservative.

Steps to success with potted plants

- Select the largest container possible and fill it with special potting compost formulated to retain water.

- Choose drought-tolerant plants that flower continuously or look good without flowers.

- Water the container as often as needed and add a slow-release fertiliser at planting time, so the plants never go short of food during the growing season.

Modern materials

It is now possible to buy convincing terracotta and wood lookalike pots made from plastic in a range of sizes and designs. They are lighter than the genuine article, easier to move around and often less expensive. Although frost-proof, plastic pots can become hard and brittle over time, especially if exposed to bright sunshine for long periods.

If you want to create a traditional-looking garden, a stone urn or trough is an ideal addition, but can be extremely expensive. A good alternative is to buy one made from reconstituted stone – these look as good, are as heavy and nearly as frost-resistant as the real thing. Alternatively, you could buy concrete pots. These take longer to weather, but you can speed up the process by painting their surface with a liquid manure or yogurt – this encourages the growth of algae and mosses.

Similarly, instead of buying a heavy and expensive lead trough for a traditional garden setting, choose a fibreglass lookalike; these are just as strong but a fraction of the weight and cost. Fibreglass containers come in a range of colours, such as burnished bronze and copper, which will look fantastic in a modern garden. So, too, will shiny metal containers made from galvanised steel.

Which plants?

Most garden plants grow perfectly well in containers, so choose your favourites. Bear in mind, however, they should look good from a distance as well as up close.

Plants that produce compact, neat growth, have attractive foliage and flower over many months are ideal. If choosing plants for a sunny patio, select ones that are drought-tolerant – look for those with thick waxy leaves such as *Echeveria*, grey hairy leaves such as *Helichrysum petiolare*, or spiky foliage like yucca or agave. Such plants are more likely to be able to survive short periods without water.

For areas in light shade, choose shade-tolerant plants, such as hostas and fuchsias. Moisture-loving plants such as impatiens can be grown successfully in pots provided they are well watered.

Don't use plants that are prone to pest or disease attack, or those that suffer badly when they run short of water. Campanulas and mimulus, for example, don't recover well if they are allowed to dry out. Avoid, too, permanent plants that produce a spectacular show for a few weeks, but are dull the rest of the time. Fast-growing plants, such as climbing roses also should be avoided; they will get too big and need a lot of training and support.

FIRST-TIME GARDENER'S BEST BETS

 Scented plants for containers *Cheiranthus*, cosmos, herbs such as thyme (pictured below), hyacinth, honeysuckle, *Houttuynia*, jasmine, lilies, scented-leaf pelargoniums, old-fashioned pinks, sweet pea, sweet William and tobacco plant.

 Shrubs *Aucuba japonica* 'Crotonifolia', box, *Euonymus*, hebe, laurel, lavender, *Mahonia x media* 'Charity', *Nandina domestica* 'Firepower', *Pernettya mucronata*, pieris, pittosporum, skimmia, *Viburnum tinus* 'Eve Price' and vinca.

 Perennials Agapanthus, bergenia, diascia, *Dicentra spectabilis*, erigeron, *Euphorbia characias* 'Wulfenii', *E. myrsinites*, hosta, helleborus, *Ophiopogon planiscapus* 'Nigrescens', *Sedum spectabile*, *Zantedeschia aethiopica* 'Crowborough'.

 Trees *Acer palmatum* 'Atropurpureum' or 'Bloodgood', *Betula pendula*, dwarf conifers, holly (variegated varieties), *Laburnum alpinum* 'Pendulum', *Pinus mugo* 'Gnom' and *Salix caprea* 'Pendula'.

 Grasses *Carex morrowii* 'Evergold', *C. riparia* 'Variegata', *C. stricta* 'Bowles' or 'Golden', *Festuca glauca*, *Hakonechloa macra* 'Alboaurea', *Milium effusum* 'Aureum', *Miscanthus sinensis* 'Variegatus' or 'Zebrinus', *Molinia caerulea* 'Variegata', *Phalaris arundinacea* 'Picta', *Stipa gigantea* and *S. pennata*.

planting containers

Most of the new containers you buy will be ready for planting immediately, but some new pots don't have any drainage holes. Before adding any plants, check to see if you will need to drill the base. This is a fairly straightforward if the containers are made from soft plastic or wood. Simply drill three or four equally spaced 1-cm holes in the base. If they are fibreglass, terracotta or hard plastic, however, before drilling attach some adhesive tape to both inside and outside surfaces to prevent cracking or chipping. Use a variable-speed drill on a low setting to make neat holes. Start with a small carbide-tipped drill bit, then use larger ones until the holes are the right size.

Acclimatising new plants

In frost-prone areas in spring, certain tender plants, such as summer annuals and tender vegetables, which have been raised indoors, should be acclimatised to the growing conditions outside before they are planted. This means slowly exposing them to the harsher conditions over a period of time. Make sure that the garden center has done this before you buy your plants.

You can use pots year after year. Once the display is over, carefully empty out the old plants and soil – saving as many plants as you can (see page 121) and reusing the compost in your garden. Clear as much debris from inside the pot as possible, then wash it thoroughly inside and out with soapy water using a scrubbing brush to remove stubborn roots, stains and algae. This will help prevent any carryover of pests and diseases. Rinse and allow to dry before using again.

Before planting, gather all the materials you need. Set out the new plants, in their pots, in formation on the ground. If you are planting seasonal displays, such as summer bedding, you could use a soil-less multi-purpose potting compost. For long-term or permanent planting schemes, use a loam-based compost; this will maintain its structure for longer and is heavier so it will provide extra stability for any top-heavy plants. If you want to grow acid-loving plants, use a special acid compost (known as ericaceous compost) instead. Bear in mind that large containers are very heavy once planted, so it is a good idea to position them before planting.

Planting a simple container

To prepare the pot for planting, cover the drainage holes with one or two large crocks or stones **(1)** to prevent compost from falling out. Fill the container with soil, breaking up any lumps with your fingers. Keeping the rootball intact, add each plant in turn, making sure each is upright and planted at the same depth as in its original pot **(2)**.

Firm soil lightly around each plant and push slow-release fertiliser tablets into the soil to feed the plants for the first growing season. As a finishing touch, cover the surface of the compost with a layer of fine gravel or pebbles. This will help prevent weeds, reduce water-loss through evaporation and provide an attractive finish. Water thoroughly and let it drain.

Planting windowboxes or troughs

The easiest way to create attractive windowbox displays is to plant a series of removable plastic trough-shaped containers (called liners) that fit snugly inside. This will save you having to lift or detach a heavy stone trough or wooden window-box each time it needs replanting. A windowbox should be fixed securely on a sill using special brackets and rust-proof screws, and you can then slot in your plastic liners once they have been planted.

This system allows you to create a continuous year-round display of colour using successive selections of potted plants in a series of liners.

To prepare a liner or windowbox for planting, cover the drainage holes with a couple of pieces of broken pot (known as crocks) or large stones to prevent the soil falling through. Change the display to fit in with the time of year:

Spring Half-fill your windowbox with fresh compost and position bulbs, such as dwarf tulips or daffodils in small groups at the correct depth (see page 60). Top up with soil, then plant bedding plants, such as brightly coloured poly-anthus, double daisies or forget-me-nots with trails of ivy cascading over the edges.

Summer For long-lasting, easy-care displays in sun-drenched spots, choose drought-tolerant plants such as the trailing verbena, gazania, *Helichrysum*, both upright and ivy-leaved pelargoniums and petunia. In lightly shaded spots, choose impatiens, spider plants, fuchsia and *Lamium*.

Autumn and winter Combine winter-flowering pansies, with red-berried skimmia, silver-leaved curry plant and variegated vinca. If you have a large planter, then add some ornamental cabbage or kale for a dramatic foliage contrast.

Planting a layered container

Using both bulbs and plants in a container can enable you to extend the season of the display. You will need a variety of bulbs, one large potted plant and a few small filler and trailing plants.

1 Prepare your planter as for the simple container, opposite. Place your first set of bulbs in groups towards the side of the container, then cover with a layer of compost. Now add the second set of bulbs and cover them with a layer of compost. Ensure that each type of bulb is planted at the correct depth and the right way up (see page 60). Once the second layer of bulbs has been planted, add more compost to your container, leaving 5–10 cm of space at the top.

2 Now, add your largest plant, making sure it is upright and planted at the same depth as it was in its original pot. Tease out any circling roots around the rootball to encourage them to grow into the new soil. Next, position the small filler and trailing plants around the large one.

3 Firm compost lightly around the roots of each plant and push slow-release fertiliser tablets into the soil to feed the plants for the first growing season. Cover the surface with a layer of pebbles or fine gravel and water thoroughly.

planting hanging baskets

For splashes of summer colour, nothing beats hanging baskets They can have a dramatic effect all around the garden but perhaps are most effective when sited around the patio or when used to brighten up fences or walls. If you choose the right plants and keep them well fed and watered, the glorious displays can last for several months.

Choosing a basket

There are two main types of hanging basket – open-mesh wire baskets and solid-sided plastic baskets, both of which are available in various shapes and sizes. Wall-mounted versions of both types of basket are also available.

Most First-time Gardeners will find the more conventional wire-frame baskets very easy to plant. They can look decorative when the plants are positioned along the sides as well as in the top. Wire baskets do, however, need to be lined with moss, plastic or other liner (see right) and need frequent watering, often as much as twice a day during hot weather. This is because the liner is exposed to the air, which causes the compost to dry out.

Water evaporates very quickly through a wire-frame basket. To reduce the need for watering, you can incorporate water-holding granules, available at garden centres, in the compost. Or you can create a water reservoir in the base of your chosen container to retain water so that roots can absorb it before it runs off. Keep in mind that baskets will be heavy when the reservoir is full, so make sure they are firmly secured.

Basket liners

To hold in the compost in a wire basket, you will need a liner between the frame and the compost. You can buy readymade mats for lining, made of natural or synthetic materials. Coconut fibre mats are widely available. Or you can make your own liner from moss or conifer clippings. Choose any material that doesn't detract from the plants, and which will resist decay when wet.

Buying a preplanted basket

Many garden centres or nurserymen sell ready-planted baskets in spring and autumn. You should select your basket as early as possible so that you get the best choice and combination of plants. If buying a display of tender plants in spring, but you cannot provide frost protection, ask the garden centre if it could look after it for you until after the threat of frost has passed in your area (see page 160).

Green tip

Efficient watering
Baskets need to be kept moist at all times if the displays are to last throughout the summer. Stop water running off the edges when you water by sinking a small pot rim-deep in the centre of the basket and fill this each time you water. The water will then remain in place long enough to be absorbed by the soil, reducing run-off.

FIRST-TIME GARDENER'S BEST BETS

Plants for full sun
Begonia, *Bidens ferulifolia*, *Brachycome mulifida*, *Convolvulus sabatius*, *Diascia integrimma*, felicia, French marigold, gazania, heliotrope, nasturtium, osteospermum, pelargonium, petunia, portulaca, sanvitalia, sutera and verbena.

Plants for light shade
Chlorphytum, *Cineraria maritima*, *Glechoma hederacea* 'Variegata', fuchsia, *Helichrysum petiolare*, impatiens, ivy, lamium, *Lysimachia nummularia* 'Aurea' and *Plectranthus forsteri* 'Marginatus'.

Trailing plants
Acalyphya, alonsoa, pendulous begonia, bidens, brachyscome, convolvulus, diascia, glechoma, helichrysum, ivy, lotus, lysmachia, parochetus, trailing pelargonium, petunia, plectranthus, ground-cover roses, scaevola, sutera and verbena.

Planting a wire basket

Planting your own hanging basket allows you to choose a combination of plants that may not be available in preplanted baskets. For small baskets, it is a good idea to choose one large central plant and a selection of trailing plants (see plant lists, above). Plant winter baskets densely because they will not put on much growth after planting.

1   Line your basket with your chosen material (see left). Loose lining material, such as conifer clippings, will need to be lined with a piece of perforated black plastic to stop the compost falling through. It is also worth placing a small piece of plastic or an old saucer on top of other types of liner to act as a water reservoir.

2   With larger baskets, half-fill the basket with compost and then make holes in the liner so that you can plant the sides. To make planting easier, wrap the top-growth of the plant in a strip of plastic to protect it.

3   Thread it from the inside through the hole in the liner until the top of the rootball butts against the liner and the top-growth of plant is sticking outside. Remove the plastic and untangle the stems of the plant. Repeat with the others

until the sides are planted up. Then plant the top of the basket, starting with the main specimen plants and finishing off with the edging and trailing plants.

4   Add compost around the rootball of each plant and firm gently. Top up with compost and push pellets of a slow-release fertiliser into it – this prevents having to feed the plants regularly during the growing season.

caring for container plants

Plants in containers are completely dependent on your care. They are crammed together in a small space with a very limited amount of compost in which to root. This means they are in competition with one another for the available water, nutrients and growing space. It is important, therefore, to choose plants that grow at similar rates and require similar amounts of water and nutrients so they all have an equal chance of thriving. Check the plant labels for this information when you buy. Plants that grow at similar rates will also produce more balanced displays that will remain looking good longer.

Feeding and watering

If plants run short of nutrients or water, they will be put under stress; growth and flower production will slow down and they will become more susceptible to attacks from pests and diseases.

After about six weeks in fresh compost, plants will start to run short of nutrients. To ensure a sufficient supply, insert slow-release fertiliser tablets into the compost at the time of planting or later. These tablets provide a full range of the nutrients the plants need over a set period of time – anything from a few weeks to several months, depending on the type used (see packet for details). Fertiliser tablets are coated in a resin that releases more nutrients as the temperature

and moisture levels increase. This means that the plants get exactly the right amount of feed they need all the time. An alternative solution is to use a high-potash liquid feed, every other watering.

Watering is more of a challenge to get right. It can be incredibly time-consuming if you have a lot of containers to water. During hot spells and in summer, containers may require watering more than once a day. One way to cut out the guess-work of watering and make the task easier is to invest in an automatic watering system that supplies

Easy-care patio collection
This drought-tolerant combination of potted succulents and cacti make an easy-care permanent feature on a sun-drenched patio. The hand-painted containers add a primitive art theme, which is particularly striking.

Five ways to cut down on watering

- Plant large containers, if possible – oversized pots and baskets hold a much larger volume of compost, which means your plants will require watering less often.

- Combine plants that have the same watering requirement in each container.

- Choose drought-tolerant plants that are well adapted to surviving long periods without water (see page 117).

- Line the sides of porous terracotta pots with plastic to stop moisture from evaporating.

- Use moisture-retaining granules, which absorb water that plants can draw from when they need it.

a regular amount of water to each container via a series of small plastic pipes (see photo, right).

The best time to water

The amount of water a container needs depends on its size and material, the number and type of plants it contains, where it is positioned, the time of year and the prevailing weather conditions. The best way of checking to see if a container needs watering is to push your finger into the compost about 2 cm below the surface to check whether the soil is moist. If it feels dry, the container needs watering; if not, test it again the next day. You can also get moisture meters from garden retailers to test the water content of compost.

When you water a container, it is important to water it thoroughly so the whole rootball is soaked – not just the surface. Try to apply water gradually, so that it has enough time to soak into the compost. Stop when you see the water starting to trickle from the drainage holes at the bottom of the container.

If the surface soil of a container dries out completely, it can be hard to get the water to soak in. Stop water from running off by breaking up the surface with a handfork, or add a drop of washing-up liquid to the watering can to break surface tension of the water.

If the entire rootball has dried out, it can shrink away from the pot so that water runs down the insides of the pot and out of the drainage holes, without ever wetting the compost. If this is the case, stand the container in a bowl of water until the roots are thoroughly soaked.

Watering equipment

The type of equipment you need depends on the number of containers you have to water. If you have just a few pots, you can use a watering can or garden hose. Spending time watering gives you the opportunity to inspect the plants on a regular basis, so you can spot and deal with any pests or diseases early. For hanging baskets, consider investing in a hose-lance, which will both extend your reach and save a lot of bending and stretching.

If you have many containers, an automatic watering system will save you lots of time. The water is delivered via a network of tubing that is attached to the water supply. You can regulate the amount of water each container receives by adjusting the nozzle at the end of each tube. The water supply can be switched on and off by hand or made completely automatic by

Watering made easy
Install an automatic watering system with adjustable nozzles that can be set to deliver exactly the right amount of water to each container of plants. Check nozzles from time to time to make sure they are still working properly.

attaching the tubing to a timer that has been fitted to the outside tap. Bear in mind, however, that you still have to check the soil in each container from time to time to ensure there are no blockages in the system.

getting better displays

The plants recommended in this book will generally perform well if you keep them properly watered and fed. However, displays can still be improved with a bit of occasional care. If, for example, a plant starts to overwhelm some of its neighbours or is getting over-grown and messy, trim it back using scissors or secateurs. Cutting back lanky growth also encourages a plant to become more bushy.

Bedding and border plants

Check plants regularly and pick off fading flowers to keep the display neat and to encourage the plant to produce more blooms; this technique is known as *deadheading*. Even annuals that continue to flower when old blooms are left on the plant will waste energy producing seeds at the expense of future displays. To deadhead

More flowers

Remove fading blooms from bedding to tidy up the plants and promote flower production. Pick off large, fading blooms individually.

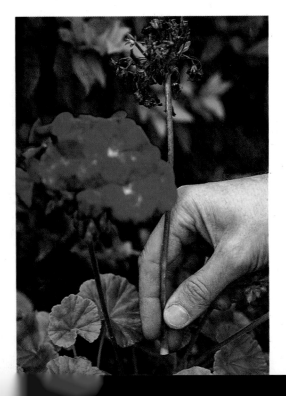

Caring for your plants during holidays

If you cannot find a willing neighbour to water your plants, use the following tips to get your plants through the holiday period unscathed. If you are away for just a few days, move your containers into a sheltered spot in the shade and water them well. For longer trips, lay out a plastic sheet on a level surface and raise the edges to create a large water reservoir. Cut 5 cm wide strips of capillary matting (available from garden retailers) and poke these through the drainage holes of each pot so that they are in contact with the compost. Then stand the containers on bricks on top of the plastic sheet so their capillary matting wicks stick out out like short tails. Water each container thoroughly until water trickles out the bottom and then fill the reservoir with water. Each pot will then draw water from the reservoir via the wick.

bedding, simply pinch off the fading flowers between your finger and thumb just above the next bud or leaf. If a plant produces a lot of tiny flowers, deadheading may be impractical, but it might be worth trimming the whole plant lightly with shears when it begins to look tattered. It is also worth tidying displays of flowers to remove unsightly yellowing foliage.

When watering and dead-heading, keep an eye open for early signs of attacks by pests and diseases. Sickly looking leaves, unusual holes or spots and colonies of tiny insects on new growth or the undersides of leaves are common signs. If the problem is not severe, pick off and dispose of affected leaves and rub off colonies of insects using your fingers. If the problem is severe, use chemical control.

Later in the season, containers fed by slow-release fertiliser tablets may start to run out of nutrients, reducing flowering and slowing the overall growth of plants. If the performance of your plants starts to fade in late summer, give them a boost by applying a high-potash liquid fertiliser every couple of weeks until the end of the season.

Permanent container plants

Trees, shrubs and other permanent plants will need watering through-out the year. During the winter, give the soil a thorough soaking about once a month. It is also worth turning these containers occasion-ally to prevent lopsided growth. This is particularly important if the container stands next to a wall or fence. Turn the pot about 90 degrees once every two weeks from spring to the autumn. Some permanent shrubs benefit from an annual light pruning to keep their shape well balanced. Do this during the dormant season (from autumn to spring) for deciduous plants and in spring for evergreens.

As plants grow, you will need to repot them into larger containers using fresh loam-based compost. Carefully tip the plant from its old pot and remove any loose soil, then repot it into a slightly larger container, making sure that the plant sits at the same level in the compost as it did before. If it is impractical to repot a large perman-ent display, simply remove the top 5 cm of soil from the container and replace it with fresh loam-based compost instead.

Patio clean up

Keep your paving looking good by giving it a thorough annual clean. Sweep up accumulations of dirt and clean stubborn stains and slippery algae (you can rent a pressure washer to make this job easier). If algae is severe, especially near steps, use an algaecide to control it.

Remove weed seedlings by hand or apply a patio or path weed killer to deal with large areas. However, before you spray, make sure you cover up nearby ornamental plants with a plastic sheet and leave the sheet in place until the spray has dried completely.

Overwintering containers

Potted plants are more susceptible to winter cold and wind than those grown in the garden. Plants that are too tender to survive outdoors in winter will need to be moved to a frost-free place, such as a cool porch. Even hardy plants will need some protection in severe weather.

Roots Protect roots from freezing by insulating containers in layers of bubblewrap. Alternatively, sink your pots rim-deep in border soil and cover the rim and compost surface with an insulating layer of soil or shredded bark.

Plants Protect the top-growth from cold by wrapping in a double layer of garden fleece, secured with string. Even when conditions are above freezing, some evergreens, such as conifers, are susceptible to damage from cold winds. Move such plants to a sheltered spot or protect with fleece.

During cold winter weather, protect tender climbers and shrubs trained against a wall. Make an insulating blanket of dry leaves or straw and netting. Remove all protection in spring.

Reusing container plants

Don't be in a hurry at the end of summer to throw away old plants from your containers. You will find that many can be used for next season's display.

Hardy perennials and shrubs can be planted out in your garden, unless you want to use them in a new container scheme. Sift through the old compost for bulbs and plant any that are firm to the touch. Trim any tattered leaves from plants such as ivy and vinca before transplanting to the garden.

You can also save tender perennials such as geraniums over the winter to include in displays the following year. Cut back the stems to about 5–10 cm using a pair of secateurs (1). Then, place the root of the plant in a box of moist compost (2). Repeat this procedure with the other plants and pack them into the box (3). Store in a frost-free place until spring.

creating a private terrace

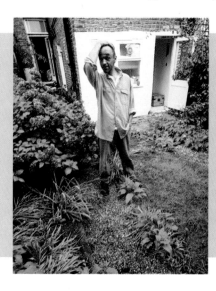

In the heart of the city, Scott's shady garden is overlooked by neighbouring properties. He wants to create an intimate garden in a contemporary design that will reflect its urban setting. He is looking to provide a quiet sanctuary for restful contemplation as well as be somewhere he can entertain his friends, but he does not want to feel boxed-in by high fences. The soil is very poor so he will either have to spend a lot of time and effort improving it or grow plants in containers and raised beds filled with fresh topsoil. He likes plants, particularly those which stimulate the senses with attractive fragrance and interesting textures, but his busy lifestyle means that he has little time to look after them.

A simple patio

The northwest-facing back garden receives sun for a few hours in the afternoon and early evening, and less during the winter months. Due to this, Scott decided that he wanted to base his design around a paved patio to make maximum use of the available space, bordered by a selection of delicately scented and textural plants that require little maintenance. Raised beds seemed a good choice as they take far less time to look after than lots of potted plants.

Mediterranean-style

Scott liked the idea of a simple Mediterranean-style patio area and opted to cover it with frost-proof tiles in a split-level design. He decided to choose pale-coloured tiles to reflect as much of the available light as possible, making the garden brighter. In order to soften the appearance of stark tiles, it is best to employ a variety of shades. Scott selected small terracotta tiles and mixed them with large pale yellow-coloured ones to create a clean, contemporary feel in his garden. If you are buying a variety of garden tiles for your patio, it is important to ensure that they are of the same thickness to make laying easier.

Scott cleared the site of the existing vegetation and then he levelled the area. He then marked out the patio area and covered it with a 15 cm deep foundation of dry concrete mix. This was carefully levelled and then consolidated with a plate vibrator (available from tool-hire shops) and allowed to harden. Scott then laid the tiles on top. As a functional detail, he decided to leave the terracotta tile in the middle of the patio loose. Beneath the tile, Scott installed a hidden slot that he could use to anchor his garden umbrella or his rotary washing line.

Planting pockets

Scott wanted to include plants to soften and add interest to his patio, so he decided to include random planting pockets. To do this, he removed several of the smaller tiles along with their foundations underneath and replaced the area with topsoil. He then planted the pockets with aromatic ground-hugging thymes, which, when walked on, filled the air with their pungent scent. He also left a planting strip between the two levels of his terrace, which was filled with aromatic plants and topped up with gravel.

Raised boundaries and borders

To create a quiet and secluded atmosphere and to prevent the terrace from being overlooked by neighbours, Scott extended the boundary walls upward. He did this by fixing it has been pressure-treated with a wood preservative to prevent rotting or is naturally rot-resistant.

To make the raised beds, Scott constructed a series of sturdy box-like structures and bolted them to the walls along each boundary. The wooden frames were supported at each corner by 7.5-cm-square fencing posts that were concreted into the ground; the sides were then clad in 2-cm thick boards. Once complete, Scott lined the inside of the boxes with heavy-duty black polythene to prevent soil from washing out between the cladding timbers. Next he filled them with good-quality topsoil and allowed them to settle. He then topped them up again with soil and added some plants. After planting, Scott covered all the raised beds with a 2-cm thick layer of gravel to reduce the need for watering and to suppress weed growth.

Sensual planting

Scott chose a range of aromatic herbs including sage, rosemary, thyme and mint to plant in the raised beds, combined with plants that have textural foliage such as furry lamb's ears, artemisia and mullein as well as silvery cotton lavender (*Santolina*). He trained scented climbers, such as jasmine and clematis, to cover the trellis and added a backbone planting of compact evergreens such as clipped box. Architectural plants such as phormium and globe artichoke were also included.

Patio full of plants

An intimate yet spacious patio was created in a very small space using deep raised beds overflowing with flowers and foliage. By covering the surface of the soil with a 2-cm layer of gravel, watering and weeding were kept to a minimum.

2-m posts to the low brick walls using expansion bolts and screwing a 1-m-high trellis to the posts. As a finishing touch, he topped each post with a matching finial.

Scott was worried about the patio feeling enclosed, so he raised the beds along the three boundaries. The raised beds on either side were 1-m high and deep. To increase the sense of space in his small garden, Scott cut the section along the end of the garden, furthest from the house, lower and set it back further than the others. This created an illusion of depth as well as a stepped effect to the raised beds, which were emphasised by the posts at each corner.

He then created another step on the sunny side of the garden where part of the raised bed was converted into an intimate double seat. All the beds were built from rough-sawn wood bought from the local fencing specialist. When buying softwood for use outdoors, you must make sure that

using containers in the garden

Jenny enjoys growing plants in containers, but wants to try something different. She would like to use containers more creatively, so that they add interest to all parts of her garden. Jenny already owns a lot of different sizes and styles of container that she wants to incorporate. She would also like to make the most of an existing raised terrace situated next to the house.

Using containers effectively

The great thing about containers is that they can be moved around. This means you can alter the appearance of your garden by simply substituting one style of container for another or mixing and matching containers in different parts of the garden. To create effective displays, it is important to develop a theme, as an uncoordinated group of different pots made from a variety of materials and containing completely different plants will not rest easily on the eye.

Jenny liked natural materials so she decided to create a collection of different-sized containers made from wood and terracotta, and placed them beside a seat on a sunny path. She filled them with a range of sun-loving Mediterranean plants to complete the effect. Jenny is not afraid to experiment; she coordinated a selection of varied containers placed outside the back door by planting them with bedding of similar flower colours and foliage textures.

Mix and match

In a formal setting, matching containers can be very striking. A pair of terracotta urns, for example, filled with an identical planting scheme, standing on either side of a doorway or garden gate, can be dramatic. Similarly, a series of identical pots filled with the same flowering plants running up one side of a series of steps helps accentuate the change of level. Jenny tried this with two pairs of matching but different-sized containers, to create the illusion of space in her small front garden. Each of the large containers was planted with two identical conifers and placed in the foreground, while the smaller ones were filled with similar-looking, but smaller, conifers and placed further away. This created the illusion of depth when viewed from the road outside her house.

Using the same-sized containers in an informal setting can look a bit regimented. However, you can break up the uniform appearance by standing some on upturned pots or bricks to create a change in level and scattering pebbles in front to provide a contrasting shape and texture.

Containers to catch the eye

In common with many gardens, Jenny's plot lacked focal points for attracting the eye. Containers, both planted and empty, are ideal for this purpose if used in moderation. Choosing the right pot for the setting is important if it is to be effective, and you must decide whether it is the plants or the pot that will be the focus of attention. Jenny had a beautifully ornate container that she wanted to accentuate. She planted it with a simple unassuming scheme of white marguerite daisies so that the container and not the plants it contained remained the point of focus. Further down the garden, she grouped a collection of elegant urns with a bright green backdrop of leafy hardy geraniums and colourful roses to good effect (pictured below).

The surroundings can have a significant impact on whether a container display has the desired effect. As a rule, displays of vibrant colours need a light-coloured or plain background to have the most impact, while pastel shades often look most effective if given darker surroundings. Jenny made the most of all her left-over containers by filling them with colourful bedding plants and grouping them together to create a virtual border along the edge of her raised terrace. The brilliant flowers contrasted well against the pale stone of the wall and the paving.

Plant selection

When choosing plants, look for ones that offer more than just flowering interest. Keep the colour scheme simple and stick to a theme. Jenny chose plants to suit the style of her containers. In decorated Oriental-style pots she stuck to a simple single-subject planting of bamboo – Japanese maple would also have looked effective. In terracotta containers, fiery displays of geraniums and gazania worked well.

Jenny also used plants to provide a seasonal change to her scheme. She moved containers into prominent positions while they were looking their best, and changed her display regularly. She did this by planting plastic liners that fitted snugly inside a decorative container. She then regularly swapped the liners to keep the display consistently good. A simpler option for a large container is to plant the rim with permanent edging plants and to slip in different flowering interest for every season. You could start with a camellia and spring-flowering bulbs, for example, and follow with lilies in early summer and then cannas when the lilies fade. You could try adding an aster for a splash of autumn colour and a flowering evergreen over the winter months to complete the year-round display.

Backing winners

Pale stone walls and paving provide a neutral setting for the vibrant colours of summer bedding (left); an all-green backdrop of hardy geranium foliage (below) is a good contrast for the elegant lines of terracotta urns.

Setting the scene

Collections of pots look most effective when linked by a common theme. Alongside a garden bench on a sunny path, Jenny arranged wood and terracotta containers planted with drought-tolerant bedding, such as geraniums, gazania and curry plant, to good effect (left).

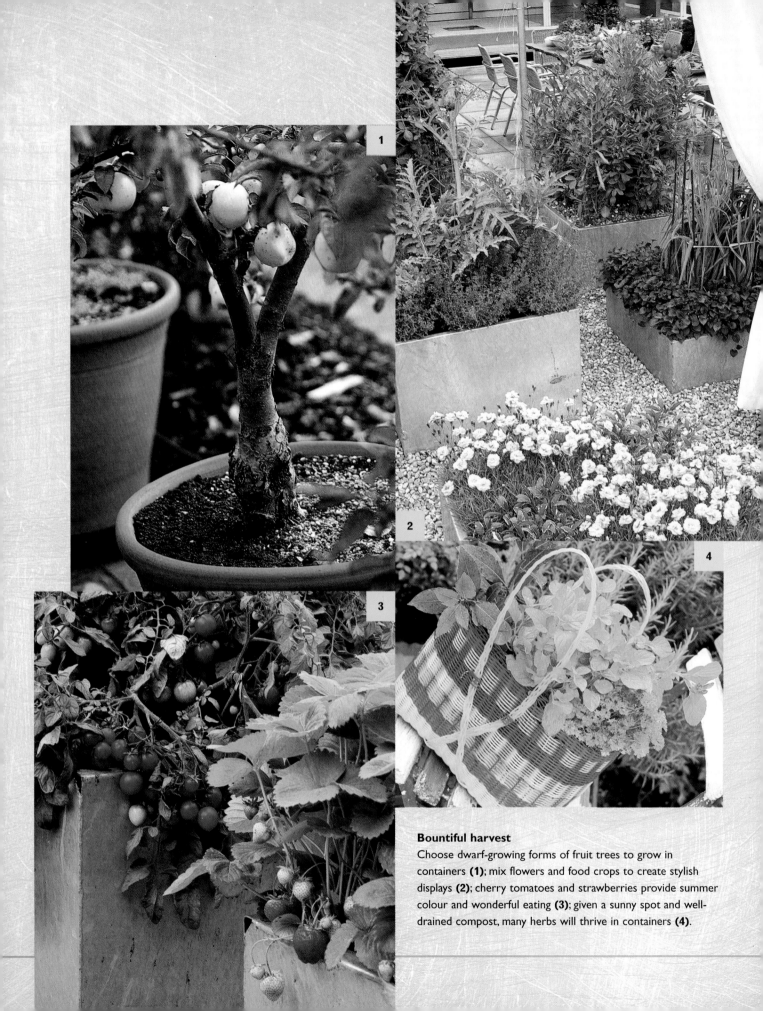

Bountiful harvest
Choose dwarf-growing forms of fruit trees to grow in
containers **(1)**; mix flowers and food crops to create stylish
displays **(2)**; cherry tomatoes and strawberries provide summer
colour and wonderful eating **(3)**; given a sunny spot and well-
drained compost, many herbs will thrive in containers **(4)**.

A kitchen garden
in and around the patio

You don't need a vegetable patch or a large backyard to grow fruit, vegetables and herbs in your garden. Many popular foods can be raised successfully in containers of all shapes and sizes on the patio or elsewhere in the garden.

Nothing can beat the flavour of freshly picked fruit and vegetables. It is also highly satisfying to be able to grow and harvest your favourite foods. The best crops in containers for the First-time Gardener to start with are those that are easy to grow, don't take up much space and will give reliable yields – many herbs and salad crops, such as radishes, lettuce and tomatoes, give excellent results in containers.

Growing your own herbs

Many popular herbs thrive in containers on the patio because they like well-drained soil and sun (see page 128). A few, such as mint and parsley, prefer moisture around their roots in a lightly shaded spot, so are best grown in the border. A word of warning, however. Mint is invasive and can become a weed problem unless its roots are restricted. The easiest way to do this is to plant it in a bottomless bucket sunk into the border. Leave 5–10 cm of the rim showing above the ground to prevent the runners from spreading into the surrounding border.

Vegetables in containers

On the patio, choose varieties of vegetables with attractive foliage or flowers. Ruby chard, for example, with its bright red stems and glossy green foliage, is as striking as any flowering plant. Runner beans are also easy to grow, but will need a supporting wigwam of canes or trellis. Their flowers are either red or white: both are very attractive.

To produce tasty baby vegetables, grow salad crops and root vegetables such as carrots and beets about 2–5 cm apart either in a border or in a container. Harvest carrots when they are about 1 cm across and baby beets at about twice this size.

To get good results with vegetables in containers, you will have to pay careful attention to watering and feeding. This may mean watering more than once a day in warm weather. Give leafy vegetables a balanced liquid fertiliser with every watering. Throughout the growing season, fruit- and pod-bearing vegetables, such as tomatoes and beans, should be given a weekly liquid high-potash feed, such as tomato fertiliser, which promotes flower and fruit production.

Among the tastiest crops from the garden are new potatoes, and these are fairly easy to grow in containers. Choose an early variety such as 'Concorde', 'Dunlace', 'Maris Bard' or 'Pentland Javelin', and grow the plants in a large tub or plastic dustbin half-filled with compost or topsoil. Top up the compost as the shoots grow, making sure that at least 5 cm of shoot remain, above the soil. Repeat until the container is full of compost. When the potatoes reach about the size of a chicken's egg (put your hand in the compost to check), tip out the container and harvest the new potatoes.

Patio fruits

Most fruit trees require sunlight to flourish and can be grown successfully on and around a sunny patio. Dwarf forms of fruit trees can be grown in large tubs, but must be kept well watered from the time they blossom in spring until the crop is harvested in the autumn. Sun-loving patio peaches and nectarines are particularly worth trying. It is also possible to grow grape vines in containers, but they do need a sturdy support and careful pruning. Use a stable container with a wide base, as tree fruits and grape vines become top heavy when the fruits swell.

Strawberries are well-suited for being grown in containers, even hanging baskets. By selecting varieties that fruit at different times you can get crops from early summer to mid-autumn. The season can be extended if you can provide protection early in the year, with the first crop in mid-spring (see page 128).

growing herbs in containers

Herbs vary in colour, shape and texture, so they can be combined to make very attractive container displays. On the patio, shrubby herbs such as rosemary and bay look effective trained into decorative shapes. Bay in particular lends itself to being pruned and trained into various conical or pyramid shapes or even grown as a mini-tree with a clear trunk and a ball-shaped head of foliage.

Remember, large containers will be very heavy once they are filled with compost and plants, so put them in position in your garden before planting. Wooden containers, such as rectangular Versailles tubs or half barrels, can be fitted with outdoor castors that make moving them around the patio a lot easier.

In a large tub, surround the base of a shrubby herb with variegated sages and thymes that will cascade over and soften the edges. Another herb worth growing in a large container is lemon verbena, which produces a wonderfully stringent scent and flavour.

Keep herbs growing well

Most sun-loving herbs are drought-tolerant and need watering less frequently than other container plants, so that if you already look after a few containers the extra work will be minimal. They don't require much food either. A half-strength dose of houseplant food once a month during the growing season is quite sufficient.

Keep herbs looking good and producing lots of new growth by trimming regularly with scissors or secateurs. If they are allowed to get leggy, trim them right back to encourage a new flush of foliage.

Recycling growing bags

Growing bags that have been used to produce a crop of tomatoes or peppers can be recycled by planting them with herbs that are used in large quantities, such as parsley, chives or mint. Make sure there are plenty of drainage holes cut along the side of the growing bag about 1 cm from the ground. Water sparingly and feed with a half-strength houseplant feed every two weeks.

Old growing bags also are useful for producing a crop of early strawberries in April or May – up to ten can be planted in one growing bag. Pot up new plants and keep outside until January. Then plant in the growing bag and move to a cool greenhouse. Good varieties to try include 'Cambridge Favourite', 'Tamella' and 'Elvira'.

Steps to success with herbs

- Select easy-to-grow herbs and plant them in well-drained soil.

- Choose the herbs that you use most often for kitchen and household purposes.

- Position the container in full sun in a convenient position, so the herbs can be harvested easily.

Planting a windowbox

A windowbox is one of the most convenient ways of growing herbs. During the winter the container can be placed indoors on a south-facing kitchen windowsill to provide fresh herbs all-year round.

Herbs, such as chives and basil, that are used in large quantities are best plunged rim-deep into the soil while still in their pots, making replacement a lot easier when the herb has been used up. Sow chives thickly like mustard and cress in a pot of compost, and use them while young.

1 Cover the bottom of the windowbox with a layer of crocks to improve drainage. Then fill the container with potting compost.

2 Plant the herbs, starting with the central ones. Choose clump-forming and mat-forming herbs like marjoram and sage and avoid using tall herbs such as fennel. Top with a layer of pea gravel and water the box well.

Herbs in a strawberry pot

A deep strawberry pot with cupped planting pockets around the sides is a good way of growing a number of herbs in a small space. Soak the strawberry pot thoroughly and cover the drainage holes with crocks. If you live in a high rainfall area, put a 5-cm deep layer of drainage material, such as gravel, in the bottom of the container to help improve drainage. Fill the container up to the first planting pocket with compost. Then position the first plant before adding more compost around the rootball and firming it gently with your fingers.

1 To make watering easier, place a 15-cm-long drilled plastic tube in the centre of the pot so the top is level with the rim and fill the tube with some gravel. Then top up the container with more compost and plant the rest of the planting pockets.

2 Plant up the top of the container and then mulch with a 1-cm layer of fine gravel as the finishing touch, making sure the compost is covered right up to the plant. Water well.

FIRST-TIME GARDENER'S BEST BETS

Containers in full sun
Basil, bay, borage, chives, coriander, dill, fennel, marjoram, rosemary, sage, tarragon and thyme.

Hanging baskets
Basil, marjoram, nasturtium, sage, thyme and winter savoury.

Containers in light shade
Apple mint, bergamot, chervil, chives, lemon balm, parsley, sage, salad burnet, spearmint and sweet Cicely.

Windowboxes
Basil, chervil, chives, marjoram, nasturtium, parsley, sage, thyme and winter savory.

FAQs – HERBS IN POTS

Q What's the best way of buying herbs?

A You can buy herbs in spring as vigorous young plants. Pot them up immediately using well-drained compost. If you're on a tight budget, many herbs including basil, borage, chervil, chives, coriander, dill, lemon balm and parsley, can be successfully raised from seed. Sow in spring.

Q Which herbs should I start with?

A Choose the herbs you like and use a lot in cooking. The most popular are sage, mint, thyme, parsley and marjoram, followed by chives, rosemary, lemon balm and fennel.

Q What kind of container do I need?

A You can grow herbs in almost any container, although small pots will require watering more often. Ideally, choose a container over 20 cm in diameter but windowboxes, tubs, strawberry pots, growing bags and even hanging baskets can be used. Terracotta is ideal for most herbs, but use non-porous plastic for moisture-loving dill, fennel and coriander.

Q How do you get the best flavour?

A The flavour of sun-loving herbs such as rosemary, thyme and tarragon can be intensified if you grow them in full sun and water sparingly. Feed them with a half-strength house-plant food about once a month during the growing season.

Q How long will the herbs last?

A Annual herbs such as borage, chervil, coriander and dill will last one season. Hardy perennial herbs such as chives, fennel, lemon balm, lovage, mint and oregano will last several years, while shrubby herbs such as rosemary, bay and thyme can be grown for many years.

Water features

Water features have an atmosphere and charm all their own. Adding one to your back garden will open up a whole new world of gardening opportunities. Nothing else quite captures the soothing ambience of the sight and sound of moving water. You don't need to have a large plot or have years of experience to create a beautiful water garden. With modern starter kits, a simple pond or moving water feature can be put together in just a few hours.

Water features can take many forms. Which one you choose should reflect the style of your garden and the atmosphere you are trying to create. In a formal design, for example, you could use either a traditional square, rectangular or round pond, but if you are trying to create an air of informality, a simple kidney-shaped or irregular pond would be a better choice.

A conventional pond brings light, colour and movement to the garden. It should be in proportion with the rest of the garden, so the size and shape of the pond will be determined to some extent by nearby features and your garden's overall layout. Choose a sunny site to get the best reflections. To successfully integrate the pond into your garden's design, aim to echo existing lines and shapes in the garden and create an area of transition using lush planting schemes.

In a modern garden design, creative water features have become a key ingredient. Made from unconventional materials, such as old watering cans, stone sinks and washboards, they can be used to add drama and give a central focus to the garden, or offer a sense of discovery and humour when hidden from view to be chanced upon by the casual visitor. Wildlife ponds have also become popular. If well planned and properly looked after, they will become a magnet for wildlife and home to a wide range of native plants and animals.

small water features

The First-time Gardener will find small water features ideal because they are easy to construct, require little time to maintain and are safe for children. There are various types available in kit form to suit almost any garden, but if you want to be more creative or tailor a feature to fit in a specific spot in your garden, then you can build your very own water feature easily from widely available materials. Small, reliable submersible pumps enable you to create a water feature in almost any size container.

Bubbling fountain This is the simplest and perhaps the most versatile of small water features. Its simple shape is easy on the eye and its gentle sound creates a relaxing atmosphere. A bubbling fountain consists of a single burbling spout of water that splashes over a pile of rocks, through the centre of a millstone or another decorative centrepiece to create a soothing yet enticing sound **(1)**. A small fountain looks effective as a raised feature or when sunken into the ground where it can be used as a focal point – try placing one near a seating area, for example, or subtly hidden from view elsewhere in the garden where it can be heard but not seen.

Bell fountain The domed shape and sparkling appearance of a bell fountain make it ideal for the modern garden. The spout protrudes from the rocks or water feature and water is forced through a thin nozzle to create a dome-shaped water jet. Like a bubbling fountain, it can be installed in the ground, but is perhaps even more eye-catching when placed in a large pot or raised bed so it becomes the focal point of your garden (see the page opposite).

Wall fountain A traditionally styled wall mask, such as a lion's head or gargoyle spitting water **(2)**, is an eye-catching way of adding moving water to a formal setting. It can be combined with a pond or simply aimed into a reservoir concealed with pebbles. Novelty wall masks can be used to add humour and drama wherever it is wanted.

Unusual features Don't be constrained by convention, you can use all sorts of household items to create unusual small water features. For example, this child's watering can **(3)** has been fitted to the outlet pipe of the pump to make a wonderfully modern fountain with novelty appeal (see also page 134).

Choosing a pump

Low-voltage submersible pumps are very easy to install. The size of pump you require will depend on the height to which the water is to be raised (known as lift) and the amount of water flowing through (known as flow rate). The lift is the distance between the surface of the water in the reservoir and the nozzle outlet of the cascade. For a small water feature you will need a flow rate of around 540 litres per hour, but for a fountain or water spout, such as a wall mask, look for a pump which can deliver around 770 litres per hour. To supply sufficient water for a water cascade and waterfall look for a pump that will produce 1200 litres per hour. Check the packaging for information.

1
2

3

Making a miniature container pond

A miniature pond makes an attractive water feature for any patio or balcony. They are very easy to create in a half-barrel or any other large waterproof container. They are ideal for growing a range of dwarf aquatic plants (see FAQs on page 137). However, a miniature pond is unsuitable for fish because the water temperature fluctuates too much. Even a miniature pond full of plants will need to be covered with an insulating layer in winter to prevent it from freezing solid. Alternatively, drain the pond in the autumn and keep the plants in a bucket of water in a cool but not freezing place over the winter.

- Position the barrel on a firm level base. If it is a genuine hand-crafted half-barrel it will seal itself as the wood becomes saturated. If not, you will need to line it with black polythene or a flexible pond liner.

- Half fill the barrel with water. Then trim the liner (1) so it is just below the rim. Fold the top 1 cm over neatly and fix it to the inside of the barrel using a staple gun or tacks.

- Place a 1-cm layer of pea gravel (2) over the base to protect the liner and top up with water.

- Leave it for a week to check for leaks and to allow chlorine to disperse. You can now add any planted aquatic baskets (3).

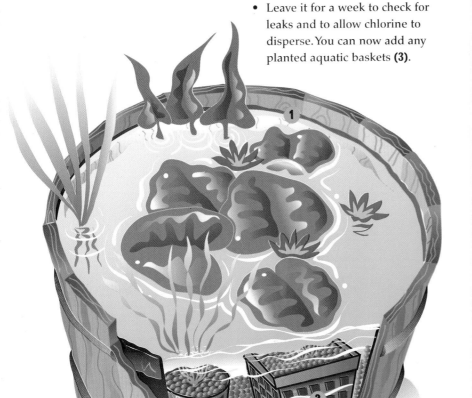

Bell fountain in a pot

You can buy container water features in kit form or create your own from scratch. When self-contained in a pot, a water feature can be moved around to change the focal point of your garden – to draw the eye to seasonal features, for example.

- Select a container that has a base at least 30 cm wide and is deep enough to hold the pump covered with at least 10 cm of water. The smaller the container, the less water it will hold so you will have to top it up more often. Bell fountain kits often contain a float to indicate whether the reservoir needs topping up.

- If you have chosen a porous container, such as terracotta, line it with thick black polythene or flexible pool liner, or stand a waterproof plastic pot (without drainage holes) inside the ornamental porous pot to create the reservoir.

- Position the pump in the bottom of the container, so that the outlet nozzle is roughly level with the rim. Cut a piece of plastic-coated, heavy-duty mesh using a pair of bolt-cutters until it is the correct size to lodge just below the rim on the inside of your container. Then cover the mesh with a layer of pebbles.

- Fill the container with water, then plug the pump in and adjust the flow rate of the pump until a pleasing fountain is achieved and all the water falls back into the container.

Wonderful ways
with water

Imaginative water features lead the way in contemporary garden design. No longer are you restricted to a simple pond or fountain: with a little creative thought you can give life to a modern work of art.

Water features have much to offer the First-time Gardener who wants to impose individuality and personal style on a garden environment. The interplay and juxtaposition of water, rock and plants has the power to produce evocative atmospheres, particularly if the water feature is accompanied by restful sounds and hypnotic motion. A creative water feature can add subtle humour, provoke spontaneous thought, even spring a surprise on the casual visitor, and in a city can mute the passing traffic.

All the active water features pictured here are based on the same simple construction outlined on page 132. You don't have to buy an original piece of art to be stylish – with a little imagination you can use practically any materials you have on hand, from a pile of log slices to pieces of old junk lying around the garden. Bear in mind, however, that the different elements need to be connected by a theme.

Natural contrast
Some materials and shapes have a natural affinity, while others seem to be poles apart. This underlying linkage is often used to create effective designs in good contemporary gardens. The bronze heron spouting water from the security of a reed bed (see the page opposite), for example, contrasts completely in colour and texture with its surroundings, but both sit comfortably together. In a comic undertone, the bird stands guard over the very fish that its wild counterparts would find a tasty meal.

This idea of contrast can be turned on its head by combining the most unlikely materials that have a distinctly common theme. The metallic water chute, opposite, is an excellent example. It has a formality of shape that is at odds with the natural flow of water, yet the sparkling cascade and watercourse connect well with the vertical galvanised monolith.

The surprise element
Every garden benefits from the surprise element – the unexpected sound or view which makes you sit up and take notice. Still water features are particularly useful for this purpose, because they can be hidden out of sight to be chanced upon seemingly by accident. Bear in mind they do need to be discovered to be effective, so don't camouflage them completely.

Another good design technique is to take advantage of natural human curiosity by providing enticing glimpses of a feature or statue associated with water, or using the sound of moving water to hint at the existence of a pool. The water itself can then be completely hidden from view.

Adding a touch of humour
Light-heartedness is a particularly effective technique in contemporary garden design. The pond at top left, for example, is dominated by a spiral of large white pebbles on a bed of slate. The curving shape draws you in as it threads its way relentlessly to the centre of the feature, creating a visual whirlpool effect so adding virtual movement to a static scene.

Humour doesn't have to be surreal to be effective. The bronze swimmer at bottom right, which seems to be emerging from a barrel to spout water at passers-by, is a more literal comic touch which works really well. It is particularly effective, however, when the water spout is intermittent. The rest of the time, the water can gently cascade and circulate from one barrel to the next.

Water enlivens a contemporary garden
A spiral of white pebbles suggests a visual whirlpool **(1)**; light and dark are united in this silver water chute edged by black grass **(2)**; the bronze heron stalks the margins of its pond **(3)**; and a spouting swimmer adds a comic touch **(4)**.

building a new pond

A conventional garden pond **(1)**, stocked with plants and fish, has much to offer the First-time Gardener. If well designed and constructed, it makes a wonderful year-round feature. If you build the pond large enough, it will require little maintenance because a natural equilibrium will be reached. With a surface area of 12 square metres and a maximum depth of about 1 metre the temperature of the pond water will not fluctuate greatly and so is less likely to produce problems such as green water (see page 138).

Raised ponds

A raised pond **(2)** is one that is constructed on top of the ground in a raised bed or free-standing container. Although less popular than a conventional pond, it offers several advantages. You don't have to dig a hole or get rid of the excavated soil. The water and any wildlife the pond contains is raised

1

Steps to success with water features

- Choose a style and size that reflects the design and layout of the garden.

- Site it in the open where it will be most appreciated, well away from nearby trees and buildings that will cast dense shade or drop leaves in the autumn.

- Choose the right combination of easy-care aquatic plants so the pond becomes largely self-sustaining.

up where it can be appreciated more easily. Moreover, the pond is easier to care for because you do not have to bend as much. If you have young children, a raised pond with sides at least 45 cm high is also a safer

option than a conventional sunken pond. A variety of raised ponds are now available in kit form.

Using a preformed liner

Most ponds are built using a pond liner. There are two main types: preformed rigid liners and flexible liners that are supplied as a sheet that can fit any shape. The easiest way to build a standard pond is to use a rigid liner made from either plastic or fibreglass. Although quite expensive, rigid liners are simple to install. They last about 15 years and you can be sure of the end result. Mark the outline on the ground then dig a hole sufficiently deep and wide following the liner's contours. Line the hole with sand, then position the liner and check that it is level in all directions. Carefully fill around the sides with sand making sure there are no gaps, before filling the pond with water.

2

Installing a free form pond

To create a pond in the shape of your choice, you will have to use a flexible liner. There are two main types: plastic, which is cheapest but punctures easily and only lasts about five years; and rubberised (PVC, LDPE or butyl) which is stronger and more durable. Even though it is relatively easy to build a pond, it does take a fair amount of effort to install, so if you don't feel up to digging, seek help.

- First, choose a suitable site for your pond (see FAQs, below). Then, mark out the desired shape using bamboo canes for straight lines and a hose for curves.

- Once you are happy with the shape, dig the hole so the main part of the pond is at least 45 cm deep and the shelves around the edges that support the marginal plants are around 25 cm deep. Make sure that the sides slope slightly inwards and check the levels carefully.

- Remove any sharp stones, then cover all surfaces with a 5-cm layer of sand. On a warm day, lay out the flexible liner over the hole and partly fill it with water. Gently pull at the edges of the liner to remove creases, before topping it up with water. Trim the liner to leave a 15-cm overlap on all sides, then cover the overlap with your desired edging such as rocks, pebbles or a mixture of bricks and plants. Finally, stock the pond with plants and fish.

FAQs – SETTING UP A POND

Q What is the best position for a pond?

A Choose an open, sunny site away from overhanging trees and the dense shade cast by buildings. Also check that there are no underground cables or pipes to worry about if you are sinking a pond into the ground. Above all, position it somewhere it will be appreciated, taking into account what will be reflected in the water.

Q What size pond is best for a beginner?

A A mini pond can be the size of a half-barrel, but a conventional pond with plants and fish should have an area of at least 5 square metres (around 50 square feet) — the equivalent of an 2.1 x 2.4 m (7 x 8 ft) rectangular pond.

Q How deep should it be?

A At least part of a small conventional pond should be about 45 cm deep. Larger ponds should have a deep water area of between 60 and 90 cm. To grow shallow-water plants at the edge of the pool, you will need a 30-cm-wide shelf about 25 cm below the surface. The walls of the pond should slope slightly inward.

Q What are the best plants for a small pond?

A Choose miniature waterlilies, such as *Nymphaea pygmaea* 'Helvola' (yellow) or 'Alba' (white), and shallow-water plants such as the corkscrew rush, zebra rush, water lettuce, variegated iris, pickerel weed, frog bit, miniature reedmace and water forget-me-not.

Q Which fish should I buy?

A If your pond has a surface area of over 12 square metres, choose brightly coloured goldfish. They are cheap and easy to look after, but most important of all, they will swim close to the surface where they can be seen.

adding plants and fish

Fish add movement and colour to a pond and the plants help to integrate the feature into the surrounding garden landscape. Plants are also important for maintaining a natural balance in the water, so the pond becomes largely self-sustaining. Choosing the right combination of plants is important because this will not only affect the ornamental appeal of the feature but dictate how much time you will have to spend looking after it.

Pond plants can be grouped into three types: those that are planted in the shallows around the edge of the pond, known as marginals; those that cover the surface; and submerged plants that can be scattered across the floor of the pond. The submerged plants produce oxygen while using up the nutrients in the water that would otherwise encourage the pond water to turn green with algae. The floating plants also help prevent algae by effectively preventing sunlight penetrating the water.

To work out how many of each type of plant you need, calculate the surface area of the pond then allow ten bunches of submerged plants per square metre and introduce sufficient floating plants to cover at least one-third of the surface area. Add a combination of marginal plants to give flowering interest throughout the growing season.

Planting your pond

Use a special aquatic planting baskets which have wide bases for stability and micro-mesh sides to prevent the soil washing out into the water. Older styles of baskets with lattice-work sides should be lined with hessian before filling with soil. Do not use standard potting compost because it will release soluble plant food into the water, encouraging algae. Special aquatic compost is available. Marginal plants can be planted on their own in small baskets or in groups in a larger one, but waterlilies should be planted individually.

Adding fish

Do not add fish until the plants have become established. To give fish sufficient room to grow, do not add more than 50 cm of fish per square metre of surface area. Fish need to adjust gradually to the temperature of pond water, so to prevent distressing the fish you need to leave the fish in their bags and float them on the surface of the pond for about three hours. This will enable the water inside the bag to cool slowly until it reaches the same temperature as the pond water. Do this during the evening, then after the designated period, open the bag and allow the fish to swim away.

FIRST-TIME GARDENER'S BEST BETS

Marginal shelf
Acorus calamus 'Variegatus', marsh marigold (Caltha palustris 'Flore Pleno'), corkscrew rush (Juncus effusus 'Spiralis'), Iris laevigata 'Variegata', pickerel weed (Pontederia cordata), Typha minima, umbrella grass, zebra rush (Schoenoplectus subsp. tabernaemontani 'Zebrinus').

Submerged plants
Curled pondweed (Potamogeton crispus), goldfish weed (Lagarosiphon major), hairgrass (Eleocharis acicularis), hornwort (Ceratophyllum demersum), willow moss (Fontinalis antipyretica), water buttercup (Ranunculus aquatilis) and water milfoil.

Surface-floating plants
Cape pondweed (Aponogeton distachyos), fairy moss (Azolla caroliniana), floating heart (Nymphoides peltata), frog-bit (Hydrocharis morsus-ranae), water chestnut (Trapa natans), water hyacinth (Eichornia crassipes), waterlily, pictured left (such as Nymphaea odorata 'Sulphurea', N. 'Rose Arey', N. pygmaea 'Helvola', N. pygmaea 'Rubra'), water lettuce (Pistia statiotes) and water soldier (Stratiotes aloides).

Green tip

Preventing green water
If you want to avoid using special chemicals to clear ponds of algae, simply place a pad of barley straw (available from garden retailers) on the pond surface before the algae has a chance to build up. You can also use loose barley or wheat straw – apply 25 grams in a pond that contains about 2 cubic metres of water. As the barley or straw decomposes, it releases an anti-algae chemical into the water.

Positioning waterlilies

Thread two cords through the mesh of the basket and use these to lower the waterlily to its correct position. Dwarf forms of waterlily should be placed with about 10 cm of water above the basket and other forms where there will be 30–45 cm.

Lowering the basket should be done in stages; by standing the basket on various sized blocks you will give the leaf stalks time to grow. Alternatively, trim off the fully expanded leaves and lower the plant to the correct depth straight away. The emerging leaves should then naturally grow up to the water's surface.

Where to position your water plants

Different types of aquatic plants require particular depths of water to thrive, so need to be placed in the most suitable area of the pond. Marginal plants which have roots submerged, but stems and flowers held above the water's surface, are placed on a special shallow shelf at the edge of the pond (1). Deep-water plants, such as waterlilies, are placed in the deeper areas (2), so that their leaves float on the water's surface, and submerged plants are scattered across the bottom of the pond.

Planting a basket

The best time to plant aquatic plants is while they are actively growing between spring and autumn. Keep the roots moist at all times by placing them in a bucket of water until you are ready to plant.

Use a special aquatic planting basket with a wide stable base and open-mesh sides rather than other types of container. Choose one that will fit on the marginal shelf of your pond (see above) and, if necessary, line it with some hessian to prevent the soil from escaping. Then cover the base with a layer of special aquatic compost.

Next, position the plant in the centre of the container and fill in around the roots with compost (1). Firm down well. Now, cover the surface of the compost with a 1-cm layer of fine gravel and firm again (2). The gravel will help to prevent fish from stirring up the soil and muddying the water.

Before placing the basket in the pond, you need to remove any trapped air. This prevents the compost bubbling up when the container is lowered into the pond. To do this, submerge the planted basket in a bucket of water until the strings of air bubbles stop emerging from the basket. Then place the soaked aquatic basket into the appropriate position in your pond.

wildlife ponds

It is quite possible to turn a new or existing pond into a haven for wildlife by including a few simple design features.

The edging materials of a pond are important for attracting wildlife. They should be natural and provide a safe route to and from the pond. A gently sloping beach of pebbles or slate scree is ideal and should be used on at least one side to give easy access for the wildlife and shallows for birds to drink and bathe. Grass turfs laid up to the water's edge can look good, but may turn the water muddy. Avoid paving, which gets too hot for amphibians to cross in summer. Do not site your pond near to your patio or house, because it will be a breeding ground for many insects, including mosquitoes.

Use a thick and lush planting along the margins and outside the pond to obscure the edges and provide a seamless transition into the surrounding garden. Choose native plants where possible, but make sure they are not too invasive or grow too big for your pond. Allow clumps of grass to grow longer around the pond and heap up at least one pile of logs to provide extra cover. A large log can be partially laid into the pond to provide a convenient perch for birds and a gangway for amphibians.

If you are building a wildlife pond from scratch, include some deep water areas – at least 60 cm deep, but preferably 90 cm deep. These areas will remain cool even during the summer months and will be deep enough to protect pond creatures during winter. Do not stock a wildlife pond with fish as they will eat many of its inhabitants.

Plant all the aquatic plants in baskets to keep them within bounds (see page 139); submerged plants are the exception, which can be scattered over the floor of the pond or planted into the sediment layer.

Maintaining a wildlife pond

If you choose the right plants, a wildlife pond should require little maintenance. Be prepared to allow some algae growth and common pond weeds such as blanket weed and duckweed, but do not let them take over. Keep more invasive plants in check by removing them from the pond and cutting them back using secateurs in spring or the autumn (see page 139).

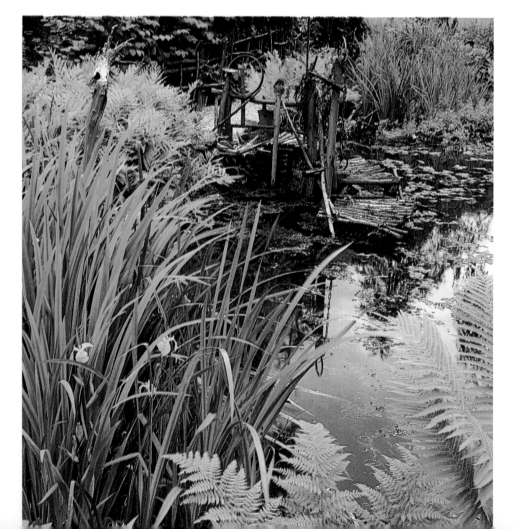

Take a closer look
Visiting wildlife can be studied at close quarters if you incorporate a viewing platform, using a material such as decking, when designing your pond.

Natural setting
Situated in a natural dip and
surrounded by a bog garden filled
with moisture-loving plants, this pond
is in a perfect spot.

FIRST-TIME GARDENER'S BEST BETS

 Marginal shelf Bog bean
(*Menyanthes trifoliata*), lesser
reedmace (*Typha angustifolia*),
flowering rush (*Butomus umbellatus*),
water mint (*Mentha aquatica*), water
plantain (*Alisma plantago-aquatica*).

 Floating plants
Fairy moss (*Azolla filiculoides*),
frog-bit (*Hydrocharis morsus-
ranae*), water soldier (*Stratiotes aloides*),
water hawthorn (*Aponogeton distyachos*),
waterlily (*Nymphaea alba*).

 Submerged plants
Curled pondweed
(*Potamogeton crispus*), hornwort
(*Ceratophyllum demersum*), water violet
(*Hottonia palustris*), water crowfoot
(*Ranunculus aquatilis*).

 Bog garden
Variegated Japanese rush (*Acorus
gramineus* 'Variegatus'), *Astilboides
tabularis* (syn. *Rodgersia tabularis*), *Astilbe
chinensis* 'Pumila', *A.* 'Gnom', *A.* 'Perkeo',
cuckoo flower (*Cardamine pratensis* 'Flore
Pleno'), variegated meadowsweet (*Filipendula
ulmaria* 'Variegata'), *Gunnera manicata*, *Iris
ensata*, variegated yellow flag (*I. pseudoacorus*
'Variegata'), *I. sibirica*, *Lobelia* 'Queen Victoria',
Lythrum virgatum 'The Rocket', *Lysimachia
punctata*, *L. nummularia* 'Aurea', *Ligularia
stenocephala* 'The Rocket', golden groundsel
(*L. dentata* 'Desdemona'), *Rodgersia aesculifolia*,
R. pinnata 'Superba', *R. podophylla*, ornamental
rhubarb (*Rheum palmatum* 'Atrosanguineum'),
R. 'Ace of Hearts', kaffir lily, (*Schizostylis
coccinea*).

Creating a bog garden

A bog garden goes hand-in-hand
with a wildlife pond, but can work
equally well with more ornamental
water features. Filled with moisture-
loving plants it naturally bridges the
transition between pond and the
rest of the garden. Alongside a
wildlife pond a bog garden also
provides a rich habitat for the
creatures that live around and visit
the pond.

If you have naturally moisture-
retentive soil, simply add plenty of
well-rotted manure before planting.
If not, you will have to create an
artificial bog garden using a flexible
pond liner. If you are building a
pond from scratch using a flexible
liner, you can make the bog garden
at the same time using a piece of
the same liner.

- Dig a hole 30–45 cm deep and up
to 2 metres across. Smooth the
surface and remove any
protruding stones, then line the
hole with about 2 cm of sand.

- Lay the liner on top of the sand,
then make 1-cm holes in the liner
spaced every 65 cm across the
bottom of the bog garden.

- Fill the liner with a rich moisture-
retentive soil made from one part
well-rotted manure to three parts
good garden topsoil.

- Trim the liner to leave a 15-cm-
wide flap on all sides, then cover
these with large pebbles.
Alternatively, bury the edges and
cover with gravel, turf or paving
stones.

- Scatter 50 grams per square
metre of general-purpose
fertiliser over the soil, then plant
the bog garden starting at the
centre with the largest plants and
finishing at the edge. For best
effect, make sure the plants along
the pond side overhang to
obscure the edge.

- Bog gardens must be kept
constantly moist, so it is worth
your while installing an automatic
watering system (see page 119).

a garden with natural balance

Kevin and Joanna Gibb have recently bought an old house with a long narrow garden that has been completely neglected. They would like to redesign the space so that it feels less claustrophobic. They want to include a modern formal water feature as well as a secluded area for sitting, with some storage space for outdoor furniture and garden equipment. Joanna wants the garden to exhibit a modern style but to retain many of the original plants; and Kevin would like the design to be innovative with plenty of intrigue and a few surprises.

A question of space

When designing a long, narrow garden it is important that you don't emphasise the plot's shortcomings. Dividing a garden into sections or 'rooms' with an open water feature in the centre can increase the amount of light and feeling of space. Also, a series of parallel lines used across the plot would make a long, narrow garden seem much wider.

Deciding that the necessary construction was beyond their abilities, Kevin and Joanna employed a professional garden designer to ensure their ideas and aspirations were realised in a coordinated and well-thought-out plan. The resulting garden consists of two rectangular courtyards linked by stepping stones that run through a central pool and water feature.

Hot and cool courtyards

Lines of bricks have been used to define the boundaries of each courtyard. The 'hot' courtyard, at the far end of the garden, is the only area that catches the sun and has been slightly sunken to improve privacy. The low retaining stone walls are made from small granite blocks and have had soil pressed into the cracks allowing flowers to seed themselves naturally and create a more harmonious effect.

Nearest to the house, the 'cool' courtyard is made all the more relaxing by the gentle sound of water. This cascades from the copper monolith water feature with novel drip-fed containers filled with small aquatics. A living screen of ivy, jasmine and Virginia creeper adds to the seclusion, making it an ideal place for contemplation or entertaining.

The formal geometric pool is ingeniously integrated into its surroundings by blending the rock and water elements. The granite blocks and recycled slabs used in the access path continue into the pool, appearing to float on the surface of the water. No mortar is used between the blocks, which form a 'tadpole maze' of watery corridors. Clam-like carved pods, that were inspired by the seedpods in the film *Alien*, stand alongside the pool and open out to form single seats with back supports (see the picture at right).

Building the water feature

The overgrown plants were removed from the area and the pond design was marked out on the ground using pegs and string. The whole water area was excavated, firmed and covered with a sheet of flexible butyl rubber. Retaining walls that form the formal pool were built up and the main water feature elements positioned (pictured left). The flexible liner was then trimmed and the paving laid, starting with the spaced granite blocks and recycled slab stepping stones.

You don't need to start from scratch to create a stylish and practical garden. Even a dramatic makeover like this can make intelligent use of plants, such as the leaning pear tree and climber-clad fences, that were part of the original garden. Indeed, incorporating existing plants with thought into a new garden plan will help to give the design an established look, providing instant maturity and credibility.

Practical storage

The design cleverly incorporates a storage shed in the middle of the garden without making the garden seem smaller. This is achieved by extending the roof of the shed, which, combined with the existing leaning pear tree, forms a feature gateway linking one garden courtyard to the other. To soften the overall effect, the extended shed roof has been covered in turfs of meadow grass dotted with wildflowers such as buttercups, daisies, clover, cranesbill, fritillaries, ragwort and dandelions. The grass is kept moist by automatic watering and needs cutting just twice a year

using a pair of shears. At ground level, the two courtyards are linked by all-weather, ground-covering materials including gravel, recycled slabs and granite blocks.

Planting themes

A modern theme is achieved by planting eye-catching specimens with bold outlines such as loquat, yucca, ornamental onions and acanthus with ornamental grasses of contrasting softness. The foliage theme continues into the margins of the pond where dwarf reedmace are planted as a visual counterbalance to the saucer-shaped floating leaves and flowers of the dwarf waterlilies.

The greening effect was continued at every level, with lush planting of walls and fences, which helped to obscure the boundary line and add to the sense of space within the garden. In the shady corners, ferns have found their perfect niche, and climbers sprawl upwards and along the ground to cover the surfaces and provide extra seasonal colour.

Perfect balance
Equal areas of light and shade have been achieved in this practical yet innovative design. The dramatic copper monolith (below) stands out against an evergreen back-drop of ivy. Carved elm planters filled with miniature aquatic plants are drip-fed with water by an underground pump.

a watery retreat in the country

Greg and Sarah Black have busy lives in the city. Wanting to get away from it all on weekends and holidays, they bought a house in the country with plenty of land on which to create a natural retreat. They want an informal garden where nature is the dominant element and where they can relax. Neither of them have much free time, so it will have to be able largely to look after itself. Their property boasted a natural pond which was fed by an underground spring, but it was completely overgrown and needed an overhaul.

The natural garden

To achieve the Blacks' dream of creating a functional garden with ornamental appeal that blends perfectly with the countryside, the design had to take into account the garden's immediate natural surroundings. It was decided that the garden design would become progressively more natural and wild the further away you got from the house. Greg wanted to keep at least a small area of well-manicured lawn outside the French windows, but the grass further away from the house was allowed to grow longer and, therefore, needed cutting less often. This basic principle was applied to all the different elements of the garden design.

Spring-fed pond

If it is neglected, a pond becomes a tangled mass of growth as the more vigorous plants swamp their neighbours. Some plants that are essential for maintaining the natural balance in a pond cannot compete with the other plants and soon die out. This is precisely what had happened to Greg and Sarah's pond.

Since the pond was fairly small and could not be seen from the house, Greg decided to take the opportunity to have it enlarged – he wanted it to form the central focus of the garden's wildlife theme. This was a big job, so instead of doing it themselves, they opted to bring in professional contractors with earth-moving equipment. Before the contractors arrived, Greg removed a few of the better-behaved aquatic plants including a large clump of iris that could be reintroduced after the pond was enlarged.

The contractors reshaped the pond so it had sweeping curves and a long 30-cm-deep shelf running down both sides. This shallow area was planted with marginal aquatic plants (see page 138), which like their roots in water but prefer their leaves and flowers to be held well above the surface. To maintain the natural appearance, native aquatic plant species were introduced.

Pond weeds, such as blanketweed **(1)** and duckweed **(2)**, can be a problem in small ornamental ponds but they are tolerated in the Blacks' wildlife pond. If you spot these two species in your pond, and you notice that they are covering large areas of the surface, scoop out as much as possible using a fine-mesh fishing net.

Boggy patch

On the side of the pond furthest from the house, Greg and Sarah planted moisture-loving bog garden plants so that the pond integrated faultlessly into its surroundings. Along the grassy access paths that lead to and from the pond, they sowed a wildflower mixture of grass seed and added clumps of container-grown purple loosestrife (*Lythrum*) and meadowsweet (*Filipendula*) to complete the transition.

Water meadow

The low-lying ground adjacent to the pond remained very wet for most of the year, so the Blacks decided to make it into a water meadow feature filled with wetland species, such as Sarah's favourite, snake's-head fritillary. To create this type of feature in your garden, the ground needs to be thoroughly prepared, then sowed with a special wetland soil mixture of grasses and wildflowers. Sarah chose ragged robin, cowslips and snake's-head fritillaries and then added further drifts of fritillaries as bulbs in the second year. The grass was allowed to grow long, only to be mowed twice a year, with a meandering country path cut through the area so weekend visitors can lose themselves among the hazy grasses and busy bees – the perfect antidote for a hectic city life.

From the house, the water meadow stretches away into the distance to merge with the surrounding fields and hills. Beyond the water meadow, the property was partly bordered by a mixed hedge. This was improved by planting native species around it which bear heavy crops of winter berries to feed the resident wildlife.

Butterfly borders

The other end of the country path in Greg and Sarah's garden starts close to the house. It was decided to border this with a simple combination of massed sedums, asters, butterfly bush and lavender. A sweetbriar and honeysuckle-clad fence was added to run behind. This created a heady mixture of scents in spring and summer, and was alive with pollinating insects and butterflies.

expert tips   Dividing aquatic plants

If you have a pond, it is important to split up any overgrown aquatic plants to keep them vigorous and flowering well.

The old baskets in Greg and Sarah's pond were damaged by shoots and roots growing through the sides. So the baskets had to be cut from the plants to avoid damaging the plants' roots. The plants and their roots were then divided carefully into clumps using a sharp garden spade making sure each clump had plenty of healthy roots and shoots. Several healthy looking sections from the outside of the clump were selected to be replanted in new aquatic baskets (see page 138) and the rest were put on the compost heap.

Ornamental touch

To add a sense of spectacle to the pond, a floating fountainhead was installed, powered by a submersible pump. It is switched on only when Greg and Sarah, or their visitors, take a stroll down the country path or sit by the water.

keeping it looking good

spring •

early summer •

late summer •

autumn •

winter •

spring

patios & containers

ESSENTIAL TASKS

Water Keep watering winter containers as required. Remember that plants protected by the eaves of your house or situated by a wall or fence will need watering more often.

Plant Hanging baskets and other containers can be planted with tender summer bedding during late spring, after the danger of frost has passed.

Feed plants Push slow-release fertiliser tablets into the soil of permanent plants and when planting seasonal displays to keep them well fed all season.

Uncover pots Containers that were wrapped to protect them from winter cold can be unwrapped during mid- to late spring.

Save water Cover the surface of planted containers with a layer of pebbles or fine gravel to help conserve moisture during the summer months.

Plant hanging baskets p. 116

TROUBLESHOOTING

Tidy up Remove any dead flowers and leaves from winter containers to keep them looking their best. Clear heavy snow from container plants. Sweep the patio.

lawns

ESSENTIAL TASKS

Mow When the weather is fine and the grass is dry, mow your lawn. The grass will be lush, so collect the clippings and place on the compost heap.

Flowering lawns Leave the foliage of bulbs growing in the lawn for six weeks after flowering has finished. This will give the bulbs time to build up sufficient food reserves to flower well next year. After this period, the leaves can be cut back and the lawn mowed as normal.

Feed Give your lawn a boost during late spring using a spring-formulation lawn fertiliser. If weeds or moss need to be tackled, use a combined lawn treatment.

Plant new lawn Sow seed or lay turf as soon as soil conditions allow (see page 44).

Neaten lawn edges Repair damaged lawn edges (see page 47) or lay a mowing strip (see page 49).

Kill weeds Pull out weeds by hand or use a dab-on weed killer. For a widespread problem, apply a selective weed killer once the lawn starts growing.

Remove moss Control moss by raking vigorously; improve drainage for permanent control.

TROUBLESHOOTING

Improve drainage Spike your lawn with a garden fork. Make rows of holes at least 7.5 cm deep every 5–10 cm across the soggy area. Fill holes with sharp sand. If the whole lawn is affected, hire a mechanical spiker to do the job.

Improve drainage p. 47

beds &
borders

ESSENTIAL TASKS

Get pruning Cut back late- and early-flowering shrubs (see page 182), including early-flowering clematis. Quick-prune shrub and bush roses by trimming shoots back by about two-thirds (see page 184). Prune dead, diseased and weak growth from climbing roses.

Get pruning p. 182

Plant If the weather is mild, plant bare-rooted trees and shrubs while they are dormant. Late spring is the ideal time to plant evergreens, hardy perennial flowers and summer-flowering bulbs.

Provide supports Prevent top-heavy perennials from collapsing when in full bloom by placing supports around the emerging shoots. Use bamboo canes and string or wire supports that are available from garden centres.

Feed permanent plants Apply a general-purpose fertiliser or well-rotted manure around shrubs and trees. Scatter 25–50 grams per square metre over the shrubbery or about 25 grams around individual plants.

Divide flowers Large clumps of herbaceous perennials can be divided during mid- to late spring to keep them vigorous and flowering well (see page 70).

Deadhead bulbs Remove the fading flowers from plants, such as daffodils, but leave flower stalks and leaves to die naturally for six weeks after flowering.

TROUBLESHOOTING

Slugs and snails Protect susceptible border plants such as delphiniums and hostas by scattering a few slug pellets around before the new shoots emerge.

 ponds

ESSENTIAL TASKS

Feed fish Start feeding when the water temperature begins to rise and the fish become more active. Feed sparingly at first, but more regularly by late spring.

Tender plants During late spring, replace tender floating plants that were removed from the pond the previous autumn and kept somewhere frost free.

Feed plants Push special aquatic fertiliser tablets into the compost of established aquatic plants. Keep the tablets toward the centre of the basket to prevent nutrients from leaching out into the water and encouraging the growth of algae.

Divide large plants Some shallow-water plants and many bog garden plants will need to be divided every few years to keep them flowering well (see page 145).

New plants Add new plants during mid- to late spring. Plant in flat-bottomed aquatic planting baskets using special aquatic compost (see page 139).

TROUBLESHOOTING

Rotting leaves Remove netting covers and scoop out any wind-blown leaves before they have a chance to sink to the bottom and rot.

early summer

 ## patios & containers

ESSENTIAL TASKS

Water Plants should be watered as required, which may mean watering twice a day in hot, dry weather. Move containers to a shady spot to reduce the amount of water they need. Consider installing an automatic watering system if you have a lot of containers to maintain (see page 119).

Plant Plant hanging baskets and other containers with tender summer bedding during early summer, if not already done. Line porous terracotta with polythene and use drought-tolerant plants to reduce the need for watering (see page 117).

Automatic watering p. 119

Feed plants If you didn't insert slow-release fertiliser tablets when planting in spring, container plants will need feeding about six weeks after they were planted. To improve flowering displays, apply a high-potash liquid fertiliser every other watering.

Tidy containers Remove fading flowers to tidy displays and encourage further flower production. Also, remove any dead or yellowing leaves.

TROUBLESHOOTING

Weedy areas Hand-weed gravel, patios and other paved areas, or use a commercial weed killer. Cover nearby ornamental plants with polythene or upturned buckets and leave in place until the spray has completely dried.

 ## lawns

ESSENTIAL TASKS

Keep in trim Mow the lawn regularly. This may mean cutting twice a week while the lawn is growing strongly. Clippings can be left on the lawn to feed the grass if they are less than 2 cm long, otherwise put them on the compost heap.

Neaten edges Trim the lawn edges each time you mow for the cleanest effect, but you can reduce this to every other mowing if you are pushed for time. To get a really neat appearance, pick up the clippings after edging. This will also prevent them from rooting in the border and becoming a weed problem.

Worn areas Over-sow patchy lawns or re-seed (see page 44). Frequently used areas can be reinforced with heavy-duty plastic mesh (see page 48).

Wildflower meadow Areas of spring-flowering meadow can be cut once the plants have finished flowering and shed their seed. Check the seedpods to make sure the seed has been scattered before you mow.

TROUBLESHOOTING

Weeds Remove individual weeds with an old kitchen knife and weaken patches of coarse grasses by mowing regularly. If the whole lawn is weed infested, apply a selective weed killer.

Brown grass Don't worry if your lawn turns brown in summer due to lack of water, it will soon regain its green appearance when the rains come. But if you want to keep it green all summer, apply 1 cm of water twice a week using a sprinkler.

beds & borders

ESSENTIAL TASKS

Harden off seedlings Tender bedding and vegetables need to be acclimatised to the cooler environment outdoors before they are planted. Place in a coldframe or in a sheltered spot for a week or two prior to planting in their flowering position.

Replace bedding Spring annuals that have come to the end of their display should be replaced with tender summer bedding that have been acclimatised.

Trim hedges Trim fast-growing ornamental hedges, such as privet, in early to mid-summer. Prune informal hedges after they have finished flowering.

Mulch beds Apply a 5-cm-layer of wood chips, compost, or other organic material around shrubs, perennials and bedding to smother weeds, conserve moisture and improve soil.

Pruning Cut back shrubs that flower as soon as the display has finished (see page 182).

Frost damage Severe frost can kill exposed tips of many plants, so you need to cut out dead stems. To check if it is dead, scrape away a little bark with a fingernail; if it's creamy-yellow or green it is alive, if it is brown it's dead.

Check supports Make sure all tall perennial plants that are prone to flopping over while in flower have been securely staked.

Deadhead flowers Remove dead flower heads from rhododendrons and azaleas after flowering has finished. Continue deadheading late varieties of daffodil and tulips, leaving their foliage to die down naturally. Deadhead roses to improve the display.

TROUBLESHOOTING

Spray roses Mildew, blackspot and rust can seriously weaken susceptible varieties. Spray with fungicide every two weeks to keep these diseases at bay.

Pest patrol Watch out for tiny insects on the new growth of many plants including roses. Wash off small colonies with soapy water; spray severe outbreaks with a suitable insecticide.

 ponds

ESSENTIAL TASKS

Top up reservoirs Regularly top up the water reservoirs of small water features, especially if the weather is hot or windy.

Plant Early summer is the best time to plant tender aquatic plants after the threat of frost has passed. It is also a good time to revamp neglected ponds (see page 144).

Water bog garden Keep the compost in the bog garden moist, but not waterlogged. In hot weather, it may require watering every day, so it may be worth your while installing a seep hose to make watering easier or plumbing it into an automatic watering system.

Plant aquatic baskets p. 144

Improve displays Remove faded blooms and yellowing stems and leaves using a pair of scissors or secateurs before the dying growth falls into the water and rots.

TROUBLESHOOTING

Green water Prevent the water from turning green with algae by placing a barley straw pad in the pond.

late summer

 patios &
containers

ESSENTIAL TASKS

Water Continue to water plants as required.

Feed Give all container plants some liquid fertiliser every other watering.

Holidays Arrange to have a neighbour or friend water all container plants each day while you are away. If you are away for a short period of time you could set up a temporary watering system instead (see page 120). If you are away a lot, consider installing an automatic watering system.

Take cuttings Prepare cuttings from tender perennials as insurance against any winter losses of plants to be left outside.

Tidy plants Continue to tidy up displays by removing dead flowers and leaves. Use a pair of secateurs to trim back over-vigorous plants from time to time to prevent them overwhelming their neighbours and spoiling the balance of the display.

TROUBLESHOOTING

Pest alert Watch out for aphids in the buds and shoot tips of container plants. Wash off small colonies with soapy water; use a ready-to-use insecticide to deal with more severe outbreaks.

Disease check Plants in containers are usually more susceptible to diseases, such as powdery mildew, if they run short of water. Remove any badly affected leaves and spray the rest of the plant with a suitable fungicide. Pay particular attention to keeping all containers well watered.

Take cuttings p. 180

 lawns

ESSENTIAL TASKS

Mow and edge Keep mowing your lawn regularly. Clippings can be left on the lawn to feed the grass if they are less than 2 cm long, otherwise put them on the compost heap. Continue to trim the edges of the lawn every time you mow.

Holidays Ask a neighbour to mow the lawn for you if you are away for more than a week during the summer months; the edge trimming can wait until you return.

Edge the lawn p. 47

Heavy wear Lawns can suffer from excessive wear and tear during the summer holiday, especially under children's play equipment and areas used for ball games. Either move the play equipment around to spread the wear more evenly or reinforce the worn patches using heavy-duty plastic mesh before the damage is done (see page 48).

TROUBLESHOOTING

Weeds During prolonged dry spells, the grass may stop growing, but weeds don't. They will flower, set seed and then spread if you let them. Stop this from happening by running the mower over the lawn once a week to remove the flowers.

beds &
borders

ESSENTIAL TASKS

Pruning Cut out one stem in three from summer-flowering shrubs after they have finished flowering. Prune the sideshoots from wall-grown pyracantha to a few leaves to enhance the display of berries over the winter months (see page 185).

Plant bulbs Autumn-flowering bulbs such as colchicums, hardy cyclamen, nerines and autumn crocus should be planted during mid-summer.

Trim hedges Give hedges their final trim. This will allow any new growth time to mature before the onset of winter.

Water There is no need to water established plants, but it is essential that any plants added this spring or early summer are kept watered through their first growing season. It is also worth watering bedding, such as fuchsias and busy Lizzies, as well as leafy and pod-producing vegetables during long, dry spells.

Tidy borders Remove dead heads and yellowing leaves. Also cut back straggly pansies and untidy leaves of perennials, such as hardy canesbill, which will produce a fresh mound of attractive foliage and may produce another flush of flowers.

Take cuttings Remove semi-ripe cuttings of shrubs (see page 180) to increase stocks. Also take cuttings from not-so-hardy shrubs, such as hibiscus, myrtle and olearia, so that you have ready replacements for any losses caused by winter cold and wet.

TROUBLESHOOTING

Save water Prevent moisture loss from the soil by adding a layer of organic material (known as a *mulch*) around trees, shrubs and climbers.

Disease check Inspect perennial flowers for powdery mildew disease. Spray affected plants that have not flowered with a suitable fungicide (check instructions on the packet). Those that have finished flowering can be cut back and the diseased leaves disposed of. New disease-free foliage will then be produced.

 ponds

ESSENTIAL TASKS

Top up ponds Continue to top-up ponds and water features as necessary. Do this often so that the temperature of the pond remains more or less constant and the fish are not distressed.

Feed fish Continue to feed fish regularly throughout the summer.

Tidy plants Continue to remove fading flowers and yellowing stems and leaves from plants before they fall into the pond to rot. Thin out floating plants if they are covering more than two-thirds of the pond's surface area and scoop out dense growths of submerged plants using an old colander.

TROUBLESHOOTING

Gasping fish During hot and thundery weather, the oxygen levels in still water are depleted and fish can often be seen gasping at the surface. If you have a fountain or cascade, switch it on to oxygenate the surface water. If not, use water from a hose to do the same job.

Duckweed Like tiny seedlings floating on the surface of the water, duckweed can soon multiply to cover the entire pond. Use an old colander to scoop out as much as you can.

Blanketweed Use a rake to scoop this rapidly growing weed or twist the thread-like growths around the end of a bamboo cane. Leave the weed on the side of the pond

Duckweed p. 144

to give any pond creatures the chance to get back into the water. Then add the dry weed to the compost heap.

autumn

patios & containers

ESSENTIAL TASKS

Plant winter displays Patio containers, hanging baskets and windowboxes can be planted with hardy plants, including colourful foliage, berries or flowers. Use winter bedding plants, such as pansies for intermittent blooms over several months and dwarf bulbs to give displays a colour boost in spring.

Plant winter displays p. 115

Tender plants Move containers filled with permanent tender plants into a frost-free place. If your garden only gets light frosts, almost-hardy container plants can be overwintered successfully outside. Move them to a sheltered spot and wrap the pot with a double layer of bubble wrap and the plants with a double layer of garden fleece. Leave an opening so the plants can be watered if necessary.

Clear out containers Pots and tubs containing summer displays should be emptied and the pots cleaned. Salvage as many plants as possible, reusing hardy plants, such as ivy, in winter displays and over-wintering tender plants, such as pelargoniums, in a frost-free place. Cut back plants and store them in boxes or take cuttings (see page 180) if space is limited.

TROUBLESHOOTING

Frost-proofing Some garden containers, notably those made from terracotta, are not reliably frost-proof. Empty and move to the safety of a shed or garage any that are susceptible to frost damage in your garden.

lawns

ESSENTIAL TASKS

Mow Continue to mow your lawn until it goes dormant.

Edge Continue edging your lawn to keep it looking neat. Consider adding a mowing strip, if not already done in spring (see page 49).

Clear leaves Fallen leaves should be cleared from the lawn regularly. If they are allowed to remain for more than a week, the grass underneath will suffer. Use a wire rake to collect leaves for the compost heap. For larger lawns, consider renting or buying a leaf sweeper which will clean up leaves quickly.

Feed Apply an autumn lawn fertiliser to give your lawn a boost, particularly if it suffered heavy wear during the summer.

Plant bulbs Daffodils and crocuses can be planted in small areas near the edge of the lawn to create an attractive display next spring.

Create a mowing strip p. 49

Rake If necessary, remove the dead and decaying stems that build up within the grass (known as *thatch*) using vigorous strokes with a wire rake.

TROUBLESHOOTING

Moss To prevent moss in shaded areas, you will have to reduce the amount of shade or replace the grass with more shade-tolerant groundcover plants.

Bare patches Sow grass seed to thicken up patchy grass or re-sow bare patches (see page 44).

beds & borders

ESSENTIAL TASKS

Lift tender bulbs Tender plants such as gladioli need to be lifted and stored somewhere dry and frost-free in frost-prone areas.

Get planting Plant spring bulbs, woody plants and winter flowers. Trees, shrubs and climbers should be watered thoroughly and planted at the same depth as they were in the container (see page 102). Plant bare-root specimens immediately.

Tender plants To ensure tender perennials produce displays year after year, keep them frost-free over winter. Box up a selection of your favourite plants in soil that is moist and place in a frost-free garage (see page 121). Alternatively, take cuttings (see page 180).

Clean borders Remove the dying top-growth from herbaceous plants and protect the central root (known as the crown) of not-so-hardy types with a blanket of leaves or straw held in place with netting. Leave dead stems of grasses to provide architectural interest to borders, especially on frosty mornings.

Tie climbers Check climbers and wall shrubs to see if they are well secured. Tie any stems that need it.

Dig vacant ground Areas that you intend to plant next spring should be cultivated during the autumn so that the frosts can break down any large clods over the winter. If your soil is light and sandy, leave digging until the spring.

Hardwood cuttings Now is the time to take hardwood cuttings from many shrubs (see page 181).

TROUBLESHOOTING

Protect climbers Give borderline-tender climbers a protective double layer of garden fleece or a layer of insulation made from straw held in position by fine-mesh netting. This will prevent them from dying during the cold weather.

ponds

ESSENTIAL TASKS

Clear ponds Remove any dead or dying foliage from plants growing in the shallow areas by cutting stems back to about 2 cm above the surface of the water.

Feed fish Give your fish a high-protein feed to allow them to build up sufficient reserves before winter.

Divide large plants Remove baskets of large plants from the pond and divide them up using a sharp spade, before replanting and replacing in the pond (see page 139).

TROUBLESHOOTING

Net ponds Prevent fallen leaves from blowing into the pond by covering it with a fine-mesh net. If your pond is too large or if wind-blown leaves are the main problem, it is worth putting up a 65-cm-high netting barrier around the pond to catch the leaves. Clear accumulations of leaves as necessary.

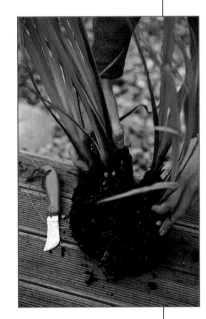

Divide large plants p. 139

winter

patios & containers

ESSENTIAL TASKS

Water Keep watering all containers filled with plants if compost is not frozen. Containers under the eaves of your house or shed and those next to walls tend to receive less rain and so require watering more often. Don't forget to check plants that were wrapped up in the autumn, as they will need occasional watering too.

Protect winter displays Small pots and hanging baskets may require protection in moderately cold winters because they contain a relatively small amount of compost that is more prone to freezing. Wrap pots in bubble wrap to protect the plant roots. In cold areas, move susceptible plants to an unheated porch or garage or to the shelter of a thick hedge.

Tidy displays Remove dead flowers and foliage from winter containers to improve the displays and prevent them from rotting.

TROUBLESHOOTING

Protect from snow Some evergreen shrubs, especially conifers, are susceptible to damage by large accumulations of snow. If heavy falls are forecast, either wrap the conifer with soft string to prevent it from being pulled out of shape, or be prepared to knock snow off before damage is caused.

Protect winter displays p. 121

lawns

ESSENTIAL TASKS

Mow Avoid walking on your lawn while it is wet or frosty. Mowing may be necessary throughout winter in very mild areas, but elsewhere the grass will practically stop growing.

Clearing leaves Keep clearing leaves that blow onto the lawn during early winter. Do this at least once a week if you have a lot of deciduous trees in your area.

New lawns In mild-winter areas, where the soil is not too wet, you could lay grass turfs in early winter. Otherwise, it is better to wait until spring.

Mower maintenance Clean and maintain your mower (see mower instructions for details). Check that blades are in good condition, clean and wipe with an oily rag to stop them from rusting while in storage. If you are getting it serviced, make an appointment now because service centres will be very busy come the spring.

Tool care Clean and sharpen all tools. Wipe metal surfaces with an oily rag before storage.

Overhanging plants Shrubs and trees that are starting to overhang the lawn or cast deep shade can be pruned back or thinned. The plants will not suffer so much stress at this time of year and you will be able to see where to make the cuts more clearly.

Clearing leaves see p. 168

TROUBLESHOOTING

Lawn protection Keep pets from using the lawn as a toilet to prevent dead spots in spring.

beds & borders

ESSENTIAL TASKS

Check supports Take the opportunity to check the condition of supports while climbers are dormant and leafless. Make repairs as necessary and loosen any constricting ties.

Check roses Check woody plants such as roses after a hard frost or severe winds and refirm the soil around their roots if they have become loosened.

Early sowings If you have the facilities to grow plants somewhere frost-free until the end of the spring, sow sweet peas during late winter. For nearly all other flower crops wait until early or mid-spring before sowing (see page 178).

Boundary repairs Check walls and fences to see if they are in need of repair, especially if they are used to support a climber. Carefully take down climbing plants and protect them with polythene before applying wood preservative or repointing crumbling mortar.

Feed birds Place bird food out in a cat- and squirrel-proof bird table. Feed birds nuts, seeds, suet and fruit, and give them fresh water every day. Once you start feeding, keep it up all winter because the local bird population will come to depend on you.

TROUBLESHOOTING

Clear leaves from roses Wear thick gloves to gather all fallen leaves carefully from bush and climbing roses or use a leaf sweeper to make the job easier. This will help prevent disease from infected fallen leaves from carrying over to next year's new foliage.

ponds

ESSENTIAL TASKS

Remove the pump Remove submersible pond pumps and clean thoroughly before storage. If your pond contains fish, replace the pump with a low-voltage pond heater (available from specialist suppliers), which will keep at least part of the surface ice-free all winter.

Clear leaves Continue to clear up wind-blown leaves from around the pond and netting so that they cannot find their way into the pond, rot and foul the water.

Feeding Continue to feed fish with a high-protein fish food until the weather turns really cold and the water temperature reaches 10°C (50°F) – once this occurs, the fish become less active.

Winter protection Cover small water features with bubble wrap. Protect small ponds by covering with planks and laying insulation materials over the top.

Ice-free hole Fish ponds need to have at least part of their surface kept free of ice to allow toxic gases produced by decaying plant materials at the bottom of the pond to escape from the water. If your pond freezes over, melt a hole using a saucepan full of hot water. Never smash a hole in the ice because the shock-waves may kill the fish.

TROUBLESHOOTING

Big freeze When sub-zero temperatures last for a period of time, use a hose to siphon off a 5–10 cm of water from below the ice-sheet on the pond to prevent it getting any thicker. The trapped air under the ice-sheet will act as an insulation layer and help prevent the pond surface from freezing over again.

gardening basics

know your garden climate

The climate in your garden is determined by several factors. The most important is the geographical location of your garden: how far north it is, its altitude and distance from the coast.

Coastal gardens tend to have more rain and experience less extremes in temperature than those inland. Local geographical factors such as hills and lakes also can have a significant influence on the climate in a particular area.

What plants can you grow?

Temperature, sunlight, rain and wind are the main factors that affect the plants you can and cannot grow.

Temperature Plants vary greatly in their ability to tolerate high and low temperatures, so it is essential that you choose varieties that are able to cope with your garden's conditions.

Apart from your garden's geographical position (see chart opposite), air temperatures are affected by the lay of the land. A garden with a slightly north-facing slope, for example, will be slower to warm up and quicker to cool down than a garden with a slight south-facing slope, which captures more of the sun's energy.

The temperature of the soil is affected by the type of soil you have: sandy soil warms up quickly while heavy clay soil takes its time. Dark-coloured soils also warm up more quickly than light-coloured soils.

Tender plants, such as summer bedding, are very susceptible to damage and easily killed. Even a plant considered hardy can be damaged if the cold period is prolonged, very severe or occurs just after the plant has put on new growth in spring. It is essential that all tender plants are protected from frost. The easiest way to do that is not to plant them out until the last likely frost date in your area (see chart for rough guidelines). If a frost is forecast after planting out tender plants, cover them with a double layer of garden fleece to protect them. If you are caught by an unexpectedly late frost, cover affected plants early in the morning with sheets of newspaper to slow down the rate of thawing, because this is when most of the damage to plant tissue occurs.

Sunlight This obviously increases temperatures, so the more sunshine a garden gets, the warmer it will be. Any south-facing areas in your garden will provide a warm growing environment. Many plants like sunny conditions and do best in a site that gets direct sunlight for most of the day. Others, such as rhododendrons (1), are adapted to growing under trees and so prefer a partially shaded site.

It is important to assess how much sunlight each part of your garden receives, and then choose suitable plants for each area.

Rain Water is essential for plants to survive and most is supplied by rainfall. Levels of rainfall vary considerably from area to area. There are also variations in how much rain falls from month to month throughout the year.

All areas experience periods of drought, which put plants under stress and if prolonged, can kill them. If you live in a drought-prone area, choose plants that have evolved to reduce water loss. Plants which have gray, hairy, glossy, needle-like or thick succulent leaves, such as *Echeveria* (2), will do well in these conditions.

Wind The dramatic damage caused by strong winds is all too obvious, but even a light breeze has an effect on plant growth.

Air movement is beneficial as it reduces the incidence of disease and helps plants to keep cool. Wind is not a problem in most gardens, except in exposed, windy sites. A steady breeze, however, reduces humidity and increases evaporation of water from the plants' leaves, which means the plants need more water to compensate. This can put the plants under stress, especially during prolonged drought – reducing growth and potential yields from fruit and vegetable crops. Fortunately, it is very easy to protect plants from the effects of wind by putting up windbreaks that help to slow down the air movement.

In some gardens, currents of air are accelerated by the funnelling effect of buildings or natural weather patterns. Wind damage is particularly severe on the coast, as the air is laden with salt. Use salt-tolerant shrubs such as *Pittosporum* (3) to help shelter coastal gardens.

AVERAGE MINIMUM WINTER TEMPERATURES IN WESTERN EUROPE

ZONE	AREAS COVERED	TEMPERATURE
1	Coastal Portugal, south-west coast of Spain, southern Greek islands, Crete	5°C (40°F)
2	Southern Portugal, northern Portugal, coastal southern Spain, coastal eastern Spain, Balearic Islands, Mediterranean coastal France, Sardinia, Sicily, south coast of Italy, northern Greek Islands	0°C (32°F)
3	Coastal and southern England, coastal Wales, coastal eastern Scotland, coastal and southern Ireland, western and coastal France, central Portugal, southern and eastern Spain, central Italy, central Greece	-5°C (23°F)
4	Central England, central Wales, lowland Scotland, central Ireland, Netherlands, Belgium, Luxemburg, northern Germany, western Denmark, central France, northern Spain, northern Italy, northern Greece	-10°C (14°F)
5	Highland Scotland, highland Spain, highland France, Switzerland, Austria, eastern Denmark, western Norway, southern coastal Sweden, central and eastern Germany, highland Italy	-15°C (5°F)
6	Eastern Norway, central Sweden, Pyrenees and alpine France, alpine Italy, alpine Switzerland, alpine Austria, alpine Germany	Below -15°C (5°F)

planning a garden redesign

You may want to redesign your garden for a number of reasons: if you have moved into a new house, for example, and inherited a design from the previous owners that doesn't suit your particular needs; or if your circumstances have changed and you require different features in your garden, such as a safe play area for children. Whatever your situation, the first step is to draw up a scale plan of your existing garden. This will give you an accurate vision of what your garden can accommodate.

Making plans

First make a rough sketch of your garden, then use a measuring tape to measure accurately the position of major features such as the house and garage as well as any boundaries. A 3-metre retractable tape is suitable for measuring a small garden, but for larger areas use a 30-metre surveyors' tape (available from do-it-yourself stores or rental shops). Measure and jot down any changes in level, both from front to back and from one side of the garden to the other. Now sketch the location of permanent plants such as trees and large shrubs and other large features that may be present, such as a shed, pond or pergola. To get accurate measurements of the position of each feature within the garden, measure its distance from two fixed points of reference, such as two corners of the house.

Using the measurements that you recorded on the sketch, draw up an accurate plan on graph paper. Make it reasonably large – a scale of 2 cm to 1 metre is ideal for most gardens. Include on the graph paper all the features you intend to keep in the final garden plan, then add all the other features on an overlay of tracing paper or a sheet of clear acetate placed on top.

On a sunny day, note which way is north (use a compass if you are unsure) and how the shadows fall across the garden. Use different colours to indicate different levels of shade. For example, use red for areas that are shaded in the morning, orange for areas that are shaded in the evening, and yellow for any areas that stay shady for most of the day. Transfer these shaded areas onto a second overlay.

Also note any obvious problem spots where plants struggle to grow, such as deep shade next to the house or under the canopy of a maple tree, boggy soil that stays wet for long periods or soil that dries out too quickly in summer. Finally, take a soil sample and check the acidity levels in different areas using a simple pH kit (see page 166).

Area of overgrown lawn and neglected shrubs

Large trees and overgrown shrubs create areas of dense shade

Fence

Grass path

Wall

Brick paved patio area behind the house

Make the most of existing features

Assess the existing garden and consider which, if any, of the features you want to retain. In this garden, most of the large shrubs were overgrown and had to be removed to allow more light into the house. Two compact evergreens, however, were retained to give the new design a sense of maturity.

Existing tree

Bench

Topiary spheres

Focal-point empty container and lavender

Paved area in geometric design with beds built in

Seating area under a pergola

Flower border

Compost piles

Bench

Fence

Grass path will be replaced with a brick one

Area to be laid to lawn

Wall

A pergola will run along one side of the patio area

Patio area for container plants

Plan out the key elements on paper

Sketch out your ideas to see how the different elements fit together in the new garden design. Start with the boundaries, paving and other ground covering materials, then add other features such as seats and garden structures.

The plan should now contain enough information for you to finalise the position of features, decide on planting schemes and develop your garden design with confidence. The graph paper layout can be used as many times as you want to try out a variety of ideas. Cut out shapes in coloured paper to represent different features, such as a shed, patio area or pond and try them out in different positions around the garden. Don't be afraid to change your mind: a well-designed garden usually goes through several revisions during the planning and building stages as unexpected problems or new ideas emerge. Building features such as patios and ponds, however, are difficult and costly to alter once work has begun, so make sure you have considered everything before committing yourself.

trying out your ideas

Before you make any changes to your garden, it is worth marking it out to help you visualise the overall effect. Straight lines such as the edges of a patio or formal pond are easy to mark out with pegs and string, but to create the sweeping curves of a new border or lawns a rope or garden hose would be more suitable. If you want further reassurance, you can try mocking-up other key features. For instance, you could use bamboo canes and string in the place of arches and other garden structures to see what impact they have on their surroundings.

Creating the new garden

Your garden will be viewed and accessed from your house, so plan the design from this viewpoint.

Changing boundaries It is always a good idea to start with the garden boundaries because they can have a great influence on the style and feel of the design. Boundary fences and walls are difficult and often expensive to change, although if totally inappropriate for the garden design you are hoping to create, they can be disguised with paint or camouflaged with relatively inexpensive trellis and climbers.

In this garden, a new wall was built to provide privacy. It was made from salvaged bricks to match the materials used in the house. If you want to change a boundary wall or fence, check there are no planning restrictions on height or materials before you begin.

Decorative paving Patios designed for sitting in the sun or enjoying outdoor meals need to be carefully positioned if they are to be successful. So it is a good idea to establish where you are going to have your patio before you add any other features to your plan.

In the garden featured, the overgrown lawn area was paved over to create a low-maintenance patio in a

modern geometric design. Small beds for planting form a circular shape around the large terracotta pot, which provides a focal point. To minimise the impact of so much paving in a relatively small garden, the design combines different paving materials and uses plants to soften the harsh outlines.

Covering the ground The influence of a grassy lawn or other ground covering on the appearance of a garden is often overlooked by the beginner. Here, a well-proportioned lawn has been shaped to complement the overall design of the garden. It provides a natural open space that is restful on the eye and offers the opportunity for creating attractive vistas, even in a small garden like this.

Special features Desired garden features such as arches and pergolas should be included on your design plan, along with practical features, such as a shed or compost heap. Bear in mind that some features, such as a pond or areas for growing herbs and vegetables, need an open,

sunny location. The pergola in this garden is a decorative feature with a practical function – a table and chairs have been placed there and a small candelabra provides soft lighting for evening entertaining.

Using garden dividers Dividing a garden up into 'rooms' is a useful design technique for disguising the size of a garden. It also allows you to combine different styles. Here, a picket fence has been retained to separate the area for growing herbs

Planting plans

A detailed planting plan was drawn up for each border taking into consideration how much sun each area receives. The ground was thoroughly dug and cleared of weeds before the plants were due to arrive, so they could be planted immediately.

and vegetables from the pergola and mini-orchard. Anything that breaks the direct line of sight can be used as a garden divider – hedges and fences work well in large gardens, while trellis and rustic fence panels are suitable in a small one.

Borders and plants Like other features, beds and borders should be in proportion to the rest of the garden design. Do not make them too wide unless you provide access, such as stepping stones, through the middle to carry out routine maintenance. In this garden, a balance of deciduous and evergreen plants that offer more than one season of interest was chosen to give the garden year-round appeal.

Focal points

The two main points of focus in the garden were both combined with fragrant plants to help soften their appearance. The pergola was planted with climbing roses and colourful clematis, while the large terracotta urn was surrounded with lavender.

understanding your soil

Soils vary in quality and fertility. The easiest way to grow a satisfying garden is to accept your type of soil, and select only those plants that will thrive in these conditions. Garden centres and catalogues are packed with adaptable plants, and also offer many for conditions like dry shade, very dry soil, heavy clay soil, or wet areas. (See below for advice on assessing your soil.)

If your soil has been damaged – the topsoil removed during building works, perhaps, or the soil compacted by heavy equipment – you will need to make major changes to loosen it or increase fertility. Otherwise, it is unlikely to support the healthy growth of plants. If you have less than ideal soil, consider building raised beds.

Digging in well-rotted manure, or compost, and applying organic matter as mulch, supplies nourishment to the micro-organisms that thrive in the soil. These tiny creatures create the food for the roots of plants, and improve soil drainage.

Assessing your soil

If you have a new garden that is completely bare or an area of a garden you intend to replant, it is worth checking that the soil is in good shape before you start.

Dig several 60-cm-deep holes over the area and check the soil profile – that is, the two layers of soil. The top layer (called topsoil) contains most of the nutrients and supports most of the plant growth. It is usually about 15 cm deep and is often a darker colour than the second layer of soil (called subsoil).

To test the drainage of your soil, fill each hole with 10 litres of water. If it drains away completely within 24 hours, all is well. If not, you will have to dig the soil (see right). If the

How to test your soil

Different plants require a certain type of soil to grow healthily: some love acid soils, others thrive in more alkaline conditions, while most prefer a neutral or slightly acid soil. You can test the pH (the level of acidity) of your soil very easily using a soil test kit (available from garden retailers), which tells you whether your soil is alkaline, neutral or acid. To get an accurate reading, you need to gather a sample of soil that is representative of your garden as a whole.

1   Lay out 2-metre-long bamboo canes in a W-shaped pattern over the area. Then dig small holes where the canes cross and collect soil samples from about 10 cm into the hole. Avoid contaminated areas or those that are not typical of the plot as a whole, such as around a compost heap. Mix the samples together in a clean bucket and use a garden sieve to remove stones and other debris.

2   Place a small amount of the soil into a folded piece of paper or card and gently pour the soil into the testing bottle.

3   Add water as directed on the testing kit and then shake vigorously. Allow to settle before checking the sample against the colour chart supplied.

For a more accurate analysis or an indication of the nutrient levels in the soil, send a sample to a soil laboratory. See your local directory for your nearest service.

water drains poorly, you may have to install extra drainage (ask your garden centre for advice) or grow plants in raised beds or pots instead.

Simple digging

The traditional way of overcoming poor drainage is to dig vacant areas of soil once a year. This helps to bury weeds and break up any surface compaction, allowing water to drain freely. It also allows you to incorporate organic matter, such as manure, deep into the soil where a plant's roots develop.

Different soils require digging at different times of the year. But only dig when soil conditions allow, or you will do more harm than good. You can use a spade on most soils, but if your soil is very stony, a garden fork may be easier.

Heavy soils If your soil has a high clay content, dig in the late autumn so that any large lumps of earth are exposed to frost action, which breaks the clods down.

Steps to success when digging

- Dig heavy soils in late autumn before the soil becomes too wet. If it sticks to your tools and boots it is too wet. Leave lighter, sandy soils until spring.

- Choose a spade with a handle that is comfortable and sufficiently long to prevent you from stooping while digging. Wear sturdy boots.

- Push the blade vertically into the ground and turn over small amounts of soil at a time, keeping your back as straight as possible. Take regular breaks.

Loamy soils (not clay or sandy) These can be dug any time during the winter months provided the soil is not too wet or frozen.

Sandy soils Light, sandy soils are best dug during the spring, a couple of weeks before planting.

No digging method

If you don't like the idea of digging every year, you don't have to. Take a leaf out of the organic gardeners' book – if you don't walk on the soil,

you won't cause the damage which makes digging necessary. The secret is to prepare the soil thoroughly to begin with by deep digging (see box below) and then to add a thick layer of organic matter to the soil surface once a year. Thereafter, you can simply leave the worms and beetles to do the work for you.

Deep digging

Some soils can develop hard compacted layers about 30 cm below the surface, which are impenetrable to roots. This causes shallow rooting, so that plants grow poorly and are more susceptible to periods of drought. Ordinary digging does not break up the soil at this depth, so a special technique called deep or double digging has to be employed. Even though very simple, it is hard work.

- Dig a 60-cm-wide trench with a spade to a depth of about 20 cm and move the soil to the other end of the plot being dug.

- Break up the bottom of the trench using a garden fork and incorporate some organic matter, such as well-rotted manure as you go along.

- Move back 60 cm and dig out a second 60-cm-wide trench, moving the soil forward to fill the first trench. Fork over the bottom of the second trench as before, adding the organic matter.

- Repeat this process until the whole plot has been dug, then use the soil from the first trench to fill the last trench.

improving your soil

Knowing how to feed your soil properly is one of the basic principles of good gardening and should be the starting point for every First-time Gardener.

Using organic matter

Nearly all garden soils can be improved by adding some sort of bulky organic matter, such as well-rotted manure, bark or wood chips, or home-made garden compost or leafmould (see below).

How does it work? Organic matter is broken down by micro-organisms (free-living bacteria and fungi), releasing nutrients to plants and improving growth. The way bulky organic matter benefits your soil, however, will depend on the type of soil you have. On light and sandy soils, which are very well drained,

organic matter acts like a sponge helping the soil to hold onto water. Organic matter also provides food for soil-borne creatures, such as earthworms, which burrow through the soil opening up the structure, and improving both drainage and aeration, which is of particular benefit to heavy, clay soils. This, in turn, encourages deeper roots and better plant growth.

How much should you use? The amount of organic matter you add depends on your soil type. Loam garden soils will need about a bucketful for every square metre each year, but if your soil is either especially heavy and clay-based or very light and sandy, you will need to add about ten-times this amount to see any improvement. If you don't have enough organic matter to

treat your whole garden, concentrate on areas which will benefit most, such as prominent flower borders or where you intend to grow fruit and vegetables.

When is it applied? If you are cultivating your soil, incorporate the organic matter as you dig (see page 166 for advice).

If your garden is already filled with established plants, however, simply place the organic matter on the soil's surface during the spring where it will also help to prevent moisture loss and suppress the growth of weeds. In the first year, place a 7.5-cm layer over the soil around each plant, taking care not to spread it directly against the plant's stem. Renew the mulch to this depth once a year or as needed, as it decomposes.

Making leafmould

Piles of leaves can be used to make a particularly useful and pleasant compost known as leafmould. The process is remarkably simple.

1 During the autumn, rake up any fallen leaves (provided they aren't diseased), and fill large, heavy-duty polythene sacks with them.

2 Add a few handfuls of grass clippings to the bag, water well if the leaves are dry and place the sacks in an out of the way place for a year.

The resulting leafmould can then be used as a mulch or a soil improver before planting. To make potting compost, leave the leafmould for two years, then sieve before use.

For large amounts of leaves, make a 'leafmould bin' out of heavy-duty plastic mesh held up by 4 sturdy posts. To prevent the leaves from blowing around, cover the bin with a piece of old carpet once it is full and the leaves are wet.

Using garden compost

Spread well-rotted garden compost as a surface mulch or incorporate it into the soil at planting time to improve the soil's structure.

A compost heap

If you have the space, it is a good idea to have a compost heap in your garden where you can recycle organic garden waste such as grass clippings, prunings and weeds. This makes getting rid of garden and kitchen waste very easy and provides you with lots of free garden compost that can be used to improve your soil at planting time or as a surface layer (known as *mulch*) around established plants to conserve moisture and suppress weeds. What's more, a compost heap also benefits the environment because it recycles waste materials that would otherwise end up in a land-fill site.

Making garden compost

This couldn't be easier. All you need to do is to use the right ingredients in roughly the right quantities (see below) and mix well, adding water as necessary. Then simply allow the pile to 'cook' for a year. During this period, unseen micro-organisms and garden creatures do all the hard work, turning your waste into a useful material, generating a lot of heat in the process.

Use the best ingredients if you want good results – any organic kitchen or garden waste can be used, including potato peelings and grass clippings. Don't add thorny or evergreen prunings because they take far too long to decay, and avoid adding flowering weeds because they may release their seeds in the compost heap and be spread when you use the compost. Any meats, fats and bones should also be avoided as they decompose slowly and may be smelly or attract pests. Avoid disproportionate amounts of any one ingredient or results will be disappointing. Instead, mix two parts of green materials such as non-flowering weeds or grass clippings with one part of something dry, such as straw, shredded newspaper or dead leaves to get rich, sweet-smelling compost. You can either mix the materials together before adding them to the heap or add them in alternate layers, up to 15 cm thick, until the bin is full.

Within a week, or so, the compost should heat up as the micro-organisms get to work, reaching a temperature of about 50°C (120°F) in the centre. After 'cooking' for about a year, it is ready to use.

During winter, insulate the pile with a piece of old carpet to prevent it from cooling down. You should also add a lid to prevent it from getting too wet. You can improve the consistency of your compost and speed up the composting process by turning the pile when it starts to cool. To do this, move the material that was around the outside of the pile toward the centre and spread the core of the pile on top. This is much easier to do if you have more than one compost bin side by side, because you can simply move the compost from one bin to another when you turn. If the compost becomes too dry, add some water.

Compost made easy

If you have the space, construct three compost bins side by side. One should be in the process of being filled, the second filled with decomposing material and the third being emptied of ready-to-use compost. This makes turning the compost very easy, as you can simply transfer it into the third bin when it's empty.

feeding your garden

Plants need a range of nutrients to grow well. All the essential nutrients are available in good border soil, so most plants will not need feeding every year unless your soil is poor. Plants which grow very quickly, however, such as vegetable and fruit crops, and those that put on dramatic flowering displays, such as roses, are worth feeding more regularly. Plants grown in a confined amount of soil, such as in a container, require feeding about six weeks after planting.

The most convenient way to feed all plants is by applying fertiliser. Deciding which fertiliser to buy, however, can be very daunting, because so many types are available. To be able to make the right choice, you need to know what nutrients plants need and the type of growth you are trying to promote.

Essential nutrients

Plants need a balanced diet of nutrients if they are to grow well. The three main plant nutrients are nitrogen (N), phosphorus (P) and potassium (K). They are often called the macronutrients or primary nutrients and expressed as a ratio of N:P:K on fertiliser containers. These three nutrients promote different types of growth in plants. Nitrogen generally encourages plants to grow quickly, producing lots of leaf and shoot growth; phosphorus is essential for the healthy growth of roots; and potassium promotes flower and fruit production.

Calcium, magnesium and sulphur, known as secondary nutrients, are also needed by plants, but in smaller amounts. Boron, iron, chlorine, copper, manganese, zinc and molybdenum are needed in very small quantities and are known as micronutrients or trace elements.

Applying organic matter

Using lots of organic matter in your garden, such as well-rotted farmyard manure or garden compost, is not a substitute for adding fertiliser. Bulky organic matter can, however, help to improve the structure of your soil, improving drainage and allowing more air in. If applied regularly enough and in sufficient quantities, it will also make the soil more fertile, but this takes a long time (see 'Improving your soil', page 168).

Organic or inorganic?

Fertilisers are classified as organic or chemical according to their origin. Organic fertilisers come from natural sources such as dead plants and animals; chemical (or synthetic) fertilisers are mostly manufactured, although a few, such as rock potash, are naturally occurring minerals.

The nutrients in fast-acting chemical fertilisers are immediately available to plants and useful for feeding fast-growing crops, such as vegetables, that are showing signs of starvation. However, the nutrients are easily washed out of the soil during periods of high rainfall and on free-draining soil.

On the other hand, organic fertilisers, such as fish, bone and blood, are much slower acting and continue to benefit the soil – and thus your plants – for a longer period. They release their nutrients more slowly because they need to be broken down by microorganisms before the nutrients become available to plants. The rate of breakdown varies with soil conditions: when soil is warm and moist, the action is faster than when soil is cold or very dry. Slow-release chemical fertilisers are available for similar effects.

Types of fertiliser

Fertilisers can be divided into three main groups: specific, simple and complete fertilisers.

Specific fertilisers are a good choice for the First-time Gardener, because they have been produced for a particular type of plant: for house plants, lawns, roses and vegetables such as tomatoes. They are convenient and easy to apply, but are generally more expensive than other types of fertiliser.

Simple fertilisers supply one or predominantly one nutrient. Products that supply only a nitrogen (N) boost are most common, but you

1

can also find phosphorus-only and potassium-only fertilisers. Manufacturers use various sources of these nutrients, but no matter what the source, all provide the percentage of nitrogen, phosphorus or potassium specified on the label. Commercial products include a comprehensive label that shows you the formula of major nutrients and their organic or chemical sources.

Fertilisers that contain all three of the main nutrients (NPK) are often called complete fertilisers. This does not, however, mean they contain all the nutrients necessary for healthy growth. Complete fertilisers that supply the three main nutrients (NPK) in roughly equal amounts are also called balanced or general fertilisers – they are ideal for using all around the garden to boost general plant growth.

You can also buy combination fertilisers that include a fungicide, insecticide or herbicide. The latter is often used in lawn fertilisers, to control common weeds. If you buy these products, read the label carefully to make sure the contents are safe for all of the plants in the area in which you will be using it.

Applying fertilisers

Manufacturers have devised a variety of ways to make delivering essential nutrients to your plants as easy as possible.

Granular fertilisers can be scattered onto the soil surface over the rooting area of border plants. Water areas thoroughly after applying, so that the nutrients are made available to the plants. In dry areas or periods of prolonged drought, consider applying a liquid fertiliser instead (see below).

Apply granules to the lawn using a shaker pack **(1)** for smaller lawns or a special fertiliser spreader for larger areas. For lawns covered with weeds or moss, there are special formulations that deal with these problems at the same time.

Liquid fertilisers are fast-acting fertilisers designed to promote quick growth. The balanced formulation is good for applying generally and the high-potash version is useful for flowering and fruiting crops and plants. They can be applied with a watering can, sprayer or via a special feeder that can be attached to the end of a hose.

Slow-release or controlled-release fertilisers **(2)** are coated in a special resin which releases the nutrients slowly over a set period of weeks or even months.

Making liquid fertiliser

Nettles can also be used to give bedding and vegetables a boost of nutrition during the summer. You can easily make a good liquid fertiliser from stinging nettles.

1   Wearing gloves, gather some nettles and tear them up by hand. Alternatively, lay the nettles on the lawn and run over them with your mower.

2   Place 450 grams of the chopped nettles into a 10-litre bucket of water, cover with a piece of hessian or sacking and allow to stand for two weeks. The liquid fertiliser can then be used as required, diluting it with an equal amount of water before use.

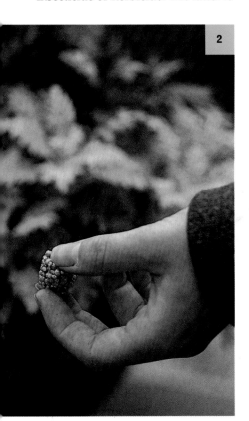

weed control

Weeds are uninvited plants growing in the wrong place. They are harmful because they compete with other plants for soil moisture, nutrients and space. If unchecked, they will smother your plants and eventually take over the whole area. In an informal garden, however, you may be prepared to allow some weeds, such as stinging nettles, to thrive to provide habitats and food for wildlife.

Annual weeds, such as shepherd's purse and chickweed, grow, flower, spread their seed and die all in one season. To prevent them from reappearing year after year, you need to remove them before they release their seeds. This is fairly easy to do if you weed regularly. Perennial weeds, such as couch grass, which live for more than one year, are more troublesome as they will spread via underground or low-growing stems that root and produce new shoots as they spread. When weeding, you must remove all the roots because many perennial weeds can regenerate from even a tiny piece left in the soil.

Green tip

Preventing weeds
Most weed problems can be prevented without using chemicals. Apply a layer of well-rotted organic matter to the soil surface around permanent plants, or plant through a special weed-proof mat called sheet mulch or landscape fabric (available from garden retailers). Any weeds that do appear should be controlled early by pulling them out by hand.

Mulch

The easiest way to control weeds is to use mulch. A layer of wood chips, bark chips, chopped autumn leaves or other organic material will smother young existing weeds. Pebbles, stone chippings and gravel can also work as mulches, but apply landscape fabric first to prevent weeds from sneaking into the spaces between stones. Mulch also keeps soil moist, cutting down on watering, and keeps the roots of plants cool. Organic materials benefit the soil by increasing the activity of earthworms and other soil organisms. As the creatures travel through the soil to feed on the mulch, they add air spaces that improve growing conditions and drainage, and work nutrients from the mulch deeper into the soil.

Weeding tools

Garden hoes and hand tools are excellent aids for removing weeds. Hand weeders are available in many styles, so experiment to find the one that suits you best. Use a long-handled hoe to weed rows of vegetables quickly. Slice off young weeds by

pulling the hoe towards you, or lift and remove clumps of bigger weeds. Shake off soil and toss uprooted weeds onto the compost heap to decompose. If the weeds have already formed seeds, avoid adding them to the compost heap, where their seeds may be spread when you apply finished compost.

Hand weeding

The most precise, but most laborious, way to weed is to do it by hand **(1)**, which is useful for dealing with isolated weeds or for removing weeds that are close to ornamental plants. Grab the weed at its base and pull. For stubborn weeds such as dock, dandelion and stray tree seedlings, give the weed a twist as you pull, to free the root.

When an ornamental border is heavily infested by perennial weeds, dig up everything in the border, so that the roots of the plants and weeds can be untangled, and then replant the ornamental ones.

Weed killers

Chemicals are an effective way of tackling weeds, but it is essential to apply them accurately, to stop them from coming into contact with any ornamental plants.

Individual weeds You can spot treat individual weeds using a dab-on applicator which allows you simply to wipe the chemical directly onto the weed. Alternatively, you can try ready-to-use weed killer sprays **(2)** which are available in hand-held spray bottles. These are especially useful for small groups of patio weeds. Spray only on still days when there is no chance of the spray drifting on the wind. If applying weed killers among ornamental plants, protect the plants with a polythene sheet **(3)** or upturned buckets before spraying. Don't remove until the spray has dried.

Treating large areas It is easier to treat large areas using a pressurised sprayer or watering can for soluble weed killers, or a special applicator for granular types. Concentrated weed killers are available as liquids, soluble powders or crystals, and need to be mixed with water before applying. Granular weed killers are supplied ready to be sprinkled.

Weeding around the garden

Weeds can appear in all areas of your garden, so it is important that you know how best to remove them.

Unused ground You can try pulling, hoeing or digging out all the weeds, but this is very hard work. You may be better off covering the area with a heavy-duty polythene sheet that will smother the weeds. But it can take up to two or three years to kill persistent perennial weeds.

For faster results, you can use a total weed killer that is deactivated on contact with the soil, so the area can be planted just a few weeks after treatment. Several applications may be needed to kill persistent weeds.

Lawns Individual lawn weeds can be removed using an old kitchen knife, a dandelion digger or other hand tool or a chemical dab-on weed killer. If the problem is more widespread, most weeds are easy to control using a selective lawn weed killer – this kills the weeds but does not affect the grass. Coarse weed grasses, however, are immune to some weed killers; to tackle these, dig up the weeds and re-sow the area with grass seed (see page 44).

Paths and patios Use a special weeding tool to hook out weeds from between paving slabs and rake gravel periodically to uproot any seedlings. Tackle severe problems with a path weed killer, which not only kills existing weeds but prevents new ones from germinating for a year. A spray bottle or watering can fitted with a dribble bar **(4)** will direct weed killer to crevices.

Mixed borders Control weeds here with mulch, which smothers existing ones and reduces further outbreaks. You can also hoe or hand weed. Spot treatments of weed killer will work, but be sure to protect neighbouring plants.

3 4

pest and disease prevention

Plants that grow vigorously will shrug off most pests or diseases. Remain vigilant, though, so you can spot problems early and take the appropriate action to ensure the affected plants are not weakened and the problem doesn't spread.

Preventing problems

Clear away dead and dying leaves promptly. Place diseased leaves in the dustbin (if you put them on the compost heap, the disease may be spread when you use the compost). Keep weeds under control, because these can act as hosts to many problems.

Buy disease-resistant plants Many disease-resistant plants are now available. Read the label of the plant or check mail-order catalogues, or information on gardening websites to find disease-resistant varieties.

Encourage beneficial insects Many species of tiny wasps and other beneficial insects attack garden pests by laying their eggs on the pest insects, or its eggs. The larvae eat the pests, but the beneficial insect adults dine on nectar and pollen. Encourage these natural enemies of pests to patrol your garden by including flowering plants to attract them. Spiders, ladybirds and lacewings also eat many garden pests. Try to avoid insecticides, which destroy beneficial insects.

Barriers Putting up suitable fencing and/or underground barriers can help to keep out deer and rabbits. Fine-mesh netting also can be used to protect vulnerable plants and crops from birds. Flying insect pests can be kept away from vegetable crops by covering the plants with insect-proof mesh as soon as they have been planted. Low-flying carrotfly can be foiled by erecting a 45-cm-high netting barrier around your crop or vegetable patch.

Traps Slugs can be trapped in dishes sunk rim-deep into the border soil, then filled with beer. Pheromone traps (available in garden centres) can be used to lure fruit tree pests, such as male codling and plum fruit moths, before they can mate. Use some corrugated cardboard to trap earwigs and pupating caterpillars, which hide in the grooves. Sticky bands that wrap around tree trunks trap wingless female codling moths, thereby preventing them from climbing the trunk and laying their eggs.

Dealing with problems

If a more severe outbreak occurs, hand-pick the insects or use mechanical means to remove them. If the pest is still not controlled, or if the problem is a disease, snip off the affected plant parts and dispose of them. If the outbreak is widespread, consider introducing a biological control or, should all else fail, you can turn to chemical aids such as pesticides and fungicides.

The first step is to identify the problem, so inspect your plants regularly to make sure you catch problems early. The chart on pages 176–177 details the most common plant problems, telling you how to spot them, how they are caused and how to treat them. If a plant starts to look sickly or foliage is being

The natural predator
You can prevent pests in your garden by encouraging wildlife that feeds on them. To encourage lots of slug-eating frogs to take up residence in your garden, add a pond or water feature.

damaged, check the plant for the culprit causing the damage. A little detective work may be needed, so arm yourself with a magnifying glass, notebook and pen.

Physical controls Pick off or rub off small colonies of insects between your finger and thumb or use a blast of water from a hose to dislodge them. Some flying pests can be encouraged to leave by simply giving the plant a vigorous shake.

Biological controls Your garden already includes many biological controls – in the form of creatures that devour pests. Birds are tops at eating insects, so attract them with feeders and birdboxes. Spiders are already busy eating pests in your garden and you may also have predatory insects at work. You can boost your population of some predatory insects by buying them at garden centres or by mail-order. If a caterpillar infestation is severe, you may want to use a product containing Bt (available at garden centres), a bacterium that kills caterpillars but not other insects. When you notice pests, give your helpers time to control the outbreak before you reach for insecticides.

Chemical controls Aim to reserve these as a last defence. Chemicals can be either organically derived or synthetic. Organic controls, such as rotenone and pyrethrins, are both effective insecticides. Many syn-

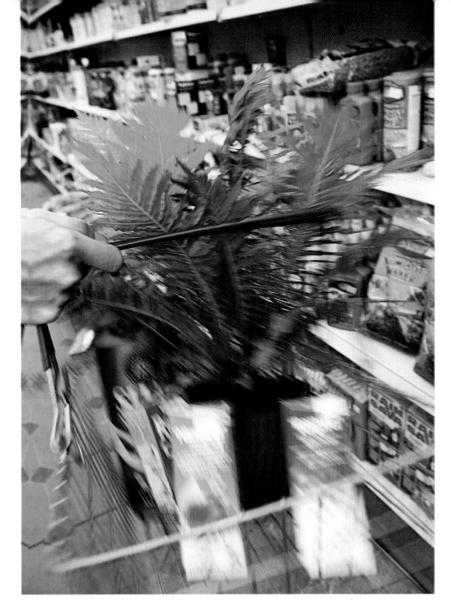

thetic chemicals are available either for specific problems or for more general use.

A general systemic insecticide is absorbed by the plant and will kill all the insects feeding upon it; a selective insecticide will kill only those insects targeted by its particular ingredients. If you are having severe aphid problems, for example,

you can choose an insecticide for those particular pests.

Disease-control products fall into three categories, depending on the way they work. Some are preventive in nature, helping to keep disease from getting a start. Others are eradicants, which control disease once it has begun. Systemic products combine both attributes.

Besides choosing a product that is formulated for your particular pest or disease problem, make sure it is safe to use on the plants you intend to apply it to. Products for ornamental plants may not be safe for use on vegetables and other food crops.

---

expert tips   Use chemicals safely

Always read the label carefully to make sure the chemical will control your particular pest or disease, and follow the instructions. Wear the recommended protective clothing and spray on a sunny, dry day when there is no wind. Wear rubber gloves when handling concentrated chemicals and wash your hands after use. Always store chemicals in their original containers and keep out of the reach of children.

problem solving

AT–A–GLANCE GUIDE TO COMMON PLANT PROBLEMS

SYMPTOMS	PROBLEM	TREATMENT
LEAVES		
Leaves have holes		
irregular holes in lily leaves, bright red beetles	lily beetle	pick off by hand
irregular notches in leaves, 1-cm-long beetles	vine weevil (adults)	collect at night
irregular holes with slime trails	slugs and snails	scatter slug pellets, collect at night, biological control
ragged holes or leaves stripped to veins	caterpillars	pick off by hand, biological control
ragged holes in deciduous trees	leaf weevil	collect at night
yellow spots turn brown and drop out leaving holes	shothole canker	spray with a copper fungicide
young leaves tattered and misshapen	capsid bugs	spray with a systemic insecticide
young leaves with small holes, shiny black beetles	flea beetle	encourage vigorous growth
Leaves marked		
black or green scabby patches (apples and pears)	scab	prune out affected shoots, spray with systemic fungicide
brown leaves often curled, dieback may occur	salt damage	avoid contaminating soil with salt or salt spray
circular or angular brown, yellow or gray spots	leaf spots	clear up fallen leaves
orange (spring) or dark brown (winter) raised spots	rust	remove affected leaves, spray with systemic fungicide
purple-black spots with yellow edges (roses)	blackspot	spray with systemic fungicide, clear up fallen leaves
scorched leaves on one side of the plant	wind damage	protect with windbreak or move to a sheltered spot
shiny, raised white spots on undersides of leaves	white blister	remove affected leaves
transparent white or brown patches	slugworms	pick off by hand
yellow or brown patches	leaf blights	cut back into unaffected growth, clear up fallen leaves
Leaves misshapen		
pale green and waxy growths	azalea gall	pick off galls, spray with a copper fungicide
raised often brightly coloured areas	galls	pick off affected leaves
rolled, sometimes with silk webbing	caterpillars	pick off by hand, biological control
shoot tips distorted, turn brown, often bark split	frost	prune out affected shoots, insulate plant next winter
small leaves, poor growth often discoloured	nutrient deficiencies	apply fertiliser
stunted leaves, distorted edges, swollen stems/bulbs	stem/bulb nematodes	destroy affected plants, clear up fallen leaves
thickened yellow margins, some curled (sweet bay)	bay sucker	pick off affected leaves, spray with systemic insecticide
tightly rolled leaves, grub inside	sawfly	remove affected leaves, spray with systemic insecticide
Leaves discoloured		
black soot-like coating to upper surfaces of leaves	sooty mould	control insects that excrete honeydew, wash leaves
discoloured foliage and stems wilt and die	wilts	destroy affected plants
discoloured areas on upper surface, gray furry threads	downy mildew	pick off affected leaves, spray with systemic fungicide
discoloured or pale leaves which often fall early	waterlogging	improve drainage
pale bands or spots	weedkiller damage	destroy badly affected plants
pale green or cream mottling, tiny insects jump away	leafhoppers	spray with a systemic insecticide
pale streaks, often mosaic, stunted growth	viruses	destroy affected plants
silver sheen, affects whole branches, leaves fall early	silver leaf	cut back into unaffected growth after flowering
tiny pale flecks, dull foliage, sometimes webbing	spider mites	cut out affected parts, spray with a systemic insecticide
white powdery coating to leaf surface	powdery mildew	spray with a systemic fungicide
yellow spots, often distorted	smut	cut out affected parts, avoid splashing water

SYMPTOMS	PROBLEM	TREATMENT
SHOOTS		
Shoots wilt		
greenfly, blackfly and other colour insects on shoots	aphids	rub off, spray colonies with systemic insecticide
poor growth, plants wilt, cream C-shaped grubs	vine weevil (grubs)	biological control
shoots die back usually from tip, leaves often wilt	dieback	prune out affected shoots into unaffected growth
shoots wilt and die, discoloured leaves	wilts	destroy affected plants
shoot tips slowly die back and remain brown	fire blight	cut back into unaffected growth after flowering
stems die back to near ground level (clematis)	clematis wilt	prune wilted stems, spray growth with systemic fungicide
tips on young trees wilt and die, tunnels in branches	leopard moth	skewer caterpillars in holes, or prune affected shoots
Shoots damaged		
flattened stems	fasciation	prune out affected stems with secateurs
bark raised and rough, often brown sunken patches	canker	prune out affected shoots into unaffected growth
shoot tips of shrubs eaten overnight, ragged cuts	deer	protect susceptible plants with suitable fencing
soft shoots grazed, gnawed bark	rabbits	protect plants with suitable fencing, use tree guards
Shoots discoloured		
bracket fungi or toadstools	wood rots	destroy affected plants, practice good garden hygiene
hard, roughened lumps present	galls	prune off affected stems
orange or red raised spots on stems	coral spot	prune affected shoots, practice good garden hygiene
spotted stems with small hard brown scales	scale insects	prune out affected shoots
stunted shoots and twisted stems	nematodes	destroy affected plants
FLOWERS		
Flowers have holes		
irregular holes with slime trails	slugs and snails	scatter slug pellets, biological control
ragged holes in buds and flowers	caterpillars	pick off buds and caterpillars, biological control
tattered holes in petals	earwigs	trap in pots filled with straw or newspaper
Flowers fail to open		
buds brown and eventually dry	balling	pick off affected flowers
buds dry up and harden (rhododendron)	leafhopper	destroy affected buds
flowers die followed by nearby leaves and shoots	fire blight	cut back into unaffected growth after flowering
greenfly, blackfly and other coloured insects on flowers	aphids	rub off, spray colonies with systemic insecticide
ragged blooms, leaves tattered	capsid bugs	pick off affected buds, spray with insecticide
swollen buds, distorted leaves	gall midges	prune off affected buds
Other flower problems		
buds and flowers turn brown early in season	frost	pick off affected flowers, protect from frost
buds fall off while apparently healthy	bud drop	water plants in late summer
flecked petals, buds may not open	western flower thrips	spray with systemic insecticide before buds open
flowers infested with shiny beetles	pollen beetle	not necessary, shake blooms before cutting
flowers stripped	birds	net affected plants or use bird scarers
no flowers, normal foliage (bulbs)	blindness	dig up and divide affected plants

growing plants from seed

Raising plants from seeds can be very rewarding, inexpensive and a lot of fun. For gratifying results, grow only fast-maturing bedding such as annual poppies, zinnias and marigolds from seed. Seed packets and catalogues will tell you how many days or weeks to maturity. Those that take a very long time to bloom are best bought as plants. Most vegetables are also easy to grow from seed.

You can sow seed directly in the garden, or in pots or seed trays. Starting seeds indoors will give you a jump on the season and provide the pleasure of gardening during early spring.

How to sow seeds

If you are planting outside, simply sow directly into well-prepared soil. Indoors, you will need seed-sowing compost and clean containers. Special seed trays are the best containers because they provide the correct depth of soil and have drainage holes. Use small trays or multipart plastic containers divided into separate cells (known as cell packs), which mean you don't need to separate seedlings into individual containers later.

Some seeds have to be kept in the dark for reliable germination (check the packets for details). Cover the planted trays with cardboard or other light-blocking material. Check for signs of germination every day and move the seedlings promptly to a warm, well-lit position once it occurs. Other types of plants need light to germinate. In this case, cover the seed tray with clingfilm or dust with a layer of vermiculite, which allows light through but keeps the seeds moist.

Sowing large seed

Some seeds are large enough to sow individually in cell trays or in pots. Fill the container with soil and make a hole to the correct depth using the end of a pencil. Drop one seed into the hole and cover with soil.

Sowing seed step-by-step

Growing your own seedlings is simple, cheap and satisfying.

1 Fill the seed tray with sowing compost, spreading it out evenly and removing any lumps. Gently firm the surface with the bottom of an empty seed tray or a tamper so that the soil is about 5 mm below the rim of the tray. Place the tray in a bowl containing 1 cm of water until the surface of the soil darkens and becomes moist. Place to one side to drain.

2 Empty a small amount of seed into the palm of your hand and then sprinkle it evenly over the surface of the soil. Aim to space the seed about 1 cm apart.

3 Cover the seed with a layer of sieved compost. Label clearly, then place in a well-lit position out of direct sunlight at the correct germination temperature (see seed packet for details on depth and germination).

Sowing fine seed

Some plants have such tiny seeds that they are impossible to pick up and sow individually. The technique described below will ensure an even distribution of seeds.

1 Mix very small seed with dry sand before sowing. This effectively 'dilutes' the seed and the light colour of the sand enables you to see how much you have sown.

2 Moisten the surface with a spray bottle and cover the container with clingfilm to prevent the surface from drying out.

Aftercare

Seedlings need warmth to germinate. The top of your refrigerator is usually suitable. You can also buy electric heating mats to place under trays for even warmer conditions. Once seeds sprout, remove the clingfilm or light-blocking covering and transfer the trays to a sunny, south-facing windowsill.

Before seedlings start to touch in the seed tray they need to be spaced out in another container using fresh compost. This is known as *pricking out*. Do this by lifting the seedlings out, holding them by a leaf and supporting the roots with the pencil or a dibber (available from garden centres). Place the seedling at the same depth into a cellular seed tray or pot filled with compost. Firm gently to hold the seedling upright. Add a light sprinkling of water.

Keep the seedlings in well-lit conditions so they remain stocky, but out of direct sunlight, which can cause scorching. Turn the containers every day to prevent lopsided growth or place aluminium foil reflectors behind the seedlings.

Trouble-shooting

Uneven germination This is caused by seed being sown at slightly different depths. Level the soil before sowing and cover seed with a thin dusting of sieved compost.

Shrivelled seedlings This is due to lack of moisture. If the soil dries out, stand the tray in a bowl containing 1 cm of water until the soil is moist.

Disease problems Seedlings can flop over after germination because of a disease called 'damping off'. Always use clean containers and commercial compost, which is free from disease organisms, and use fresh water from the tap, not from a rain barrel. Also, water seed trays by placing them in water rather than pouring water on them.

Good air circulation decreases susceptibility to damping off. Keep some space between individual pots, and avoid crowding trays altogether. Fungicides are also available for control.

FIRST-TIME GARDENER'S BEST BETS

59–64°F (15–18°C)
African marigold, alyssum, antirrhinum (l), dahlia, gazania, lobelia (l), Mesembryanthemum (d), nemesia (d), pansy (d) and phlox (d).

64–68°F (18–20°C)
Ageratum (l), cineraria (l), dianthus, French marigold, nicotiana (l) and petunia.

68–72°F (20–22°C)
Begonia semperflorens (l) and pelargonium.

72–77°F (22–25°C)
Impatiens (l), salvia (l), verbena (d) and zinnia.

l = needs light to germinate
d = needs dark to germinate

new plants from cuttings

Taking cuttings is a quick and easy way to start new plants from an existing specimen (this is known as vegetative propagating). Try taking cuttings to multiply your stock of any favourite plant. The Best Bets (right) are among the easiest, but you can have success with many other plants, too.

There are three main types of cuttings, each of which is taken at a specific time of year using growth that is at a different stage of maturity. Softwood cuttings are taken from soft, rapidly growing plants during the spring and early summer; semi-ripe cuttings are taken in summer and early autumn using stems that have started to produce woody tissue at its base

of new growth; and hardwood cuttings are taken in autumn and early winter from dormant plants that have reached their full maturity.

To root cuttings successfully you will need clean pots and cuttings compost. Semi-ripe cuttings often root better if the cut ends are dipped in a special hormone rooting powder (this is available from garden centres). A brand that also contains a fungicide will help to prevent the roots from rotting.

Softwood cuttings

These are very simple to root, but wilt easily, so they need to be kept as described below, or they will quickly deteriorate. Collect suitable material in early morning while it is

Steps to success with cuttings

3

- Before you take a cutting, ensure that the plants are healthy and prepare them using clean tools.

- Always take more cuttings than you need as some will not root.

- To stop your cuttings drying out, protect them from direct sunlight and place a plastic bag over the pot to create a humid atmosphere.

Preparing softwood cuttings

1 Use a sharp knife to trim the stem below a leaf joint so the cuttings are 7.5–10 cm long. Remove flower buds and pull off the lowest pair of leaves.

2 Insert the cuttings around the edge of a 7.5-cm pot containing moist compost.

3 Label and date the pot, then cover with a plastic bag held in place by a rubber band. This will help to stop the cuttings from wilting.

Place in a warm spot out of direct sunlight and check the cuttings regularly to see if they need watering. When new growth

appears, acclimatise the cuttings to conditions outside by first puncturing the plastic to improve ventilation and later by removing the bag completely. Then individually plant the rooted cuttings into 7.5-cm pots filled with fresh compost.

cool. Choose healthy, vigorous non-flowering shoots with three to five pairs of leaves. Trim material just above a leaf joint. To prevent it from wilting, place it immediately into a plastic bag. Then, prepare the cuttings as directed below left.

Hardwood cuttings

Some trees and shrubs are best propagated from fully ripened wood produced during the past growing season. For best results, take hardwood cuttings as soon as the leaves have fallen from deciduous plants. You need to make sure that you choose healthy stems which are about pencil thick.

Using a pair of secateurs, make each cutting about 15–30 cm long (the faster the growth rate of the plant, the longer the cutting will be)

trimming just below a bud at the base and just above a bud at the top. Make the top cut at an angle so it sheds water and makes it easier to tell which end is which. Remove all but the top three or four leaves from evergreen cuttings.

Choose a sheltered but sunny border with well-drained soil. Using a spade, make a narrow V-shaped trench about 20 cm deep. Fill the bottom of the trench with sand, then insert the cuttings into the sand 7.5 cm apart, leaving about one-third of each cutting above the ground. Refill the trench and firm each cutting in well. Water during dry spells and remove all weeds.

FIRST-TIME GARDENER'S BEST BETS

Softwood cuttings
Abelia, abutilon, clematis, cotinus, diascia, felicia, fuchsia, gazania, helichrysum, hydrangea, impatiens, marguerite, osteospermum, pelargonium, privet, *Prunus*, potentilla, verbena and wisteria.

Hardwood cuttings
Flowering currants, forsythia, honeysuckle, jasmine, philadelphus, poplar, roses, spirea, willow.

Semi-ripe cuttings
Berberis (h), buddleia, camellia, ceanothus (h), cupressus (h), cystus (h), daphne, deutzia, elaeagnus (h), garrya (h), helianthemum, juniperus (h), lavender, mahonia, olearia (h), photinia (h), pyracantha, rhododendron (h), skimmia (h), viburnum and weigela.

Semi-ripe cuttings

Many shrubs and conifers are easy to root from semi-ripe cuttings taken in mid-to-late summer. You need to wait until early autumn for evergreens, which often root better at this time.

1 Choose healthy shoots that have started to go brown and woody at the base. For those plants in the First-time Gardener's Best Bets above marked with an 'h', you need to create what is known as a heel, as follows. Gently tear the cutting material from the parent plant so that a small thin strip of woody bark, the heel, is formed. For those not marked with an 'h', you can simply make a straight cut. Use a sharp, clean knife to trim the stem just below a leaf joint so the cuttings are about 7.5–15 cm long. Cuttings with a heel should be trimmed to remove any rough snags. To

reduce the water loss from large-leafed shrubs, cut the leaves in half. To encourage rapid rooting, wound the cuttings by removing a 2-cm-long sliver of bark from one side at the base of the cutting.

2 Dip the prepared cuttings in hormone rooting powder, shake

off the excess and insert around the edge of a 7.5-cm pot filled with fresh seed and cuttings compost. Then follow the instruction from steps 2 onwards as described for softwood cuttings, left.

pruning made easy

Woody plants such as shrubs, trees and climbers may need pruning to look their best and to keep growth under control. There is a certain mystique about pruning that puts off even some experienced gardeners, but don't worry, pruning is a very simple technique as long as you follow a few basic rules.

The best equipment

Always use sharp, clean pruning tools. You should use secateurs for stems up to 1 cm in width and loppers for stems between 1 and 3 cm thick. If you wish to prune larger stems than this, use a special pruning saw.

Check that the blades of your pruning tools are in good condition before you begin. If cutting out diseased stems, remember to wipe the blades with a garden disinfectant between cuts to prevent spreading the disease to healthy tissue or other plants.

Simple pruning

The aim of pruning is to keep an established plant healthy. This amounts to cutting out any dead, diseased or damaged wood, known as the three Ds. Most plants do not require any more attention than this.

Simple pruning can be carried out at any time of the year. Spotting diseased or damaged wood is often easiest when the plant is in leaf. If the plant is dormant, scrape off a bit of bark with your fingernail to make sure it is dead. Living branches will be greenish under the outer bark.

Pruning shrubs

Even though most shrubs don't actually need regular pruning, it can be used to encourage more attractive displays of colourful leaves and flowers.

To prune successfully, you must know when the shrub flowers, or else you risk losing the flowering display the following year.

Steps to success when pruning

- Use sharp, good quality tools to guarantee a clean cut and reduce bruising to the plant.

- Choose a sunny, dry day to prune as wet weather makes the foliage soggy and the job unpleasant.

- Make sure you cut in the right place (see opposite).

Early flowering shrubs Shrubs that bloom in spring and early summer, such as forsythia, produce flowers on the previous year's growth. You need to prune these plants as soon as the flowers fade. Simply cut back about a quarter to one-third of older flowering shoots, cutting back to the highest new shoot or bud.

Secateurs and loppers

There are two types of secateurs: 'by-pass' **(1)** which have a scissor-like cutting action where a curved blade passes against a solid edge; and 'anvil' **(2)** which have a single straight blade that cuts against a block of soft metal or plastic. The by-pass type allows you to make cuts at any angle. Position the secateurs so that the blunt edge is higher than the sharp blade and pressing against the section to be cut off. Cuts made with the anvil type should be made square with the stem so that the pressure from the block is even. Loppers **(3)** work in the same way but are suitable for thick stems and their long handles make them ideal for high branches.

Prune in the right place

It is important to cut back a stem in the right place **(1)** in order to prevent diseases gaining access to the plant. This means making your cut where it will heal the quickest.

If you are removing whole stems from a plant, cut them off where they meet the main stem. If you only want to remove part of a stem, make the cut just above a bud (about 5 mm away) at an angle so that the cut surface sheds water. (For plants which produce buds in pairs, you need to make a straight cut so you don't damage either bud.) If you cut too far from the bud, the stub that is left behind can become infected and rot back into the rest of the stem. But if you cut too close to the bud, you risk damaging it **(2)**. Bear in mind that the position of the bud down to which you prune will determine the direction of the new growth. Therefore you should always prune to an outward-facing bud to stop the centre of a plant becoming congested with growth.

Late flowering shrubs Shrubs like buddleia that bloom from mid summer to early autumn produce flowers on that year's growth. Prune these plants in early spring just before new growth starts. Cut back last year's flowering stems or weak growth to within 2–5 cm of the old wood. Flowers will then develop from this new growth.

Shrubs with coloured stems A few shrubs, such as red-twig dogwood, are grown for their coloured stems. To encourage vigorous new growth with greater stem colour, prune these during early spring. Simply cut back the previous season's growth to near ground level to form a stubby framework of stems.

Shrubs with decorative foliage Some shrubs, such as elderberry, produce attractive foliage displays when young, which become less decorative as the plant matures. To maintain larger and more colourful leaves, prune such plants in early spring to encourage new vigorous growth each year. Do this by cutting back all of last year's growth to a stubby framework of old wood.

Grey-leafed shrubs Shrubs which produce grey leaves, such as lavender can be pruned in spring to maintain a compact habit of bright foliage. This should be done as soon as new shoots can be seen at the base of the plant. You need to cut back last year's growth to the lowest new shoots.

Neglected shrubs

You can rejuvenate an old shrub, even if you don't know what it is, using the fail-safe one-in-three method. All you need to do is cut out one-third of the stems, starting with the oldest (usually the largest) during early spring. This will encourage new growth from the base of the plant. The following two years cut out another one-third of the stems, starting with the oldest. After three years, all the old stems will have been removed and the shrub rejuvenated. See page 106 for more information about dealing with overgrown shrubs.

pruning popular plants

To make sure that all your favourite plants look their best and grow healthily, it is important that you prune them correctly and at the most beneficial time of the year.

Standard, bush and shrub roses

Recent research has shown that healthy, vigorous roses can cope with quite a lot of abuse and still flower well. Simply prune out any dead, diseased or dying growth (the three Ds), then roughly trim all the shoots back by about half. Don't worry about making an angled cut or pruning just above a bud. If you have a bed of roses, you can even prune them with a pair of shears or a hedgetrimmer.

Climbing and rambler roses

These are often confused because they both cover large areas, need support and are both early-flowering roses – they bear their blooms on growth produced last year – so should be pruned as soon after flowering as possible. They do, however, differ in height and flowering periods.

How to prune a climbing rose (above)

Cut out one old shoot for every new vigorous shoot that has been produced. Cut the old shoot back to a new shoot near the base, or to ground level if there is not one. Old stems left on the climber should have their side shoots, which flowered last year, trimmed back to three leaves.

How to prune a rambler rose (below)

If the rose produces vigorous new growth from ground level, cut about half of the stems right back to the ground. If only a few stems are produced, cut back about one-third of the stems, starting with the oldest.

Climbing roses These have strong stems, produce large flowers and reach a height of between 2.5–4.5 metres. If the variety in your garden flowers just once a year, prune it between mid- and late summer. If, however, it flowers throughout the summer, leave pruning until winter. If your climber produces attractive hips, it is worth delaying pruning until the winter anyway.

Rambler roses These tend to be old roses that flower vigorously and grow to a height of 4.5–9 metres. They are often grown along fences. They produce small flowers in large clusters once a year during mid-to-late summer and are best pruned during the autumn or early spring.

Pruning clematis

Clematis are another popular plant with a reputation for being difficult to prune, but if you know how and when they flower, you shouldn't have any problems. To work this out, simply note when your clematis is in bloom and whether the flowers

Better flowering
It is essential that clematis are pruned correctly to get a good crop of flowers every year.

are produced on soft new growth only or also on woody stems produced the previous year.

Flowers on new stems The late-summer flowering clematis bear their flowers on new growth produced during the current season. To maintain a good crop of flowers you need to encourage a lot of new growth each year. Prune these in early spring, cutting back to just above the lowest pair of plump buds. If you don't prune regularly, all the flowers will be produced out of sight at the top of the plant where the new growth is produced.

Flowers on old stems Clematis that bear their blooms on old wood need very little pruning. Simply remove any dead, diseased or dying growth (the three Ds) after flowering. If the plants become too large or have

been neglected, they can be cut back hard to just above a healthy pair of buds about 30 cm above the ground.

Flowers on old and new stems
Some popular varieties of clematis flower on both new and old wood. Regular pruning is not necessary except to remove the three Ds. If there are plenty of new stems coming from the base, however, cut back the oldest stems in early spring to just above the lowest pair of plump buds. This will help the plant to produce flowers over a longer period of time because the un-pruned stems will produce large blooms early in the season, while the pruned stems will grow to bear smaller flowers later on.

Honeysuckles
Most popular honeysuckles are early flowering – they bear their blooms on growth produced during the previous year. If you need to prune this type of honeysuckle, cut back the shoots after flowering to a new shoot lower down on the plant. This will then grow and produce flowers next year.

Honeysuckles that are late-flowering and bear flowers on the current season's growth, such as the Japanese honeysuckle, don't need pruning unless the climber has outgrown its allotted space. If this happens, cut back overgrown stems during early spring to just above a healthy bud about 30 cm from the base. New shoots will then be produced from the base and should be trained into the support.

Wall shrubs
Plants such as pyracantha that produce a fine crop of berries in the winter are worth pruning in a special way to make the most of the seasonal display. The trick is to prune in stages.

To keep the plant narrow, cut back one-third of the horizontal stems in early spring. These can be left to flower and carry a crop of berries in the autumn. Prune all other sideshoots after flowering. To help reveal the crop of berries, snip back any new growth that is hiding them to about 2 cm in late summer.

Improving displays of berries
To show off the berry displays of wall shrubs, such as pyracantha, prune back new shoots that cover up the colourful fruit to about 2 cm during late summer.

what's in a name?

The naming of plants can seem very confusing to the First-time Gardener. There are common names and totally unpronounceable Latin names. To be sure you are buying a specific plant, however, you need to know its full Latin name. To make finding the plant you want easier, many garden centres include the Latin name on labels. Catalogues may list plants either alphabetically by their common name or by their Latin botanical name.

Common names

Many wild plants have acquired a common or folk name from the local citizens who needed to refer to it regularly. This name is usually descriptive but not universally known, so that the same plant may have many common names, each known in different parts of the country. Common names often refer to a group of closely related plants rather than one particular type, making it rather ambiguous. In some cases the same common name is used in different parts of the country for very different plants.

Latin names

Although user-friendly, common names are very confusing and not universally recognised, so a system of naming plants had to be developed to enable experts and scientists to refer to a plant with the confidence that all their peers would understand exactly which plant they were talking about.

A famous Swedish naturalist called Linnaeus (1707–1778) put forward the idea of giving all plants two names that would uniquely identify them: the first word is the genus (a bit like a surname) and the second name is the species (like a first name). This two-name system was then used to name all known plants as well as new discoveries.

What Latin names mean

Although referred to as the 'Latin' name, genus names are often based on ancient Greek or have their origins in classical mythology. For example, the genus name *Chionodoxa* for the bulb glory-of-the-snow comes from two Greek words: *chion*, meaning snow, and *doxa*,

meaning glory. *Iris* is named for the goddess of the rainbow. Other genus names may honour a person – *Forsythia*, *Buddleia* and *Fuchsia*, for example, which memorialise Forsyth, Buddle and Fuchs – and still others are descriptive.

Species names are often used as adjectives to describe the colour of foliage or flower, the size of leaves, or other attributes of a particular plant in a genus: *purpureus*, for example, means 'purple', while *macrophylla* means 'large-leaved.'

Example of plant label information

Type of plant	*Evergreen flowering shrub*
Common name	*Rock rose*
Latin name	*Cistus x purpureus*
Use	*Flowering shrub for a sunny border*
Features	*A rounded frost-hardy shrub with small grey-green evergreen leaves up to 5 cm long. It bears masses of large pink showy flowers with slightly crimped edges. Each bloom is about 7.5 cm across with a darker spot at its centre.*
Height after 5 years	*1 metre*
Spread after 5 years	*1 metre*
Position	*Plant in full sun*
Soil type	*Any moderate or poor well-drained soil*
Hardiness	*Survives temperatures down to –5°C (23°F)*
Pruning	*Deadhead regularly. Prune out any dead or damaged stems each spring. Do not prune back hard.*

When two species of the same genus have been interbred to create a plant which shows characteristics from both parents, it is called a cross and the species name is prefixed by a multiplication sign (for example, *Camellia* x *williamsii* is a cross between *Camellia japonica* and *Camellia saluensis*). Where two species from different genera are crossed, a hybrid genus is produced and the genus name is prefixed by a multiplication sign (for example, x *Cupressocyparis* is a cross between the two genera *Chamaecyparis* and *Cupressus*).

If a plant's name includes more than a genus and species name, it is a subspecies, a variety or a cultivar.

Genus (the plural is genera) This is a group of one or more plants that share a range of characteristics, but can be separated from other genera by some major characteristic.

Species This is a group of one or more plants that share a range of characteristics and can be bred with one another to produce offspring that are similar to themselves. They differ from other species within their genus by one or more distinctive characteristics. Subspecies, which are indicated by the abbreviation 'ssp.' within the name, are a naturally occurring variant that is distinct from the species.

Variety and cultivar A plant which differs from others in the species by a relatively minor but distinct variation, such as the colour of the flower or whether or not it is has hairy leaves, may be named a variety or a cultivar. If the variation occurred naturally in the wild it is called a *variety* and given a Latinised third name, preceded by the abbreviation 'var.' (for example, var. *glauca*). If it is the result of selective

breeding, it is called a cultivar and given a name in a modern language that is set off in single quotation marks (for example, 'Snow Carpet'). In casual usage, cultivars are often referred to as varieties. Several plants of a species that share minor variations may be called a strain.

Botanical Latin names are occasionally changed as botanists reassess plants and reassign them to other genera or species. The genus *Chrysanthemum*, for example, has been reclassified in recent years, with some former species of *Chrysanthemum* being moved to *Dendranthema*, *Leucanthemum* and other genera.

You may occasionally see the abbreviation 'syn.' in plant names, which indicates that the name is a synonym for the chief botanical name by which the plant is referred.

Family The entire plant kingdom has been structured into a family tree according to each plant's main botanical characteristics. Genera are grouped together to form broad families. For example the family Rosaceae contains a wide range of seemingly unrelated genera including herbaceous perennials like *Alchemilla* and *Geum*, hardy shrubs like *Pyracantha* and *Spiraea*, and trees such as *Malus* and *Sorbus*.

A typical family line

Common name	Variegated holly
Family	Aquifoliaceae
Genus	Ilex
Species	*Ilex aquifolium*
Cultivar	*Ilex aquifolium* 'Handsworth New Silver'

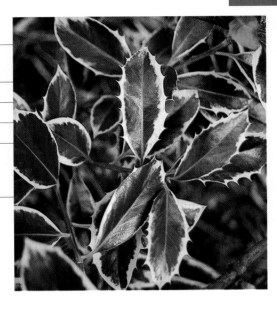

Using Latin names

Long Latin names may seem a bit daunting but don't be afraid of them: simply take them one syllable at a time. After all, you already use a number of Latin names without a hint of hesitation – chrysanthemum and rhododendron, for instance.

The Latin name, along with a lot of other useful information, can be found on the plant label. A complete label should give cultural information, such as soil, light and water requirements; cold-hardiness information (for example,'Hardy to –5°C'); special advice, such as whether a plant is invasive or poisonous; and, ideally, a photograph showing the entire plant as a mature specimen.

index

acknowledgements

Carroll & Brown Limited would like to thank Van Hague's and Country Gardens for allowing location photography at their garden centres.

Picture researcher
Sandra Schneider
Indexer
Michele Clarke
Illustrator
John Woodcock

Photography credits
t=top *c*=center *b*=bottom *l*=left *r*=right
DSR=Derek St Romaine; GEPL=Garden Exposures Photo Library; GPL=Garden Picture Library; RHS=Royal Horticultural Society Des.=Designer

2bl David Murray **8** Photo courtesy of Joanna and Richard Robinson **8/9** Photo courtesy of The Reader's Digest Association. Des. Philip Enticknap **14bl** DSR/RHS Chelsea 1997. Des. Fiona Laurenson **14br** Andrea Jones/GEPL. Channel 4 "Garden Doctors" **14/15** Jerry Harpur. Des. Isabelle C. Greene, California **16** DSR **17tr** Jerry Harpur. Des. Keeyla Meadows, California **17b** Jerry Harpur. Des. Isabelle C. Greene, California **18** Friedrich Strauss/GPL **18/19** DSR/RHS Rosemoor Vegetable Garden **19** John Glover. Tommy and Missy Simpson, USA **19** Friedrich Strauss/GPL **28** John Glover/GPL **28/29** Andrew Montgomery/New Eden/ Country Life Picture Library **29t** DSR **29b** Steven Wooster. Des. Anthony Noel **30l** DSR. Des. Johnny Woodford and Cleve West **30r** DSR/RHS Chelsea 1999. Des. James Alexander-Sinclair **32** Steven Wooster. Des. Annie Wilkes **33t** Andrew Lawson. Des. David Magson **33b** Steven Wooster. Des. Anthony Noel **34/35** Andrea Jones/GEPL Channel 4 "Garden Doctors." Des. Paul Thompson and Ann-Marie Powell **35** Andrew Lawson. Des. Andy Rees **36l** Photo by Stephen Jerrom. Courtesy Glass Garden, Inc. **36r** DSR/Hampton Court 1998. Des. Johnny Woodford and Cleve West **37t** Andrea Jones/GEPL. Des. Matthew Vincent **37b** DSR/RHS Chelsea 1999. Des. Claire Whitehouse **42/3** DSR/RHS Chelsea 1995. Des. Julie Toll **46** DSR. Des. Mark Rumary **50, 51** Andrea Jones/GEPL. Channel 4 "Garden Doctors." Courtesy of Mari Mower. Des. Dan Pearson **52t, 53** Andrea Jones/GEPL Channel 4 "Garden Doctors." Des. Paul Thompson and Ann-Marie Powell **55tl** Steven Wooster/ The Chapple's Garden, New Zealand **55tr** Steven Wooster/ Pippa Bishop's Garden, New Zealand **55bl** Steven Wooster/Growable Art Landscape Designs. Ellerslie Flower Show 1998, New Zealand. Des. Jan Latham **55br** DSR/RHS Chelsea 1997. Des. Simon Shire **58tl** DSR/ RHS Chelsea 1999. Selsdon and District Horticultural Society **58r** Jerry Pavia/GPL **60/61** Jerry Pavia/GPL **64** Gilda Pacitti **65** David Murray **66/67** DSR/RHS Chelsea 1999. Selsdon and District Horticultural Society **68, 69** Andrea Jones/GEPL Channel 4 "Garden Doctors." Des. Paul Thompson and Ann-Marie Powell **70, 71** Lynne Brotchie/GPL **72t** DSR **72cl** DSR. Chris and Stan Abbott, Kelberdale, North Yorkshire **72cr** DSR. Dr. Robinson, Howth, Dublin, Eire **72b** Andrea Jones/GEPL Channel 4 "Garden Doctors." Des./owner Nayla Green **74tr** David Murray **77** Mel Watson/GPL **80, 81t** David Murray **81b** Linda Burgess/GPL **82** DSR **83b** David Murray **84** JS Sira/GPL **85** DSR **86, 87** Andrea Jones/GEPL Channel 4 "Garden Doctors." Des. Paul Thompson and Ann-Marie Powell **88t, 89** Mark Bolton **91tl** DSR/RHS Chelsea 1997. Des. Julian Dowle and Jacquie Gordon **91tr** DSR. Mrs Maureen Thompson, Sun House, Long Metford, Suffolk **91bl** DSR. Mr and Mrs Foulsham, Vale End, Albury, Guildford **91br** DSR **92, 93** Nicola Stocken Tomkins **94bl** Gilda Pacitti **96t, c** David Murray **96b** Brigette Thomas/ GPL **99** DSR/RHS Chelsea 1997. Des. Roger Platts **100t** Marcus Harpur **100b** DSR **101** Gilda Pacitti **104, 105** Marcus Harpur/Park Farm, Great Waltham, Essex **106, 107** Mark Bolton/New Eden/ Country Life Picture Library **108/9** DSR/RHS Hampton Court 1999. Des. Ruth Chivers **109t** Steven Wooster. Des. Anthony Paul **109bl** DSR/RHS Chelsea 1999. Des. George Carter **109br** DSR/RHS Chelsea 1997. Des. Lady Xa Tollenmache **110tl** DSR **110bl** Linda Burgess/GPL **112t** John Glover **112b** Nicola Stocken Tomkins. Des. Susan Sharkey **118** Steven Wooster. Des. Sue Firth **122, 123** Andrea Jones/ GEPL Channel 4 "Garden Doctors." Des. Paul Thompson and Ann-Marie Powell **124** Nicola Stocken Tomkins. Des. Andrea Parsons **125l** Nicola Stocken Tomkins. Des. Sheila Bampfield **125r** Nicola Stocken Tomkins. Des. Katia Demetriadi **126tl** David Murray **126tr** DSR/RHS Chelsea 1999. Des. Terence Conran **126bl** Juliet Greene/ GPL **126br** Linda Burgess/ GPL **130tl** Nicola Stocken Tomkins/Hampton Court Flower Show 1999. Des. Karen Maskell **130br** Gilda Pacitti **132t** Iris Water and Design/ Pleiadian Enviromental Design Association **132c** David Murray **135tl** Nicola Stocken Tomkins/Hampton Court Flower Show. 1999 Des. Karen Maskell **135tr** Andrea Jones/GEPL Channel 4 "Garden Doctors" **135bl** Steven Wooster/Hampton Court Flower Show 1999. Federation of British Aquatic Societies. Des. Graham Robb **135br** DSR Sculpture by Dennis Fairweather **136bl** DSR/RHS Chelsea 1998 Lambeth Horticultural Society **136/137** Steven Wooster/ Himeji Japanese Garden, Adelaide, Australia **138** Gilda Pacitti **140, 141** Andrew Lawson **142** DSR. Des. Cleve West **143** DSR. Des. Johnny Woodford and Cleve West **144t/145** Andrea Jones/ Garden Exposures Photo Library Channel 4 "Garden Doctors." Garden owners Oliver Ashbee and Sarah Morgan **160l** David Murray **160c** DSR **162, 164, 165** Andrea Jones/Garden Exposures Photo Library Channel 4 "Garden Doctors." Des. Paul Thompson and Ann-Marie Powell **184/185, 186b** David Murray **187** Jonathan Edwards

Jacket Photography
Front bottom left David Murray **Back, far right** Gilda Pacitti